More Advance Praise for
The Innermost Waters

"If you think that Cape Cod fishing is just about stripers and bluefish, you're in for a nice surprise. Peter Budryk's great new book will point you in the right direction for some of the terrific trout, bass, salmon and panfishing that's available on the Cape year-round."

—Gene Bourque, Editor, *On The Water Magazine.*

"One of the BEST KEPT SECRETS of Cape Cod is the trophy freshwater fishing that anglers drive by every day."

—Barry Clifford, Treasure Hunter, Whydah Museum

Praise for Peter Budryk's
Trout & Salmon Lakes of CT and How to Fish Them

Covered Bridge Press, 2000

"Peter Budryk's new book is a terrific example of a regional fishing guide that reveals the hard-won lessons of local lore which are the keys to taking fish at any particular place and time."

"This is an important book!"

—John Merwin-Senior Editor, *Field & Stream*

"Like a trophy trout on opening day... It is the best regional fishing guide I have ever read."

"A book every outdoor writer in the state will wish he had written, and a book that many of us will use as a standard to shoot for in our own future efforts."

—Dick Alley, Outdoor Editor of *Norwalk Bulletin,*"Dean of CT Outdoor Writers"

"An awesome book! Truly beautifully done and man, is it loaded with information."

—Jim Mattingly, Publisher, *Red Book Atlas*

"Enough still water trout fishing know-how to last even an avid fisherman a lifetime."

—Rich Zaleski, Angler/Author, Host of *CT in FISHERMAN* radio show

"Clearly the most comprehensive, authoritative, and richly illustrated handbook for CT still water trout anglers ever published."

—Jim Matschulat, Three-time fly-fishing WORLD RECORD HOLDER, National Freshwater Fishing Hall of Fame

"This book is a dandy!"

—Lefty Kreh, "Dean of American Sports Fisherman & Writers."

FISHING CAPE COD'S PONDS & LAKES

THE *Innermost Waters*

BY PETER BUDRYK

AN AUTHORS GUILD BACKINPRINT.COM EDITION

THE INNERMOST WATERS
FISHING CAPE COD'S PONDS & LAKES

AN AUTHORS GUILD BACKINPRINT.COM EDITION

iUniverse books may be ordered through booksellers or by contacting:

iUniverse
1663 Liberty Drive
Bloomington, IN 47403
www.iuniverse.com
1-800-Authors (1-800-288-4677)

Originally published by On Cape Publications, Inc.

ISBN: 978-1-4917-4336-2 (sc)

Printed in the United States of America.

iUniverse rev. date: 10/23/2014

All photos by Peter Budryk except where indicated otherwise.
Interior book design by Peter Budryk with Mary Burgess of Classic Copy Printing.
Front cover photo courtesy of Jeff Capute.

Table of CONTENTS

ACKNOWLEDGEMENTS

In the process of researching and writing this book I have prevailed upon the experience, knowledge, skills, labor, time, and generosity of many special individuals, including the countless anglers, young and old, male and female, I was fortunate to meet on Cape Cod's wonderful innermost waters. For what they have given me, I am indebted. First I thank my colleagues, the authors, editors, and researchers of the sources cited in the References. My thanks are extended to the following individuals as well: Dr. Joe Sobel of ACCU Weather kindly provided me with the best available historical climate data on Cape Cod. The photo of a spectacular Cape Cod caught northern pike was wrangled for me by Gene Bourque, highly regarded Editor of ON THE WATER magazine, from a reluctant angler who was wary of giving away the store. The photo of another angler-caught MA northern pike that appears in this book was generously loaned to me by Rich Hartley of MA WILDLIFE'S Sportfishing Awards Program. Bill Byrne, MA WILDLIFE'S much honored outdoor photographer extraordinaire, allowed me to use his excellent photos of brook trout. Much of the most up-to-date and critically important scientific documentation of the status of Cape Cod stillwaters used in this book is the result of the work of Ed Eichner, lake scientist, and his staff at the Cape Cod Commission Water Resources Office. I found helpful the information on kettle ponds compiled by J.W. Portnoy and his colleagues in their National Seashore KETTLE POND DATA ATLAS. I also thank the men and women who agreed to serve on my Panel of Authoritative Cape Cod Freshwater Fishing Advisors whom you will get to know in this book. Those who were most especially generous to me were: Stan Moak, octogenarian Trout Unlimited angler who provided invaluable fly fishing information; Peter Mirick, Editor of MA WILDLIFE Magazine who shared with me a lifetime of personal and professionally accumulated knowledge regarding fishing these waters; previously referenced Gene Bourque; Mike McCaskill, proprietor, and Mark Palmer, manager of Goose Hummock Shop in Orleans; Jeff Capute, a legendary Cape Cod professional and sport fisherman whose eye- popping photographs of Cape Cod freshwater fish caught by friends, family, and himself are profusely on display in the book. Roy Leyva, MA Wildlife Angler of the Year, a fish hawk in a human skin, is a continuing source of up to the minute information on what fish are where on Cape Cod. John Tucker of MINING ORGANICS has been a steady source of help with my computer related questions. His set-up of photos, among other services, saved me much frustration and time. I am honored that Molly Benjamin, the genuine and original journalistic voice of Cape Cod fishing agreed to write the book's Foreword and Afterword. My confidence in the accuracy of the fishing information and data in this book rests upon its most crucial source, Steve Hurley, Southeast District Fisheries Manager for MassWildlife. Steve was extraordinarily generous to me with his time, knowledge, and patience, for which I am deeply grateful.

I also extend appreciation to Lance Rougeux, Executive Policy Specialist for the PA Office of Educational Technology, for helping me start the text and graphics formating. I also thank Mary Burgess of CLASSIC COPY & PRINTING for untying the Gordion knot of files I handed over to her and transforming them into an intelligible whole. Finally, I thank my publisher, Adam Gamble, for his belief in the quality of my work.

DEDICATION

With love, admiration, & gratitude for the incredible interdependency that has so enriched my life, I dedicate this book to my family, past, present & future:

– Virginia & Manuel Medeiros, & Magdaline & Alexander Budryk, my grandparents;

– Rosalie & Peter Budryk, Mom & Dad;

– William, Charlie, & Frankie, my brothers;

– Robin, Douglas, & Jennifer, my wonderful children;

– Zachary & Nathan Budryk, & Max, Riley, & Chandler Tucker, my precious grandchildren;

– and especially to Elinor, my beloved wife.

— PETER BUDRYK, ORLEANS, CAPE COD

Preface

Countless hours, weeks, and months of my research during the past five years were joyfully spent visiting, talking, recording, corresponding, and mostly, fishing with and learning from my sources, Cape Cod's most avid, successful and, where this book is concerned, sharing freshwater anglers. The recommendations of this panel of experts reflect general consensus on the top stillwaters, with enough individual variations among favored methods, baits, lures, and flies to provide range and diversity.

In one matter they were in complete and vigorous unanimity- their reverence for the Cape's beautiful and bountiful freshwaters. This reverence forced a related anxiety: in sharing their secrets, would every angler using the panel's information take individual responsibility to protect and preserve this special natural resource for future generations? In fact, that concern is the only misgiving I have had in the creation of this guidebook. Would my providing this collection of heretofore unrevealed information lead to a yahoo plundering and degradation of a fragile place? But then, this is the risk every angler takes in revealing and sharing good fishing. It is why so few anglers are forthcoming about the subject.

It also strikes me that there is a smidgen of arrogance in the assumption that others will not value and protect these waters the way I do and would want them to. In the end, I err on the side of trusting my fellow angler, as did the panel. The continued splendor of these waters will tell me whether or not our trust has been misplaced. I wager not.

In your use of this book I wish you more and bigger fish on the end of your line, joy in the splendor of where you find the fish, and the commitment to doing everything that is necessary to leave it a better place at the end of your day so that it will retain and grow in its magnificence for others in the days ahead.

Foreword

While I sit and write this, I am, along with his mother and father and the rest of our family, sitting on pins and needles. I'm waiting to meet my first grandson.

He's due to drop down from his birth-pond (his mother's womb, with a nod to David James Duncan) any day now. I wish he'd hurry up.

The concentrated attention on kids currently going on in our family has something to do with why I love Budryk's book.

For starters, it's one of the best-written pieces on how to go about fishing with kids I've ever read – and believe me, I've just about read 'em all.

Funny, isn't it, how one week you'll fall crazy in love with something (or someone), knowing that had the acquaintance been made at a different time, you might have paid no attention at all. Something about this book strikes me that way. Maybe because it's awfully close to being a how-to book.......for if there's one thing I hate to read and refuse to write, it's another freakin' how-to book.

And I won't be shy about telling you why I hate how-to books.

For one thing, their authors almost invariably take themselves more seriously than, say, Dan Rather in his "concerned" mode. I can certainly be serious, but there's that fine line somewhere that allows – nay, demands -- you to step aside and snicker at yourself once in awhile. I'd bet the farm than the worst of the How-To authors rarely, if ever, take the time to stop and smell the snickers.

And all the details! Awash, ablaze in details. If someone could become a fine artist by simply learning to describe a sunset, we'd have a lot more art in our lives. Getting a grip on an artform, and fishing is exactly that, requires grasping the whole, understanding the basics, and being free to develop one's own style from there.

Budryk's book lends itself to this greater idea of fishing. That's why you should read it.

In these pages you will find wisdom, some in the form of grand, almost-forgotten quotes from the masters such as Zane Grey.

You will find humor, the balm of life.

You will find excellent writing. Poetic even. Grab on to this description of a pickerel: "In a lake's quiver of weapons designed to keep the food chain in balance, the pickerel, in appearance as well as predatory style, with its smooth, sleek torso and dorsal and anal fins set back near the tail like matched feathers, is a well-aimed and deadly hunting arrow." Later, he mentions that pickerel "have attitude."

How great is that?

Take rainbow trout. (Take 'em all, far as I'm concerned; I seem to have an inexorable problem with rainbows in New England, the consummate hatchery fish that in real life belongs on the Left Coast. We Yankees believe in the natural order and placement of things.)
But I have lots of friends who love to fish for – and catch – rainbows. Though I regard this heresy as akin to being a New York Yankee fan, I at least understand their fondness for rainbows. Of the trout, this is the acrobat, the leapin' lizard, of the bunch.

Budryk says rainbows are "a joy to dance with on the end of the line."

How great is that?

This book is seriously well-written. Because I love good writing, I found I couldn't put it down. Me, who usually assumes I know everything about this subject, even learned a few things from inside these pages, b'gosh, and am glad to admit to same.

This fine work knows that when we go a-fishing, it's not just the fish we are after. We seek the mystery, the epic drama, the whole enchilada Dame Nature extends to those willing to get off the couch and step into her world.

Finally, you'll find here another uncommon ingredient, which is humor – the world's best condiment.

I never in a million years thought I'd ever be involved in a project to help total outlanders discover the mini-world of Cape Cod's plentiful, incredible freshwater ponds. The ponds are something about which, well, about which we simply do not speak when in the company of strangers. You know how it is, here in New England. We are raised from birth not to boast or show off.

Nor are we raised to give away the candy store, no suh.

But the ponds can take a few more people working their wondrous shorelines. They can especially do so if you have a kid who needs to be shown around and shown the ropes. All the ropes, including how to not crowd other people fishing the pond, how we are all obligated to pick up trash, how important it is to be quiet, how fishing is not about consumerism.

If any of these are your goals, this is the book for you.

Now, if only that grandson of mine would hurry up and swim downstream, well, we could get on with these things ourselves. I'm waaaaaaaaaiting..............

Molly Benjamin
Wellfleet, Mass.
August, 2003

INTRODUCTION: A Fresh Approach

The people along the sand
All turn and look one way.
They turn their back on the land.
They look at the sea all day.
FROM NEITHER OUT FAR NOR IN DEEP, ROBERT FROST, 1934

In a world class salt water fishing mecca such as Cape Cod, why would anyone want to write a book about its freshwater fishing?

Clearly and simply stated, Cape Cod's fresh water fishing is as spectacular, in its sweet-water way, as Cape Cod's nonpareil saltwater fishing is, in its briny way. Its multitude of beautiful ponds and lakes yields "double Q" fishing – quality and quantity. From pumpkinseeds to perch, smallmouth bass, largemouth bass, pickerel, trout, pike and even to Atlantic salmon, the Cape's kettle ponds never fail to delight those who have discovered them. They are truly a rich cornucopia of fishing and aesthetic pleasures as well as a wonderful alternative to fishing the Cape's saltwaters.

But discovery is key. As in Frost's poem, most anglers who live on or travel to the Cape put themselves mostly along the sand. They turn and look only one way- at the sea. They turn their back on the land, and in the process, deprive themselves of the innermost land's lakes and ponds with all their bountiful fishing and beautiful treasures.

How best to unlock this treasure trove and reveal its contents? I have fished Cape Cod for over 35 years, fortunate to own a home on this priceless peninsula. I could have relied on my own freshwater experiences and knowledge to

Another Peter, this one Peter, THE fisherman, also a fisher of men.

write this book; however, I am, after all, merely Peter, a fisherman, and most assuredly not Peter, the fisherman. As you will discover, you, dear reader, are the beneficiary of this critical distinction.

In putting together this book, like the saint, I cast a wide net. In addition to a thorough researching of this subject, instead of the holy figure along the shore of the Sea of Galilee, I consulted with today's most experienced and knowledgeable freshwater anglers. Taking my cues from the Americans native to Cape Cod- the Mashpee Wampanoag – as well as from the resourceful newer arrivals, both amateur and professional, I collected the best available and most definitive information ever to be assembled on the area's freshwater fishing.

These women and men, all with deep and wet roots in Cape Cod's well hidden and bountiful freshwater fishing, generously shared with me their hard-earned experiences, techniques and lore. What they revealed to me will enhance the success of both resident Cape Codders and the thousands of visiting anglers from nearby and across the country who, until now- largely through ignorance- have limited their fishing here to our fabled saltwaters. It is my hope that this book will provide a productive and enjoyable alternative; that is, a fresh approach.

The contents of this guidebook have been mined from my own research and experience but, more importantly, from the collective experiences of other expert anglers representing, in aggregate, well over 400 years of time fishing on the waters of Cape Cod. And this does not even count the thousands of years of fishing lore represented by the Cape's original people.

"A pond never hurries." John Merwin

Authoritative Cape Cod Freshwater Fishing Advisors

*"One fisherman may have keener eyes than another,
but no one fisherman's observation is enough."*

Tales of Freshwater Fishing, Zane Grey, 1907

> *" Time and place are everything in this broad and tidal land, Cape Cod, and it's always best to talk to locals or, better still, let one of them guide you."*
>
> Tony Chamberlain, Boston Globe, May 2, 2003

If you could spend a day fishing a Cape Cod lake with any of these people, your knowledge and skills would undergo a major growth spurt.

Since that may not be possible, I've arranged the next best thing. In this book you can read their advice on where to go, when to go, what bait, lure, or fly to tie on, and how to fish them, as though you are standing next to one of them on the sandy shores of Big Cliff Pond or sitting with one of them in a canoe on Long Pond. They will be there for you whenever you open this book. You will see pictures of many of them and you will read their time saving and fish catching tips throughout the text. You may even be lucky enough to actually meet one or another of them on a Cape Cod pond since they're almost always fishing.

Let's meet them at various places throughout this book, just as if we serendipitously happened to run into one of them on one or another of our fishing trips to a Cape Cod pond.

Glen Marshall, *Tribal Leader, Mashpee-Wampanoag Tribe*

Glenn Marshall, Mashpee-Wampanoag Tribal Leader

Glen represents the original people of Cape Cod, who have fished all of its waters from the beginning of human habitation here. The Mashpee-Wampanoag are the people who befriended the Pilgrims, teaching them

> *" The Indians are experienced in the knowledge of all baits, and diverse seasons, knowing when to fish in rivers, and when at rocks, when in bays, and when at sea."*
>
> William Wood, a member of the Massachusetts Bay Colony, 1630

There is evidence that Native Americans dredged and opened sluice ways between Cape Cod ponds as early as 2000 years ago to extend the run of herring. This one is still maintained between Gull Pond and Higgins Pond in Wellfleet.

how to catch the Cape's fresh and salt water bounty and to ward off even further privation and death over their first few years of colonization and eventually into the ultimate development of the Cape as a hub of fishing and whaling. Yet, as of this writing, the progeny of this tribe have been struggling, for years, unsuccessfully, to gain federal recognition by the Bureau of Indian Affairs.

Molly Benjamin, *Fishing Columnist, Cape Cod Times*
A former commercial fisherman, Molly has also fished the Cape's freshwaters extensively and, in her highly regarded and much awaited weekly fishing report, reflects the knowledge of many of the Cape's best anglers and bait and tackle shops. No one on Cape Cod is more in tune with what's biting/where.

Gene Bourque, *Editor of ON THE WATER, The Angler's Guide to New England magazine*
Gene, who has lived and fished on Cape Cod for over 30 years, is in a position to have experienced and to read much about its fabulous freshwater fishing from free lance and staff writers who cover the waters like a pine pollen bloom. In addition to teaching fly fishing, presenting seminars, and guiding, Gene is the author of the acclaimed FISHING NEW ENGLAND, A Cape Cod Shore Guide as well as FISHING NEW ENGLAND, A Rhode Island Shore Guide

Jeff Capute, *Mate, FISH HAWK Charter Boat, Hyannis*
Jeff is a long time Cape Cod resident who is on the water almost every day of the year, regardless of the weather, at his work or for his own pleasure. Releasing virtually all of the fish he

lands, and urging others to do the same, Jeff is one of the most highly "decorated" Cape Cod anglers, having been awarded over 150 pins for trophy fish and four gold pins for the largest fish caught during a year in MA. He is a gifted, "natural"-combining deep knowledge and endowed insticts- Cape Cod freshwater angler who not only keeps a journal but who also "fishes his brains out". His results reflect the skills and experience that have labeled this modest guy a legend. You will see many of his trophy Cape Cod fish and read his tips so you can catch your own.

Paul DuClos, *Holder of a new, unofficial largemouth bass world record: 24 pounds!*

Paul DuClos and his unofficial new world record largemouth bass .

Paul spent many years fishing and catching trophy sized largemouth bass in Cape Cod's freshwater lakes and ponds before moving to Santa Rosa, California. A member of the North American Fishing Club, Paul has caught and released over 140 largemouth bass over 10 pounds, five over 16 pounds, and his unofficial (caught, weighed, photographed, and released) new world record 24 pounder.

David Gilmore, *an Orleans native with the reputation of being one of the most prolific largemouth bass anglers on the Cape.*

Steve Halley, *Former Manager, Orvis Company Store, Quincy Market, Boston (617)742-0288 www.orvis.com*

While Steve is in a position to fish some of the best fresh waters across America, since he discovered the ponds and lakes of Cape Cod when he was 20, he now fishes them exclusively every spring and fall.

Steve Hurley, *Fisheries Manager for the Commonwealth's Southeast District, which includes Cape Cod*

Steve has been fisheries manager since 1990. Among other responsibilities, he is the person who makes all of the decisions regarding species, numbers, size, and schedule of stocked fish in all of Cape Cod ponds and lakes. No one has more theoretical and hands on scientific knowledge of the biology of the fish in the Cape's lakes and ponds. He has shared that with us for this book.

Robert Jessup, *Manager, The Sporting Life-Cape Cod, Mashpee Commons,12 Steeple St. Mashpee (508)539-0007 www.thesportinglife.com*
Rob is an expert angler who learned all his fly fishing skills from author/angler Lou Tabory who conducts frequent workshops at his brother Curt's shop.

Peter Mirick *is the long time editor of Massachusetts Wildlife, published quarterly by the MA Division of Fisheries and Wildlife, Information and Education Section.*
MA Fisheries and Wildlife Field Headquarters Westborough, MA 01581 (508) 792-7270
Massachusetts Wildlife is available at a prescription rate of $6 per year, $10 for two years. Checks or money orders only. (800) 289-4778

Stan Moak, *TROUT UNLIMITED, Cape Cod Chapter, TU 1500 Wilson Blvd,Suite 310, Arlington, VA 22209-2404 www.tu.org*
This octogenarian Brewster resident has logged many hours on Cape Cod ponds and lakes. His association with TU puts him in close and almost daily contact with other TU anglers who share hard earned information about where and how to catch trout across the Cape. You don't have to run all over; their information is here with the turn of the pages. Write or log on to the TU address above to join this fine organization committed to conserving trout and trout habitat.

Craig Poosikian, *Custom Rod Builder, Orleans (508)240-2345*
For more than 30 years Craig has fished the ponds and lakes of Cape Cod with considerable success. While he would never reveal where he catches his striped bass, he tells all here regarding his favorite freshwater haunts. His custom designed and built salt and fresh water bait, spin, and fly casting rods, tailored for every species, are much sought after by professional and recreational anglers for their own use and as gifts.

Mark Palmer, *Goose Hummock, Outfitters Since 1946, Largest Tackle Dealer in the Northeast, Orleans, Manager of Fishing Department (508)255-0455*
Mark lives, eats , and sleeps Cape Cod fishing. Walk into the Goose Hummock shop in Orleans and you will not only be greeted by a smiling and congenial man but you will also be provided with the most recent information on what baits, lures, flies, and methods are taking fish on the Cape's stillwaters.

Rod Schou, *Butterworth Map Co. Inc. Route 6A West Barnstable, MA 02668 (800) 696-2762*
Rod, who lives and fishes out of Marstons Mills, created Butterworth's Cape Cod Fishing Maps which illustrate the top 100 lakes and ponds, showing valuable depth, water type, access, species, and other information. Available at tackle stores.

Ella Schultz, *Avid and experienced Cape Cod fresh water angler*
Ella is a resident of Orleans who has spent many years fishing and catching on Cape Cod's ponds and lakes, releasing all her fish. She is the matri-

arch of a four generation family of Cape Cod anglers including her sons, grandsons, and now two great grand children.

Donald B. Sparrow, *Author & Publisher*
In his hale and hearty 80's, Don knows the olde as well as the contemporary Cape Cod, including its fresh waters which he, his children, grandchildren, and now great grandchildren fish. A CAPE COD NATIVE RETURNS,You Can Go Home Again Amusing and perceptive vignettes about people and events in a small Cape Cod town. 170 pages, 55 illustrations, $14.95 Order from Great Oaks Publishing Co. Box 1051 , Eastham, MA 02642 (508)255-2170 or d.sparrow@attbi.com

Anton "Tony" Stetzko, *Long time holder of the former world record striped bass-73 pounds- Cape Cod fishing guide, owner- Cape Copy Shoppe, 195 Cranberry Highway, Orleans, (508)255-2357*
Few ardent Cape Cod anglers don't know this man and the exciting story of his world record striped bass caught in the surf off Nauset Beach. What many do not know is his love affair with the area's fresh water fishing. Now they will.

Don Stromyer, *Owner, Red Top Sporting Goods, Inc. near the Bourne Bridge rotary, 265 Main St. Buzzards Bay, (508)759-3371*
Red Top is one of the oldest and best inventoried bait and tackle stores on (almost) Cape Cod. Anglers on and off the Cape share their success with the shop's staff who share it with us.

Walter Ungermann, *Captain, U.S. Fly Fishing Team. Owner/guide Man of War, Oyster Harbor, light tackle saltwater fishing, (508)362-1489*
Born in Centerville, a licensed charter boat captain at 18, a light line sportfishing guide on his Man of War in Oyster Harbor and during the winter out of Jupiter, Florida, Walt has done it all in the world of fishing.
He fishes salt and fresh waters over 340 days a year, having kept, to the present day, meticulous notes, observations, and diagrams of every trip on the water, including those to Cape Cod ponds and lakes since he was 9 years old. An ardent conservationist, Walt is a strong supporter of

Walter Ungerman, a Cape Cod and national fishing icon, at his fly tying table.

local, regional, national, and international efforts to preserve and conserve natural resources. His contributions and skills have brought him the position Chairman of the USA Flyfishing Team which represents this country in the Annual

World Flyfishing Championships held at locations throughout the world.

A self professed fishing addict, he says he "would fish in a sewer." This colorful and bigger than life guy, only somewhat tongue in cheek, offers "You can describe me as the best damn fly fisherman on the Cape and the rest of the planet!" Often, especially on foul weather days, he can be found on the ponds and lakes of Cape Cod, which he knows intimately.

To contact FLYFISHING TEAM USA as a possible competitor, supporter, or just out of curiosity: (561) 575-5868 or info@flyfishingteamusa.com

Ed Wanamaker, *owner, The Bait Shack, 4 Bay Ridge Lane, Orleans, (508)240-1575*

A former Alaskan fishing guide, Ed operates his bait and tackle shop at the intersection of Route 6A near the Underground Mall, a convenient location for anglers fishing Nickerson State Park ponds or heading out to the waters between Brewster and Provincetown.

Our panel of authoritative Cape Cod fresh water advisors have opened up their treasure trove of hard earned and time tested tips to help us shorten the learning curve and catch more fish. We can repay their generosity by heeding their plea that we all honor the rare and fragile beauty of the Cape and its fresh waters, practicing catch and release and leaving no trash along the shores or in the water.

MEET OTHER EXPERTS AND THEIR TIPS THROUGHOUT THE BOOK.

Ed and several staff at the Bait Shack.

Cast 1:

WHAT ARE PONDS AND LAKES?

"East and ahead of the coast of North America...there stands in the open Atlantic the last fragment of an ancient and vanished land."

THE OUTERMOST HOUSE, BY HENRY BESTON

Lakes are born, they exist for a period of time, and then they die. In Massachusetts, there are many thousands of lakes and ponds. On Cape Cod, there are various estimates of the number of stillwaters, ranging from a few hundred to over 1,000.

According to the Cape Cod Commission's Pond and Lake Atlas, completed in May, 2003, the Cape "has 994 ponds covering nearly 11,000 acres. These ponds range in size from less than an acre to 743 acres (Long Pond, Brewster/Harwich); with the 21 biggest ponds having nearly half the total Cape-wide pond acreage. Approximately 40% of the ponds are less than an acre.

Ponds of a certain area are 'waters of the Commonwealth of Massachusetts' and, therefore, **are owned by the public**. The area of these **'Great Ponds'** is either **20** acres or **10** acres depending on which portion of Massachusetts General Law is reviewed (Chapter 131, Section 1 or Chapter 91, Section 35, respectively.) In 1933, the legislature designated **164 Great Ponds on Cape Cod."**

It is probably safe to say that, on Cape Cod, there is at least one accessible and fishable stillwater for each day of the year. Doubters of these numbers need only be on the Cape when the leaves are off the trees and previously hidden and unseen waters, like mushrooms after a rain, come into view, and to understand why, because of their plenitude, some of them are simply numbered rather than named. Pond # 14 in Falmouth is a little jewel of a fishing spot.

Great Pond, Truro, a classic Cape Cod kettle pond.

> **FISHING IN CLEAR WATER:**
> *Fish are much harder to catch in clean, clear water like that in most Cape Cod ponds and lakes. If the water is also calm, it is even more difficult. Under these conditions, fish can see us at a distance, every disturbance is magnified and so are the baits, lures, flies, leaders, swivels, hooks and lines. This calls for smaller baits, tiny lures, light lines, long small diameter leaders, and small hooks. Longer casts, well beyond where you think the fish are, is advised. Also, fishing at dawn, dusk, and night, especially during calm spells, will put some odds on your side.*
>
> ADAPTED FROM THE FISHERMAN'S CATALOGUE, VLAD EVANOFF

What is the difference between a lake and a pond? Ponds are shallow and/or clear enough that light is able to penetrate and thereby support plant growth along their total bottom. While there will be vegetation around its edges in the shallows, the deep bottoms of true lakes receive so little light that vegetation cannot grow along its bottom. So depth and its effects are the factors that distinguish ponds from lakes-ponds are shallow, lakes are deep. Despite this distinction, the folks who named the still waters in America were not limnologists, scientists who study still water. The early Americans, including Cape Codders, labeled a body of water a lake or a pond depending on whatever they felt they wanted to call it, limnology be damned. Since most of the Cape's still waters that carry "pond" in their name are quite deep, they are, technically, "lakes". Cliff Pond is a *deep* lake. Pilgrim Lake is a *shallow* pond. Nevertheless, they'll keep their pond and lake names; the distinction mostly makes for interesting trivia.

> *"In terms of geology, most of the Cape is a gigantic glacial deposit composed of sand, gravel and rock rubble. It has been an island since 1914, when the completion of the Cape Cod Canal cut it from the mainland. Covering approximately 350 square miles, the Cape is dominated by fire prone habitat composed of pitch pine-scrub oak forest..*
> *Extensive residential development has occurred near many ponds. Fortunately, public access sites have been acquired on many ponds, affording us all the chance to fish them. Virtually all of the ponds on the Cape are natural kettle holes. These roundish, relatively sterile ponds, usually fed by groundwater and characterized by clear water, sandy shorelines and low alkalinity, are the 'footprints' of huge blocks of ice left behind by retreating glaciers. Many are deep and contain enough cold, well oxygenated water to hold trout throughout the year. Many ponds have direct or indirect connections to the sea, allowing them to support sea-run alewife populations. GAMEFISH AND PANFISH IN PONDS CONTAINING THIS EXCELLENT FORAGE BASE OFTEN DIS-*PLAY EXCEPTIONAL GROWTH RATES."
>
> (CAPITALS INSERTED BY AUTHOR.)
> STEVE HURLEY, SOUTHEAST DISTRICT FISHERIES MANAGER, MDFW

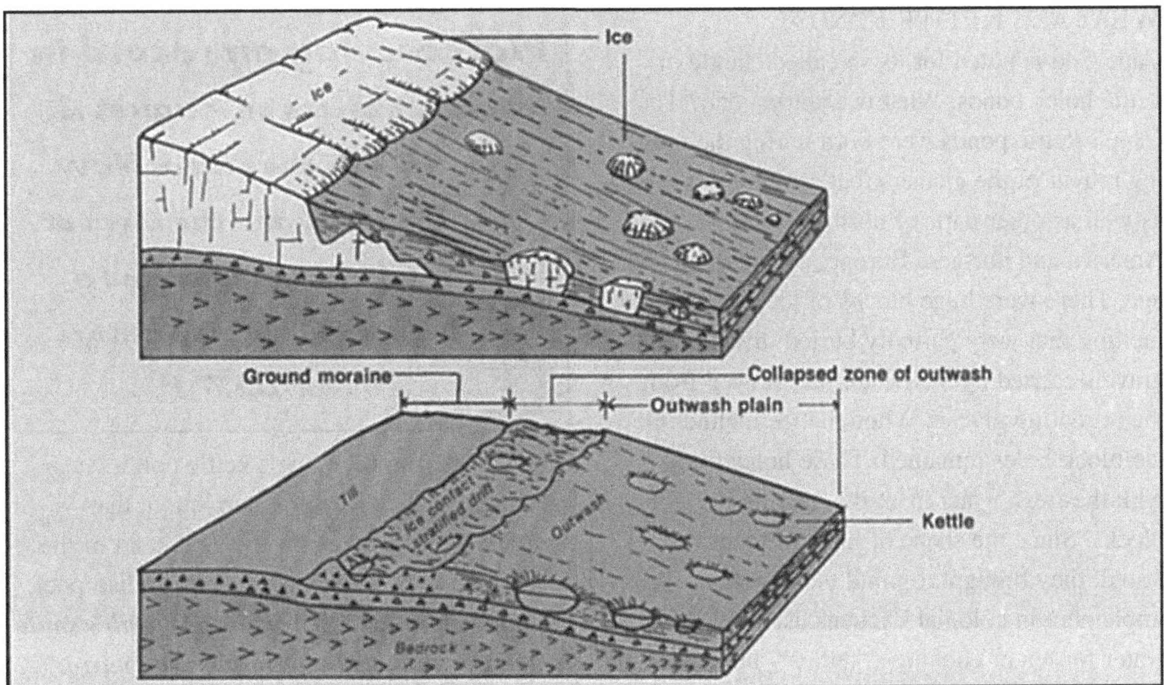

Drawing showing the relationship of buried ice to a collapsed zone of an outwash plain and kettles. (Geologic History of Cape Cod, Robert N. Oldale)

Ice House Pond, Orleans. Typical kettle pond.

WHAT ARE KETTLE PONDS?

Cape Cod is noted for its so called "kettle or kettle hole" ponds. What is a kettle pond? The Cape's kettle ponds were born during the melting retreat of the glaciers that covered this area, as well as other parts of northern North America and northern Europe, during the ice age. There were huge blocks of ice left after the melting that were partially buried in sands and gravels carried by meltwater that flowed from the retreating glacier. When the ice melted, the ice-block holes remained. These holes filled with the fresh water from the melting ice blocks. Since the shape of most of them was round, they brought to mind the common implement in colonial kitchens used to heat water for tea or cooking- "kettles"- hence, the name for such still waters. The range of depth of Cape Cod's kettle ponds is about 6 to 95 feet. The deep kettle ponds are between 10,000 and 13,000 years old, as determined by radio-carbon dating of the remains of the earliest lake organisms in the deepest layers of sediment. The outwash sands and gravels that were the repositories of kettle ponds are generally poor in nutrients, accounting for the high clarity that characterizes Cape Cod kettle ponds. There is a very special aesthetic appeal to the Cape's kettle ponds, suggesting an aura of natural perfection, that immediately captures the eye and heart of the observer. As described by the east Indian poet, Rabindranath Tagore, they are as ***"truth's smile when she beholds her own face in a mirror".***

CAPE COD POND DATA

Largest	Town	Acres
1-Long	Brewster/Harwich	743
2-Mashpee-Wakeby	Mashpee	729
3-Wequaquet	Barnstable	654
4-Great Herring	Bourne	373
5-Johns	Mashpee	338

Source: CCC GIS Dept.

Deepest		Feet
1-Mashpee-Wakeby	Mashpee	95
2-Cliff	Brewste	84
3-Ashumet	Falmouth	84
4-Long	Brewster/Harwich	72
5-Long	Falmouth	66

Source: PALS 2001 Snapshot & MDFW files

Most Common Names

Number	Name
10	Mill
9	Long
8	Flax
7	Grass or Grassy
6	Round
6	Lily

Number of Ponds/Lakes in Each Town (alphabetically)

Town	Total	# > 10 Acres (Great Ponds)
Barnstable	184	27
Bourne	73	7
Brewster	76	22
Chatham	44	7
Dennis	57	6
Eastham	23	5
Falmouth	142	23
Harwich	63	20
Mashpee	56	9
Orleans	63	4
Provincetown	31	3
Sandwich	63	10
Truro	20	4
Wellfleet	29	8
Yarmouth	70	10
TOTAL	994	165

Source: CCC GIS Dept.

(Some of the information on kettle ponds was derived from KETTLE POND DATA ATLAS, Cape Cod National Seashore, 2001)

How a Pond Changes Through the Seasons

The biology, chemistry, and hydrodynamics of a pond, the subjects of substantial research by scientists and academicians the world over, are in complex interaction at all times. But an angler need not achieve a doctorate degree in these fields to achieve a level of knowledge useful for fishing. In fact, adequate information is readily and easily available. Here, a review of how and why lake waters change over the year should be more than enough not only to appreciate the life and the environment of fish, but also to use that knowledge to advantage in fishing.

Summer

It's helpful to know that in the deep lakes of Cape Cod, as is true throughout the temperate zone, a temperature stratification, or layering, occurs. The layers are different at different times of the year. During the summer, as the surface of the water absorbs the sun's heat, it obviously warms faster than the water below the surface which is not in direct contact with the sunshine. Because warm water is lighter than cold water, the lighter, warmer surface water floats on the denser, cooler water beneath the surface.

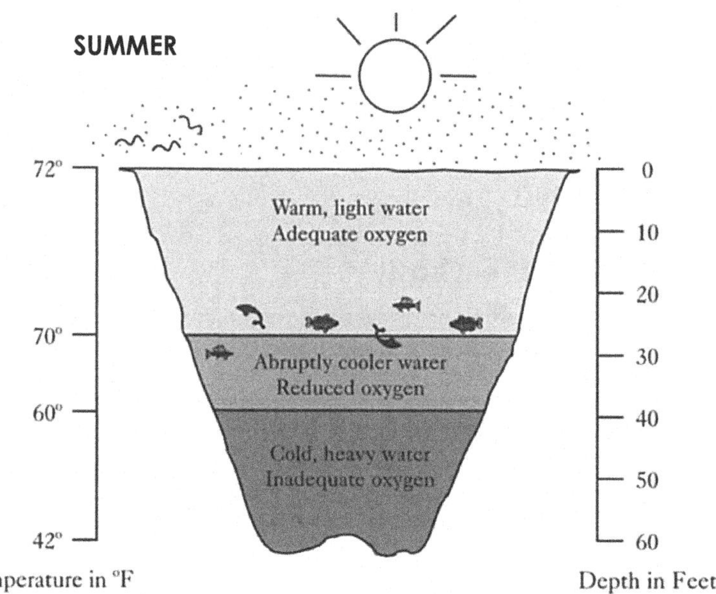

During an average Cape Cod summer, a lake will, by midsummer, develop three distinct temperature layers.

The top layer is the warmest part of the lake, with temperatures ranging from about 65-75 degrees F. As the lighter, warmer surface water gets the summer's increasing sunshine, it expands in volume and gets deeper, all the time resting on the middle layer.

At the same time, the middle layer displays two very different qualities. Because so little light penetrates to its depths, plants do not grow and it does not mix with the warm surface layer. The result is a middle layer characterized by a sudden and rapid drop in temperatures, ranging from 45-65 degrees F. The sudden temperature drop of the middle level is known as a thermocline, a decline in therm, the units of heat. This sudden cold water acts as a barrier to vertical water movement, reinforcing the layering.

The third layer, beneath the thermocline layer, obviously gets even less light and therefore no plants also. It does, however, become the gravitational depository- the lake's compost bin- for all of the lake's plants and other organic debris. The resulting decomposition increases carbon dioxide and reduces the oxygen at this bottom level. Because the thermocline above is warmer and therefore lighter, it rests on the bottom level, the temperature range of which is the lowest in the lake, ranging from 39.2-45 degrees F.

Since fish need oxygen to survive and have preferred water temperature ranges, most of them, as well as the lake's other life forms, are found at and above the thermocline and into the upper layer where food and oxygen are plentiful.

Autumn

As Cape Cod's temperatures start to drop in the fall, the upper layers of its deeper lakes start to cool. In time, the temperature of the upper layer approaches the temperature of the water in the middle-thermocline- and lower layers. The

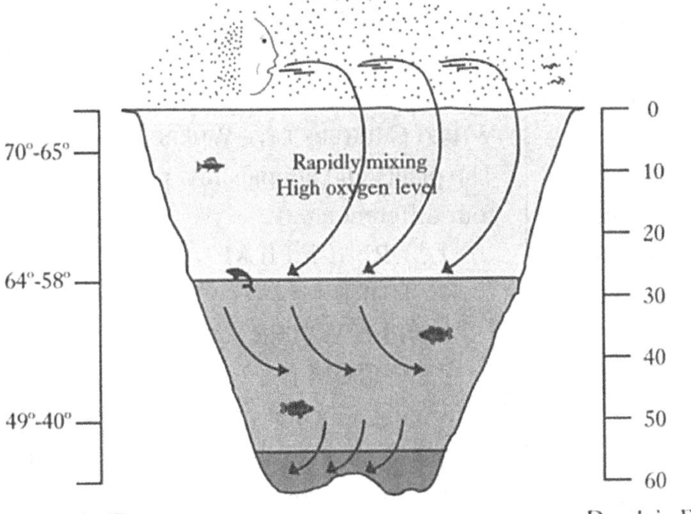

autumn winds begin to pick up and, slashing across the surface of the lakes, they assist the surface waters, now colder and heavier, to sink, causing a mixing or circulation of all waters from top to bottom. This phenomenon is labeled fall overturn. Because the temperature of the waters is equalized from top to bottom during the fall (and spring) overturn, all levels of the lake are well oxygenated and within the comfort zones of most fish which now become active and widely distributed throughout the entire lake.

Winter

Fall turnover ends and winter layering begins when the air temperatures descend in the fall. As the air and lake water temperatures drop, the cold and heavy surface water continues to sink until, near the freezing point, its density begins to decrease. Just the opposite from summer leveling, when the colder, denser water sinks. In winter leveling the colder water, due to its decreasing density/weight, rises closest to the surface and begins to freeze from the top down. When ice covers the entire lake-not an annual event on Cape Cod- temperatures range

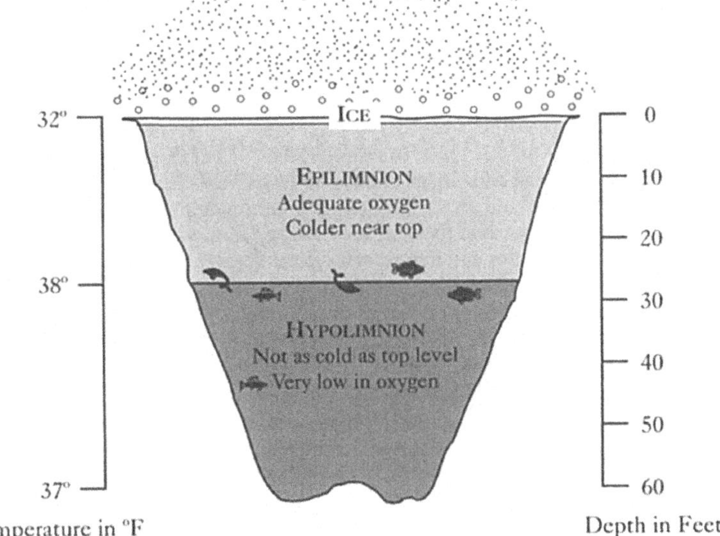

from 32 degrees at the top to 39 degrees at the bottom. Ice cover, preventing the wind from circulating the water, causes winter stagnation. Thick ice and heavy snow-rare on Cape Cod-shuts out light to the lake, and may stop photosynthesis, reducing oxygen.

Smaller, shallower lakes freeze (and thaw) first. After the autumn turnover fish feeding spree, most fish become inactive as temperatures drop and oxygen levels decline. Many of the lake's animals hibernate in the mud and debris at the bottom of the lake.

Spring

As temperatures rise in spring and the lake's ice melts, the water warms above 39.2 degrees and becomes more dense, causing it to sink. Aided by the spring winds, circulation and mixing occur –similar to the autumn- until the water temperature is essentially uniform throughout the entire lake. Again, just as in the autumn, fish and other animals are active and widely distributed.

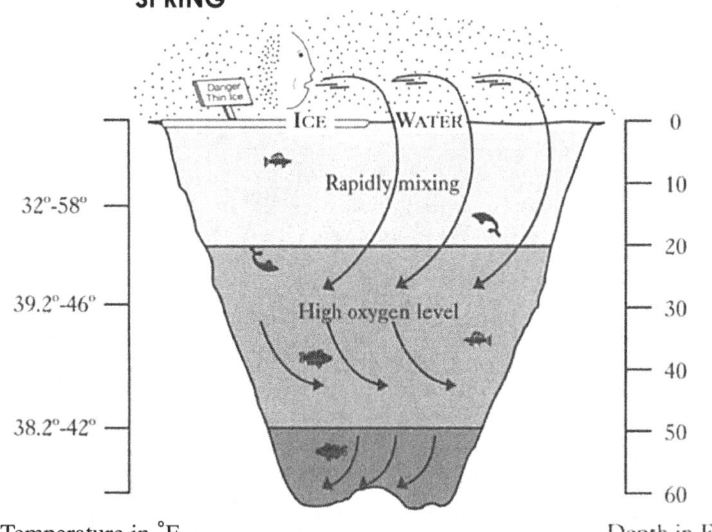

Pond Habitats:

Which Critters Live Where

The plants and animals in a pond or lake live in four different areas:

1. SURFACE FILM
2. SHORE
3. OPEN WATER
4. BOTTOM

In forming a mental picture of these zones it is helpful to imagine a bird's eye view of the water, looking down at it from high above and seeing the four zones as roughly concentric circles around the pond starting with the first ring from the shore, the emergent plant zone, then the floating plant zone further out, followed by the submersed plant zone yet further away from the shore and, finally, in the center, the eye of the pond, its bottom with no rooted plants.

1. SURFACE FILM

The surface film of a lake has the qualities of an elastic membrane and, as such, takes a specific weight to penetrate it. Light insects such as water scorpions and whirligig beetles have adapted legs and other devices that enable them to walk on the surface film without breaking through. Imagine them as Fred

Astaire and Ginger Rogers, gliding across the surface of the pond, their watery ballroom floor. Some plants and insects are adapted to life only on the upper side of the surface film. On the underside of the surface film, the larvae of some flies and beetles such as mosquito larvae and water scavenger beetles hang, without penetrating the surface above. The floating plants, upper and under surface film insects and other air breathing, floating animals are fed upon and are the prey of one another.

The pupa form of many aquatic insects such as the mayfly, damselfly, dragonfly, and frogs and water snakes comprise a broad menu of offerings to each other as well as to the lake's fish population. The surface film habitat and its critters have given rise to thousands of man made surface lures and flies designed to capitalize on this highly populated area of a lake.

2. SHORE HABITAT

Lake scientists call this area that starts at the water's edge and extends outward as far as rooted plants grow, the littoral habitat. In most of Cape Cod's ponds and in many of its shallow lakes, this habitat may extend from shore to shore.

Except where a shoreline is so swept by waves or rocky that plants cannot grow there, typically there are three distinct, concentric borders of flowering plants. The first border, closest to the shore, is called the emergent plant zone. It is comprised of plants rooted to the bottom which have stems, leaves, and often flowers above the surface. On Cape Cod's ponds and shallow lakes cattails, pickerelweed, sedges and grasses thrive in this zone. Among the stems of these plants are communities of algae, protozoans, insects, worms, snails, and small fish. Food and shelter are found in this area by many types of birds, frogs, and mammals. Since this area is so alive with various creatures, it is a prime locale to fish for virtually every species of fish found in Cape Cod's ponds and lakes.

The second border, extending a little further out into the pond, is the floating-leaf plant zone. Water ferns, duckweeds, and broad flat-leaved water lilies characterize this zone. Some snails, bugs, and mayflies lay their eggs on the undersides of leaves. Pumpkinseed, bluegills and largemouth bass spawn in this zone, their nests distinctive circles of sand and gravel interspersed among the bottom plants and debris in the spring.

The third band of vegetation, furthest away from the shore, is the submersed plant zone. Water milfoil-the plant of a thousand leaves-sends its long and bushy branches reaching up from its roots in the lake's depths. The sinuous leaves of water smartweed emerge from their roots in whorls that cluster and can form dense masses in some ponds.

Beyond the submersed zone are the dark depths of a pond or lake which may receive too little light to support plants and the process of photosynthesis. At this level, the basement of the stillwater, there are no rooted plants, just the decaying detritus of the each year's plants from the other zones.

3. OPEN WATER

Where the plant zones of the pond end, the open water area of a pond starts. Here is the area the larger fishes, turtles and birds frequent. The deep, open water of lakes supports the drifters that far outnumber all the larger lake inhabitants. They are microscopic plant life- phytoplankton- and microscopic animal life- zooplankton. Mostly algae, phytoplancton are the basic food in stillwaters. Tiny crustaceans, insect larvae, rotifers and other invertebrates comprise the zooplancton communities which, together with the microscopic plants, float about the lake like herbal seasoning and stock in a soup that feed the small plant and animal eaters in the pond. They in turn are fed upon by the medium sized carnivores, such as beetle and dragonfly larvae and small fish which capture them throughout a pond (but which favor the plant zones). They, in turn, supply food for the larger carnivores at the top of the food pyramid.

4. BOTTOM

From shore to pond center, the bottom offers a variety of living conditions and inhabitants. Snails, worms, and insects live in shallow, sandy bottoms. The bottom muds of still, quiet ponds are inhabited by mayfly, damselfly and dragonfly nymphs as well as crayfish which may shuttle to and from their preferred rocky hideaways in search for carrion, much like lobsters and crabs in salt water. In bottoms of large, deep lakes there is little to attract significant life beyond some worms, small clams and fly larvae. The bacteria of decay that are abundant on the bottom among the dead vegetation are important in returning chemicals to the life cycle of the stillwater. Throughout a stillwater, and however slowly in its depths, all dead life forms are eventually recycled.

(The Habitat section above was adapted in large part from POND LIFE, Reid, et al, Golden Press, N.Y.)

"...seasons are theatrical. Each one enters like a prima donna, convinced its performance is the reason the world has people in it."

BELOVED, TONI MORRISON

Cast 2:

BASS

> *"The honest, enthusiastic, unrestrained, wholehearted way that a largemouth wallops a surface lure has endeared him forever to my heart. Nothing that the smallmouth does can compare with the announced strike of his big-mouthed cousin."*
>
> JOHN ALDEN KNIGHT, BLACK BASS

Broad smile vies with large mouth on youngster's trophy Cape Cod bass. (Courtesy of The Bait Shack)

LARGEMOUTH BASS

Appearance: non Massachusetts native fish, they were introduced from New York and elsewhere in the 1800s. Depending on the water in which they live, largemouth bass may be mostly black or brown on top shading to mottled black with olive or grass green, silvery, bronze or white along the sides. The black back, grass green sides shading to white is the dominant coloration of largemouth bass living in the Cape's mostly clear, untinted lakes and ponds. A sometimes irregular but distinctive horizontal black band is apparent along the center of the flanks. It has an extraordinarily large mouth from which its common name is derived. Also often referred to as black bass, a name which becomes apparent when fish are taken from tannic waters. A favored fish on Cape Cod, the largemouth bass is among the most popular game fish in America.

Perfect example of a trophy Cape Cod largemouth bass, released after being photographed. (Capute photo)

Habitat: Prefer shallow, warm water bodies with weed beds and adjacent depths. Plenty of such waters can be found on the Cape. They are a prime fishing target in the summer, late afternoon into dark, when they are actively pursuing prey. Smaller fish will be taken throughout the day.

Cape Cod caught, admired, released.
(Bait Shack photo)

Size: Grow at a rate of nearly one pound per year by feeding on anything it can fit in its big mouth-crayfish, salamanders, snakes, tiny ducklings, other fish big and small.

Any fish over 2 pounds will provide good sport and the Cape produces many of these. Happily, it also provides a bonanza of fish in the 4-10 pound range. ***Minimum legal length is 12" /5 fish per day limit.***

State record: 15 pounds, 8 ounces. Sampson's Pond, Carver, 1975, through the ice.

Best methods:Generally, bass feed by hiding and pouncing

- **Live bait,** from nightcrawlers to frogs to minnows, fished 18"-2 feet below a bobber is the most reliable way to catch these fish.

-**Artificials** such as plastic worms and other soft body lures like the Sluggo, jigs with pork rind, spinner baits, floating plugs- Jitterbug, Hula Popper-swimming and diving plugs and many others all ring the dinner bell for these hungry and aggressive feeders.

-With a **fly rod** cast large floating, floating/diving, or popping flies-such as Sneaky Pete, Master Blaster-twitch with long pauses in between, and hold on for great surface action.

Tips: -To increase the chance of a 4 + pound fish, use the biggest shiner or mummichog available under a bobber.

-Better yet, save a small pumpkinseed sunfish yellow perch, or small trout imitation (á la Du Clos) to use just as you would a shiner. As a natural bait that is always on the bass's menu, you can count on some excitement from this ploy.

-If baby bunker are available in the fall, using a fish finder rig, hook the largest through the lips and cast to deep holes. Leave the reel on free spool so as not to alert the fish which will run a short way with the bait. Then engage the reel, set the hook and turn red. The action will be non stop.

Best Cape Cod Ponds:

Ashumet Pond, Mashpee/Falmouth
Wequaquet Lake, Barnstable
John's Pond, Mashpee
Long Pond, Brewster
Mashpee-Wakeby Pond, Mashpee
(Many other Cape Cod ponds, big and small, hold largemouth bass.)

East Coast-West Coast BIG!!! Bass Trivia: Paul DuClos, formerly of Seekonk, now of Santa Rosa California, practices the "big lure=big fish" theory. To call him an avid bass angler is understatement. He has caught and released almost 140 bass that weighed over 10 pounds and 4 over 16 pounds. Once in California's Castaic Lake he cast an 8 1/2 inch version of the Ken Huddleston Castaic Trout Lure. (Trout are a favored food of California's giant largemouths.) The lure was handmade, silver,with a jointed wooden body and soft plastic fins and tail. The head is equipped with a short diving lip which gets the lure down to 17 feet.

Paul proceeded to catch, weigh, photograph and release what is an unofficial new world record largemouth bass, surpassing the long standing 22 pound, 4 ounce largemouth taken from Montgomery Lake, Georgia in 1932. Paul's fish weighed an even 24 pounds.

You can see Paul and his fish on worldrecordbass.com or in the book, SECRETS of the BASS PROS, North American Fishing Club, 1998, pages 16, 17, 18.

SMALLMOUTH BASS

Appearance: The smallmouth bass is similar in body shape and general coloration to the largemouth bass. It can be distinguished from the largemouth in several ways: its mouth, when closed, does not extend beyond the eye, as it does in the largemouth; the front and back dorsal fins are connected, unlike the largemouth's which are separated by a notch. Not as potbellied as a big largemouth, the smallmouth has a more compact, athletic build. Its dark brown-black back fades to brown, bronze and olive with darker olive vertical lines along the flanks. It lacks the prominent horizontal line of the largemouth bass. Running smaller in the mouth and overall size than the largemouth, the smallmouth bass nonetheless is in a league of its own. It is one of North America's most important freshwater sport fish and is the fish of choice for many knowledgeable Cape Cod anglers. Ounce for ounce and pound for pound it outfights all other freshwater fish of equal or greater weight. It is a strong puller and continuous leaper that slaps back to the water with a resounding and startling crash. Where the largemouth is a big framed heavyweight fighter using its heft and power trying to muscle its way off the line, the smallmouth is well defined in the body, a fast and agile boxer using its rod bending diving, sprinting and acrobatic leaping to gain its freedom.

Catch a Cape Cod smallmouth bass with these dimensions and you will never forget the experience. (Courtesy of Jeff Capute)

Habitat: Prefers deep, cold, clear lakes with rocky, rubbly, gravel bottoms. It will hunt near but does not favor underwater weeds. It feeds primarily on aquatic insects, especially helgramites- the larval stage of the dragonfly- small fish, and crayfish, all of which it hunts in the shallower shorelines and mid-level depths of the lakes. Often, though not always, they are caught in the same lakes on Cape Cod shared with largemouths and of course, favoring colder waters, are often caught in trout waters.
Size: Takes 3-4 years to reach 12 inches and one pound in weight. A fish of 4 pounds is about 10 years old. ***Minimum legal length is 12"/ 5 fish per day limit.***
World record: 11 pounds, 15 ounces. Dale Hollow, Kentucky.
State record: 8 pounds, 2 ounces. Wachusett Reservoir, 1991
Best methods: -**Live bait**-worms, crayfish, minnows-under a bobber or off the bottom are most productive.
-Will strike at smaller versions of all **lures** used for largemouths. Remember that, preferring cooler waters than largemouths, smallmouths tend to hold in deeper waters.
-Try weighted deep swimming wet **flies**-Bead Head Prince, Kaufmann's Stone, Flashback Scud nymphs- and crayfish and leech imitations-Bead Head Wooly Bugger, Bead Head Muddler, Bunny Crayfish,Leadeye Leech, Soft Shell Crayfish- scooted along the bottom the way crayfish swim when avoiding attack, or slowly in short pulls like leeches swim.
Tips: -Adapt spin fishing equipment to fish flies by pinching on sufficient split shot 6-12" above the fly.
-Even in the heat of summer, if you can locate a deep hole on a lake, fish off the bottom with worms. Move around 'til you find them and you'll be into steady action.
-Salt water grass shrimp, usually available at Cape bait stores, are deadly hooked 2-3 on a hook and dropped from a boat after chumming the area.
-To chum, place a rock in a small lunch bag, deposit a handful of grass shrimp in the bag, crumple the top of the bag and drop over the side of the boat. Shortly the water will open the bag, release the grass shrimp and ring the dinner bell for the smallmouths.
-Nothing beats crayfish but they are seldom available at bait stores. Turn over rocks near shore and capture them or bait a purchased crayfish trap with fish scraps and leave it overnight in a gravely/rocky shallow. A little water under some weeds on the bottom of a small, covered styrofoam cooler will keep them alive in the refrigerator. Fill and seal a sandwich bag with some ice cubes and place it in the cooler when you head out to fish. The bag will keep them cool and, when the cubes melt, the water will stay in the bag rather than adding too much water with the bait.
Best Cape Cod Ponds:
Great Herring Pond, Bourne
Cliff Pond, Brewster
Mashpee-Wakeby Pond, Mashpee
Flax Pond, Brewster
Ashumet Pond, Falmouth/Mashpee
Long Pond, Brewster
Johns Pond, Mashpee
Peters Pond, Sandwich
Sheep Pond, Brewster
Spectacle Pond, Sandwich

Cast 3:

TROUT

> *"The legend of the trout's sagacity arises from man's conceit. If the trout can outwit us, the lords of creation, he must be superior to us in cunning."*
>
> P.B.M. ALLAN, Trout Heresy

RAINBOW TROUT

"My heart leaps up when I behold a rainbow in the sky."

WILLIAM WORDSWORTH

Appearance: Blue or green back profusely covered with black spots. Sides are silver shading to white on the bottom. Extending along the sides from the snout to the tail stem, is a pink blush to a rosy, iridescent band which distinguishes this type of trout and gives rise to its name, rainbow. The intensity of the back colors, spots, and lateral band varies with strain, age, and the chemistry of individual waters. As a general rule, the clearer lakes tend to yield a silvery fish with lighter spotting and a light blushing pink lateral band, such as the rainbow trout from the gin clear waters of **Cliff Pond, Brewster,** for example. Tinted, darker Cape trout waters, of which there are few, produce proportionately darker and more vividly crimson fish. Spawning rainbows usually darken, become more distinctly colored and may even develop a kype (hooked jaw) such as may be caught in the fall in **Goose Pond, Chatham** and other trout waters. Rainbow trout are leapers, the ballerinas of the trout family and a joy to dance with on the end of the line.

Deeply colored spring rainbow trout taken from Crystal Lake, Orleans.

Habitat: Rainbows will be found near the surface of lakes and ponds if the water temperature is below 70 degrees F. As the surface water warms, they seek their comfort zone of 56-65 F. The rule of thumb is early and late in the day and in the year, fish the upper

water columns; mid day and mid summer, fish the depths. Stocked rainbow trout tend to cruise the perimeter of a lake in search of food so they will be caught virtually anywhere.
Size: 10-12" sized stocked fish are the rule. MDFW, to their great credit, has done significant stocking of larger fish, 14-18 ", in more heavily fished lakes, supplementing the few holdovers-fish that survive and grow beyond a year- and that are a thrill to hook. Very little natural reproduction occurs. Virtually all MA trout , even some quite large specimens, are products of the excellent MDFW hatcheries and stocking program. *"If the object is to catch an award winner (minimum of 4 pounds, 20 3/4 inches long, 13 inch girth) keep in mind that our stocking crews typically release the largest trout in the lakes that receive the highest fishing pressure." Steve Hurley,* **MDFW**

No minimum length requirement. **Check the annual MassWildlife Abstracts for daily creel limits.**
World Record: 52 pounds, 8 ounces. Jewel Lake, B.C.
State Record: 13 pounds, 13 ounces. Wachusett Reservoir, 1999.
Best Methods: Generally, trout feed by cruising and searching.
-Worms, whole kernel corn, salmon eggs, marshmallows, and combinations fished on the bottom are very productive.
-Easiest way to catch stocked trout is Berkeley's Powerbait. This bait approximates the size of the pellet food used in hatcheries, is richly scented, floats above the weeds if fished on a weight off the bottom, and is irresistible to trout. Some folks feel it should be banned.
-Cast a Thomas Cyclone, Al's Goldfish, Wabler, or any number of small spoons, as well as small floating/diving Rappalas.
-Fly cast the Hendrickson, Cahill, Hornberg on top; Zug Bug, Gold Ribbed Hares Ear, Muskrat in the depths; or swim a Wooly Worm, Black Ghost, Muddler Minnow (weighted), Matuka, or bead head Wooly Bugger throughout the water column.
Tips: -Rainbow trout are partial to baits with scent. Try dabbing your bait or lure with anise (available in the spice section of the super market) or spraying on some commercially made fish scent.
-If you can net some baby alewives in

"A comet! A star! A ball of light!" The manner in which a rainbow trout fights. Seabiscuit (again), as described by daughter of jockey, Red Pollard.

the fall, gently lip hook one (from bottom up) , pinch on a small split shot 6 " above the hook, and fish a light bobber 18-36" above the bait. Rainbows can't resist these delectable, protein rich morsels.

-If rainbows are feeding on the surface but snubbing your dry flies, try smaller sizes to 20, 22, 24. Often, that will change your luck.

-Spring and fall, on a floating fly line with a 9 foot leader, 5 pound test tippet, tie on a brown or black Wooly Worm and retrieve it in steady 3 foot pulls, pause 5 seconds, pull, repeat.

Best Cape Cod Ponds: *-All Ponds in Nickerson State Park, Brewster*
Gull Pond, Wellfleet
John's Pond, Mashpee
Peters Pond, Sandwich
Shubael Pond, Barnstable
Spectacle Pond, Sandwich

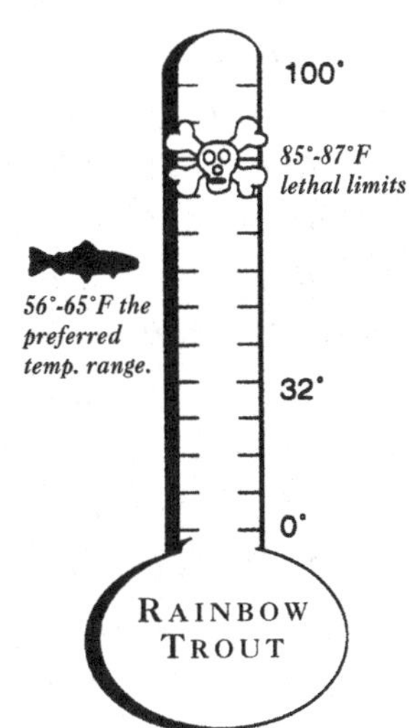

Wary brown trout that succumbed to a skilled angler's offerings. (Courtesy of the Bait Shack)

BROWN TROUT

Appearance: Its generally golden to straw colored back and sides are covered with large brown or black spots which are often surrounded by halos of color lighter than the rest of the body. A smaller number of orange or red spots intermingle with the black spots along the lower sides and lateral area. Scales of brown trout are more evident than on other trout. Big browns from the Cape's larger, deeper, clear lakes are often silvery with black Xs along the body, very similar to Atlantic Salmon, to which they are related.

Habitat: Of the trout in Cape Cod ponds, the brown is the hardiest, lives the longest, and is the most difficult to catch. As a result, stocked browns holdover (do not get caught or die from predation or other natural causes as easily as the brook and rainbow trout) to the greatest extent from year to year and, feeding almost exclusively on a diet of protein rich bait fish, they grow to substantial size. The preferred temperature range of the transplanted European brown trout is 54-64 degrees F, but they can tolerate warm temperatures in the low to mid 80s as well as more polluted conditions than the brook trout. Fortunately, most of the Cape's clean trout stocked ponds are deep enough to have a layer of cooler water even in the summer during prolonged heat waves and drought conditions. In some ways, the introduction of the European brown trout has been the salvation of trout fishing in the Northeast. Yet, for some time, not every angler was overjoyed, and even blamed the brown for the decline of the brook trout. In fact, deforestation and the resulting warming of the watershed, together with the polluting effects of the industrial revolution, rendered our waters unsuitable for the brook trout as surely as the construction of dams to harness water power in the 18th and 19th centuries destroyed much of the Atlantic Salmon habitat. More a savior than a butcher, the brown now rivals the rainbow as the most popular trout worldwide.

"The imported brown or German trout is rapidly becoming the butcher of our mountain brook beauties, fontinalis..."

TROUT & SALMON, SAGE, TOWNSEND, SMITH, & HARRIS. MACMILLAN CO. 1924

Holdover brown trout captured and then given its freedom. (Bait Shack photo)

Size: Fish are stocked at sizes ranging from 10-14 inches, with a few stocked in more popular Cape ponds in the 18-20 inch range. Because they are more likely to holdover, anglers skillful enough to outwit this wary species occasionally land fish in the 20-25 inch, 4-8 pound range.

TROUT IQ Based on the degree of difficulty in catching the three major species of Cape Cod trout, it is generally agreed that brook trout, are least difficult, followed by rainbow trout, with brown trout the most difficult to catch. Browns are the trout most likely to hold over the winter on the Cape and grow to trophy size in a couple of years. In considering the IQ of trout, any fish for that matter, it is prudent to be cautious. These animals,seemingly so low on the evolutionary scale, continue, day in and day out, to make monkeys out of anglers.

State record: 19 pounds, 10 ounces. Wachusett Reservoir, 1966.

Best methods: -Larger **minnows** hooked on a fish finder rig, in deep holes, early and late in the day are the best bet.

-**Troll** a Dave Davis spinner with a night crawler, deep, either with lead core line or monofilament, slowly.

-**Fly cast** large flies such as Turck's Tarantula, Stimulator, Muddler Minnow on top, at sunset and into dark.

Tips: -Brown trout are easily frightened; approach the lake's edge slowly, treading lightly, not talking, and keeping a low profile by trying to blend in with the background.

Rip Collins & his world record brown trout – 40 pounds, 4 ounces! Caught on a 1/32 ounce, marabou Olive Nymph. (Information courtesy of Danny Hicks, In-Fisherman. Photo courtesy of Arkansas Game & Fish Commission.)

-At dawn brown trout may be in the shallows chasing smaller fish. Try live lining shiners; casting a Wabler, Al's Goldfish, Cyclone; on a floating fly line with a 9' leader try classic streamers –Gray Ghost, Mickey Finn, Warden's Worry, Blacknose Dace-cast well ahead of sighted fish.

-Small 1 1/2- 2 1/2 inch floating/swimming Rapalas in a silver shad finish imitate a favored brown trout food.

-If fly fishing other than early or late in the day, use a sinking line with large streamers such as a Woolhead Sculpin, Egg-Sucking Leech, bead head Wooly Bugger to tempt deep water browns.

Best Cape Cod Ponds:

Cliff Pond, Brewster
Flax Pond, Brewster
Goose Pond, Chatham
Gull Pond, Wellfleet
Peters Pond, Sandwich
Scargo Lake, Dennis
Sheep Pond, Brewster
Spectacle Pond, Sandwich

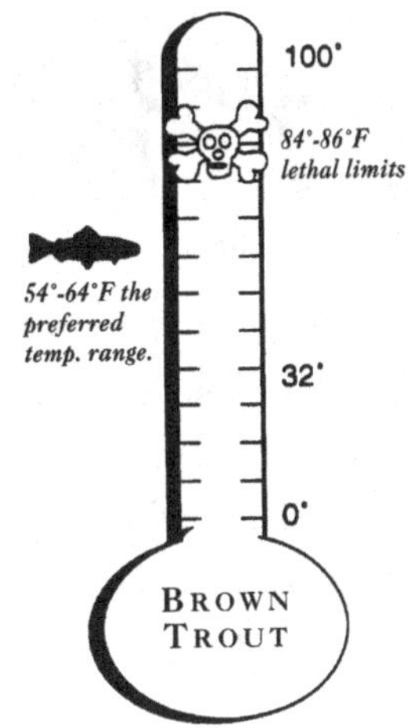

BROOK TROUT

Appearance: Thoreau wrote of the brook trout, " they glisten like the fairest of flowers." Any angler who has caught this trout in its breathtaking display of fall spawning colors can understand the special appeal of our only truly native eastern trout. The brook trout is identified by a dark back with lighter worm-like markings, yellow spots, and red spots surrounded by blue haloes along its sides. The lower fins are bright pink, orange, or red with a black border next to the white, leading edge, making a bold, dramatic contrast. In the fall, spawning colors become vivid, with males often displaying a brilliant pumpkin orange and even slashes of black on the lower flanks. Teeth are plentiful and sharp, something to keep in mind when removing hooks. The tail ,almost square, gives rise to one of its common names, "squaretail." Technically, this fish is not a true trout; it is a charr, related to the Dolly Varden and lake "trout."

A trio of dazzling brook trout (Bill Byrne photo)

Habitat: "Living in springs" is the English translation of the brook trout's scientific Latin name, salvelinus fontinalis. This captures the fish's preference for water temperatures of 57-61 degrees F, found only in clear, deep lakes, some fed by cold, underwater springs. During

New state record brook trout from a Cape Cod pond? It was eaten.

the heat of summer, they will seek out spring holes in a lake since they do not tolerate water temperatures above 68 F for any time and most will die in temperatures above 77° F.

Size: 10-12 inch stocked trout, with some of the MDFW's special 16-18 inchers stocked in popular ponds, are the norm. Comparatively, the brook trout is the smallest of the trout stocked in Cape Cod ponds. The world record is 14 1/2 pounds, less than half the record weight of the rainbow and brown trout. While brook trout of 5 pounds are commonly caught in Labrador, they get progressively smaller moving southward, and a fish over 2 pounds caught here is extraordinary and no doubt a stocked specimen.

NOTE: MDFW has been stocking Temiscamee brook trout from central Quebec.They are a wild, river strain that live longer-4+ years-and grow faster than other hatchery raised brook trout.

Cape Cod brook trout "glistens like the fairest of flowers". (MDFW -S. Hurley photo)

> *"...turned out to be the finest afternoon and evening of fishing I ever experienced, before or since. Brook trout weighing up to six pounds were congregated in enormous numbers in the gravel riffles off the foot of the island, and over the next several hours my grandfather and Donny Snowball and I caught and released hundreds. At last the trout wore me out. My casting arm ached from playing them, and as the sun lowered over the barren lands in a great wash of crimson and gold, I sat down on a boulder..."*
>
> *from* NORTHERN BORDERS, *by* HOWARD FRANK MOSHER

World Record: 14 pounds, 8 ounces. Nipigon River, Ontario, 1916

State Record: 6 pounds, 4 ounces. Otis Reservoir, 1968.

Best methods: -Noted for its gullibility, the brook trout becomes a sucker for worms in early spring when the waters are cold.

-Cast any small spoon such as a Wabler, Cyclone, Al's Goldfish, Phoebe, Daredevle and

retrieve at various speeds, occasionally stopping to let it flutter down a foot or two.
-Fly cast bright flies such as Parmachene Belle, Soldier Palmer and streamers such as a Mickey Finn or a Zonker.
Tips: -Bright is the way to a brook trout's stomach, so choose flies, lures, and baits that look like they marched in a Mardi Gras parade.
-Bright orange or red Berkeley Powerbait is double jeopardy for brook trout.
Best Cape Cod Ponds:

Great Pond, Truro
Hathaway Pond, Barnstable
Little Cliff Pond, Brewster
Mashpee-Wakeby Pond, Mashpee/Sandwich

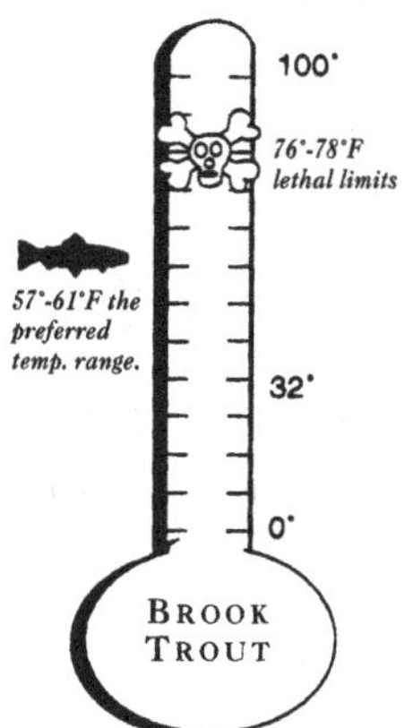

TIGER TROUT
Appearance: This sterile hybrid is a cross between a female brown trout and a male brook trout. A.J. McClane, in his Field Guide to Freshwater Fishes of North America says, "Tiger trout is descriptive not only of the color of this hybrid but also of its disposition. The progeny from this cross have tigerlike markings on their sides and are more aggressive than the parent species." Or as described in the 2000 Special Fishing Issue of Massachusetts Wildlife, "It has the base color of a brown but is covered with the squiggly vermiculations that brook trout sport only on their backs."
State Record: 9 pounds, 7 ounces. Peters Pond, Sandwich, 2004
Special Notes: -This fascinating hybrid is the product of MDFW experimentation begun in the 1950s. Thousands are now stocked across the Commonwealth with a number of Cape Cod ponds getting a generous share. They will grow to sizes larger than brook trout so the record is not expected to hold up very long.
-Tiger trout can be caught using any of the methods described for the other trout in this guide.

Annual Trout Stocking, Spring & Fall by Town

Annually, the MDFW stocks approximately 110,000 trout in the ponds and lakes of Cape Cod; 100,000 in the spring and 10,000 in the fall. Forty ponds receive the stocking and 41 streams also get a share. The ponds get the lion's share of rainbow, brook, and brown trout and, when available, tiger trout. On the following list, the underlined stillwaters are stocked in **both** the spring and fall.

All listed waters are stocked in the spring.
Those Underlined are stocked in spring and fall.

BARNSTABLE COUNTY

Barnstable: Hathaway Pond, Shubael Pond, Marstons Mill River, Lovell's Pond, Bridge Creek, Hamblin Pond

Brewster: Cliff Pond, Flax Pond, Sheep Pond, Higgins Pond, Stony Brook, Little Cliff Pond

Chatham: Goose Pond, Schoolhouse Pond

Dennis: Scargo Lake

Eastham: Herring Pond

Falmouth: Ashumet Pond, Coonamesset River, Mares Pond, Grews Pond, Deep Pond

Mashpee: Johns Pond, Mashpee-Wakeby Pond, Child's River

Orleans: Crystal Lake, Bakers Pond

Sandwich: Spectacle Pond, Peters Pond, Scorton Creek, Hoxie Pond, Pimlico Pond

Truro: Great Pond, Pamet River

Wellfleet: Gull Pond

Yarmouth: Long Pond

For stocking updates, go to www.masswildlife.org

Cape Cod tiger trout with the squiggly vermiculations of its brook trout father and the base color of its brown trout mother.

Cast 4:

PANFISH

"Fish say they have their stream and pond;
But is there any thing beyond?
And in that heaven of all their wish,
There shall be no more land, say fish."

HEAVEN, by Rupert Brooke, 1913

PUMPKINSEED, BLUEGILL, YELLOW PERCH, WHITE PERCH, CALICO BASS (CRAPPIE)

Panfish are so called due to their shape and delectability from the pan. Technically, they are of different fish families but they have at least two things in common: 1-they are relatively small and are not considered gamefish in the commonly held, though arguable, sense of the term, and 2- they taste great!

Their truly remarkable and diverse shapes and beauty, combined with their abundance in Cape Cod stillwaters, make them the fish of choice of many anglers.

They also pack a happy emotional charge-remember catching your first fish? Good chance it was a panfish of one kind or another.

"I have thus stood over them [the nests of sunfish in shallow water] half an hour at a time, and stroked them familiarly without frightening them, suffering them to nibble my fingers harmlessly, and seen them erect their dorsal fins in anger when my hand approached their ova, and have even taken them gently out of the water with my hands, though this cannot be accomplished by a sudden movement, however dexterous, for instant warning is conveyed to them through their denser element, but only by letting the fingers gradually close about them as they are poised over the palm, and with the utmost gentleness raising them slowly to the surface."

"A WEEK ON THE CONCORD & MERRIMACK RIVERS", HENRY DAVID THOREAU

PUMPKINSEED

A native species, pumpkinseed are referred to as the common sunfish; common because many anglers in the Northeast credit this as their very first fish. It is popular with children and adults for the same reasons as the bluegill.

Its pumpkinseed shape makes clear its name. Its most differentiating features from the bluegill are the red-tipped blue gill flap tipped

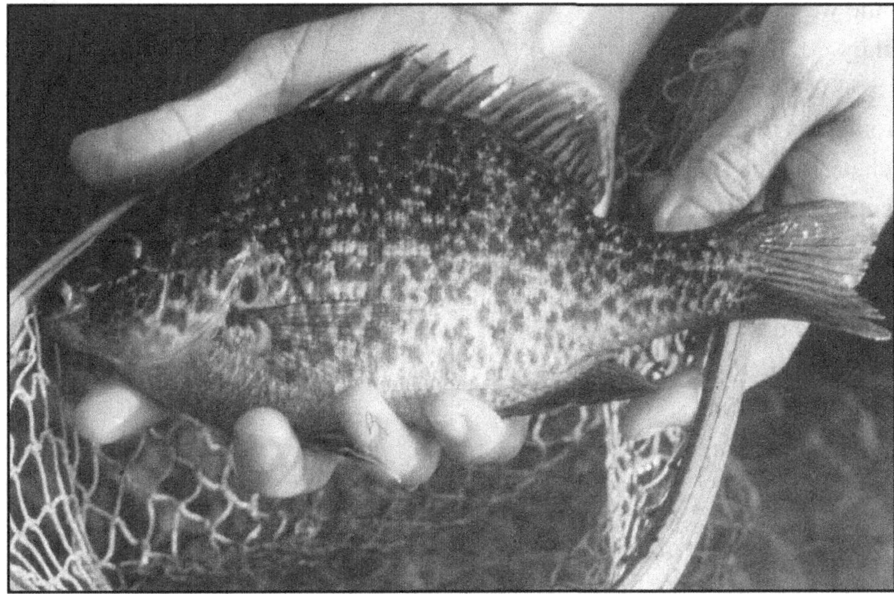
Cape Cod pumpkinseed, a bantam rooster with scales!

with red, the squiggly emerald blue lines radiating back from its snout across the eyes and across the gill cover, a yellow-orange belly, and flecks of gold across its sides, -a bantam rooster with scales ! Colorful? It's little wonder they bring a broad smile to the face of a little kid. Remember your first pumpkinseed?

Habitat: Essentially the same places that bluegills prefer. Add docks, logs, and overhanging branches.

Size: 4-6 inches, 1/3 - 1 pound, run somewhat smaller than bluegills.

State record: 1 pound, 6 ounces

Best methods: Same as bluegills.

Tips: Same as bluegills.

-If fly fishing, attach 2 feet of monofilament to the bend in the hook of a small popper. Tie a weighted wet fly, size 12 or 14, to the end of the mono. When a sunfish takes the wet fly the popper will go under like a bobber. Sometimes they'll hit the popper as well.

Top Cape Cod Ponds:

See the list next of bluegill ponds. All of those waters will contain a substantial population of pumpkinseeds.

BLUEGILL

Appearance: The bluegill is considered the most popular panfish in the USA. And for good reason. It is colorful-ranging variously from yellow but mostly to blue to dark blue- always with a totally black gill flap, with no trim (small, fingernail sized, at edge of gill where it meets the body). It is easily enticed to take myriad baits, lures, flies, and is a scrappy fighter that adds resistance to the bout by turning its broad body sideways, making it feel bigger on the end of the line than it actually is. It is delicious cooked up. A brawling, denim garbed cowpuncher in looks and behavior, this non native fish was introduced into Cape Cod stillwaters

WORLD'S LARGEST FRESHWATER FISH? A sturgeon caught in Russia weighing 2,250 pounds and measuring 14 feet.

from its natural range in the west and south.
Habitat: Not considered by MDFW to be as common on the Cape as it is elsewhere in the state, but given its prodigious reproductive capability, this will change in the near future. The bluegill prefers warm water ponds, still, weedy waters, swimming close to shore, with the bigger bluegills lurking in adjacent deeper water during the day, moving into shallows early and late in the day.
Size: 4-6 inches, 1/3 - 3/4 pound. 9" fish may be 6-8 years old . 15" maximum, up to 4 1/2 pounds, are very rare.
World record: 4 pounds, 12 ounce.
State record: 2 pounds, 1 ounce. South Athol Pond1982
Best methods: **-Bait** fishing with garden worm on small, long shank hook (less likely to be swallowed and easier to disgorge) 12-18" below a cork or plastic bobber.
-Casting and slowly retrieving or trolling a small Colorado spinner tipped with a little worm.
-Casting and slowly (just fast enough for blade to spin or spoon to flutter) retrieving or trolling a Mepps, Roostertail, Wabler, or any other small spoon or spinner.
-Fly casting small wet flies such as the Prince Nymph, Hares Ear, Olive Soft hackle. –Fly casting tiny poppers,size 10, such as the Orvis Bluegill Bug with feathers and rubber legs, any color, or a Foam Spider,twitched on top, can bring non-stop action.
Tips: -Cast and bounce retrieve tiny worm-tipped jig.

A Cape Cod bluegill, a denim clad brawler!

-Bring the fish to you by chumming. Throw a handful of crushed crackers or wetted and squeezed slice of white bread where you plan to fish. If you feed them they will come. Use sparingly or they won't want your offerings.
Top Cape Cod Ponds: Most of the waters listed in this section for all species of fish have consistently produced large trophy sized fish based on 30 years of data from the Massachusetts Division of Fisheries and Wildlife's (MDFW) Sportfishing awards pro-

gram, and information from the Division's Files.

Ashumet Pond
Falmouth Garretts Pond, Barnstable
Long Pond, Centerville
Wequaquet Lake, Barnstable
Mashpee-Wakeby Pond, Mashpee
Long Pond, Brewster
White Pond, Chatham
Great Pond, Eastham
Long Pond, Harwich
Pilgrim Lake, Orleans
Johns Pond, Mashpee
Santuit Pond, Mashpee

NOTE: Virtually every Cape Cod pond and lake in which largemouth bass are found will also have a population of pumpkinseeds and some will have bluegills. Every town on the Cape has at least one largemouth bass pond, most have several, and some have many.

Jumbo humpbacked yellow perch taken through the ice on a Cape Cod pond. (Courtesy of Jeff Capute)

YELLOW PERCH

Appearance: A relative of the popular, larger, and equally delicious Walleye, the native yellow perch has an elongated, and slightly compressed body which distinguishes the yellow perch from other panfish. The olive green and yellow alternating bands along the body set off a white belly and, together with bright orange-red fins, the end result is one of nature's most colorful creatures, a joy to behold. But only with the eyes; the fish's gill edges are razor sharp and its fins are prickly. Handle with care yourself as you remove them from children's hooks, showing them how to do it. Gently clamp down on center of gill covers with thumb and forefinger while sliding edge of palm over dorsal fin bringing it down and essentially disarming it. (I still get stabbed and cut.) Larger, "jumbo" perch have humped backs. (See photo.)

Habitat: Prefer clear, clean waters with sandy and rocky bottoms, of which there are many on Cape Cod. Prolific in reproduction, they travel in large schools of similarly sized fish. If you catch one, keep fishing in the same area.

Size: 1/4 pound fish is about 8 inches; 1/2 pound fish is about 10 inches; 3/4 pounder is about 12 inches; a 1 pound fish is 13-14 inches. From birth to about 8 inches the yellow perch is a food of choice for bass, pickerel, pike, large trout, and even jumbo yellow perch. Despite the fast action and good eating this fish provides anglers and predatory fish, some of these fish manage to live up to 11 years.

Mess of Seymour Pond yellow perch that fell for a Rooster Tail.

World record: 4 pounds, 3 ounce. Delaware River, New Jersey.
State record: 2 pounds, 12 ounces. South Watuppa Pond, Fall River, 1979
Best methods: -Garden **worms** on long shanked hooks, 1-1 1/2 feet below a bobber, as for bluegill and pumpkinseed. For the jumbo perch, replace the worm with a small 2-3 inch minnow. Pinch on a small split shot 6 " above the hook.
-Cast and bounce off bottom a small yellow Gitzit or similar tube jig.
-Fly cast a small-size 14-Hare's Ear, Soft Hackle, Montana, on a floating line, let the leader sink, then bring in slowly with little twitches. Use an intermediate sinking line with a 4 foot tippet if fish are in deeper water
Tips: - Yellow perch run you out of bait? Scale and cut a one inch football shaped piece out of the belly of a small perch. Cut one end up 1/3 of the strip to form a split tail. In opposite end insert a hook, add a split shot 6" above and cast. Bring it in, bouncing, stopping, one foot at a time. Perch will smell, feel and hit this and the bait will last longer than many other natural baits.

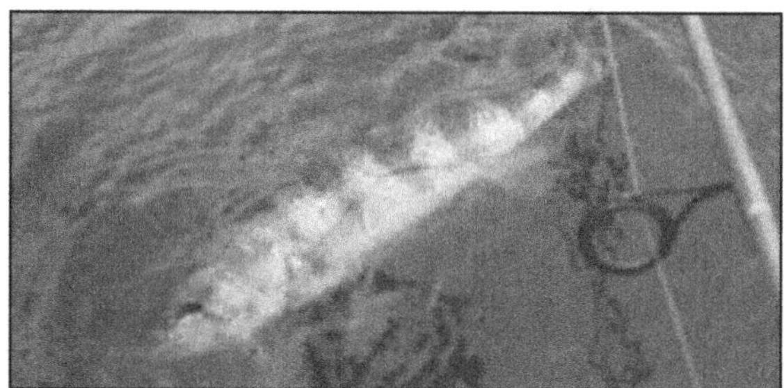

Mature yellow perch taken on grass shrimp from Seymour Pond.

-Try the small belly strip on a small jig, fished the same way.
-A productive perch tandem rig consists of a small spoon tied 8-10" below a swivel to which is also attached 6" of monofilament and a small wet fly. The eager eaters will attack the spoon while the timid takers will inhale the fly.

Best Cape Cod Ponds:

Wequaquet Lake, Barnstable
Cliff Pond, Brewster
Long Pond, Brewster
Hamblin Pond, Barnstable
Lawrence Pond,Sandwich

NOTE: Virtually every Cape Cod pond and lake with a population of largemouth or small-mouth bass will have a significant population of yellow perch.

WHITE PERCH

Appearance: Technically not a true perch, it is a member of the true bass family to which the striped bass belongs. Distinctly smaller, white perch are similar in body shape and, at times, in coloration to striped bass. Scientific distinctions notwithstanding, it is considered a panfish by anglers. When very young it has the familiar longitudinal stripes of the striped bass. As it matures the stripes fade and the body, depending on the water in which it lives, will take on a relatively uniform blackish, silver-plated, white, olive, or pewter hue. They are a prized table fish. As with yellow perch,be careful of their sharp fins and gill plates!

Habitat: White perch live in fresh, brackish, and pure saltwater. Many of those caught in Cape Cod ponds are fish that move between brackish water and freshwater via the many Cape ponds with brook, stream or river access to the sea. Many other white perch in Cape Cod ponds are landlocked resident populations.

Size: 1/2 - 1 pound, 8-10 inches are average. In some Cape Cod ponds, fish up to 15 inches and 2 pounds are frequently caught.

World record: 4 pounds, 12 ounce. Messalonskee Lake, Maine, 1949.

A Cape Cod white perch, technically a member of the true bass family, therefore related to the striped bass. (MDFW photo S. Hurley.)

State record: 3 pounds, 5 ounces. Wachusett Reservoir, 1994

Best methods: -Night crawlers on small long shanked hooks 12-18" below a bobber

-Cast and retrieve a small spinner tipped with a piece of nightcrawler

-Small, weighted wet **flies,** nymphs, streamers at the end of a 4 pound test, 9 foot leader will catch them.

Tips: -White perch do not confine themselves to the depths; they will be found throughout the water column. This dictates angling at various levels, regardless of bait, lure, or fly to find them.

-White perch, unlike yellow perch, are much more likely to take many of the top water flies listed in this book for bluegills and pumpkinseed.

-Spring fishing for white perch on any of the Cape's estuary rivers-Quashnet River, Falmouth/Mashpee; Mashpee River, Mashpee; Child's River, Falmouth; Coonamessett River, Falmouth- can produce fast fishing. Use sandworms instead of nightcrawlers.

Best Cape Cod Waters:
Long Pond, Brewster
Mashpee-Wakeby Pond, Mashpee
Snake Pond, Sandwich
Weweantic River, Wareham
Walker Pond, Brewster
Johns Pond, Mashpee
Middle Pond, Barnstable
Mystic Lake, Barnstable
Wequaquet Lake, Barnstable
Pilgrim Lake, Truro

BLACK CRAPPIE, AKA CALICO BASS

The black crappie is more commonly referred to in the Northeast as calico bass, a name derived from its mottled silver, olive and black blotched body coloration, vividly patterned tail, dorsal and anal fins, hence, "calico", and its flattened body, much larger than other sunfish, therefore more akin to a "bass" than the other sunfish. A fancy dancer,dressed for a night on the town, the beauty of this fish, edged with its diaphanous, mottled and striped butterfly- like tail and fins will make your eyes light up.

A fancy dancer, dressed for a night on the town.

Habitat: Clear still waters, preferably with underwater weed beds, sunken brush piles or logs. Usually found in large schools, especially during spring spawning period. *A non native fish introduced from the south and west, they are not as widely distributed on Cape Cod as they are in the rest of the state.*

Cape Cod calico bass, a water borne butterfly with diaphanous wings (MDFW photo S. Hurley)

Size: 6-12 inches average. Maximum 15+ inches, 2-3 pounds, rare. Prone to overpopulation and stunting, they go through cycles of abundance and scarcity.
World record: 4 pounds, 8 ounce. Kerr Lake, Virginia.
State record: 4 pounds, 10 ounces. Jake's Pond, Plymouth, 1980.
Special precaution: Thin,

papery membrane around its mouth results in lost fish if improperly played.

Best methods: - Hook small, 2-3 inch, live minnow through skin on back, pinch on small split shot 6" above hook, fished 1-2 feet below small bobber. Move to another spot if no action in 15 minutes. Once you locate a school you should catch many.

- Cast and retrieve smallest Mepps, Roostertail, 1/4 ounce Daredevl, Wabler or other small spoons or spinners.

-Fly cast size 8 or 10 Mickey Finn streamer on floating line with 4 pound test, 9' leader. Let fly sink for 5-10 seconds before starting sharp, 6" retrieve.

Tips: -With pliers, bend hook back slightly on bait rigs and jigs. This will induce more hookups in the tougher roof of the mouth and hence fewer lost fish.

-Play fish with slow, steady pressure rather than horsing them in and you will land more fish.

-In spring spawn if fish seem to be ignoring your minnow baited offering, remove the split shot to enable minnow to behave more naturally and lively. The added activity is usually enough to induce strikes.

Best Cape Cod Ponds:

Note: Calico Bass have only begun to appear on Cape Cod since the early '90s. They will become more abundant across the Cape over time. The ponds listed below are the best bets at this time and will increase and improve before very long.

Coonamessett Pond, Falmouth

Fresh Pond, Falmouth

(Lower) Shawme Pond, Sandwich

(The best near Cape Cod fishing for Calico Bass is in Agawam Mill Pond, Wareham.)

"They expect me to believe White Perch are related to this monster?"

Cast 5: PICKEREL

"The chain pickerel, the swiftest, wariest, and most ravenous of fishes, stately, ruminant, lurking under a pad at noon, still, circumspect, motionless as a jewel set in water."

THOREAU

"He ran with fire, slash, and zam!" Seabiscuit, as described by a sportswriter who could just as well have been describing the speedy fight of a pickerel. (Capute photo)

Appearance: In a lake's quiver of weapons designed to keep the food chain in balance, the pickerel, in appearance as well as predatory style, with its smooth, sleek torso, and dorsal and anal fins set back near the tail like matched feathers, is a well aimed and deadly hunting arrow. The Chain Pickerel, the type most likely to be caught in Cape ponds, has an elongated, torpedo shaped body with a flat duck bill shaped mouth loaded with sharp teeth. Its black-dark green back blends to obvious, green-gold chain links on the flanks. Be sure to have a long handled hook disgorger to avoid those nasty teeth.

Habitat: They prefer warm ponds or the warmer weedy bays of colder ponds. They lurk in the weeds or in the adjoining deeper, darker edges where they can use their explosive speed to pounce on unsuspecting prey. Their appearance in the water is menacing and can raise the hair on the back of your neck. Their bold behavior-attacking bait close to the boat or lures of all sizes-reinforces their scary appearance. They do have "attitude".

"I have caught one which had swallowed a brother pickerel half as large as itself, with the tail still visible in its mouth. Sometimes a striped snake, bound to greener meadows across the stream, ends it undulatory progress in the same receptacle." Thoreau. Monster Cape Cod chain pickerel.
(Courtesy of Goose Hummock.)

Size: 15 inches at 2 years old. 20 inches at 6 years. Seldom live beyond 6-10 years. Smaller than a pike, bigger than a red fin or grass pickerel, this native member of the pike family was the scourge of other sunfish and pumpkinseeds before the introduction of bass to Cape ponds over a hundred years ago. Despite the new guys in the 'hood, they hang tough and hefty sized fish are still regularly taken in many Cape ponds. **Minimum legal length is 15" / 5 per day limit.**
World record: 9 pounds, 6 ounces.
State record: 9 pounds, 5 ounces. Laurel Lake, Lee, 1954. MDFW states, " It remains one of the largest pickerel ever caught anywhere, and is by far our oldest standing record."

Best methods: -Minnows under a bobber fished along the edges of lily pads or at the drop offs beyond the weeds will surely attract pickerel, rocketing to the offering to beat the bass to it.
-Casting a weedless spoon such as a Johnson's Silver Minnow with a pork strip to the same areas will produce.
-Fly casting or trolling 3-5 inch rabbit strip streamers-Leadeye Leech-or feathered streamers-Moto's Minnow, Muddler, Gulley Worm-can lead to fierce, slashing strikes.
Tips: -The pickerel's sharp teeth often cut through light leaders, so if you are targeting this fish plan to use at least 12 pound test monofilament or a short piece of single strand wire leader.
-Attach a split yellow perch belly strip to a spinner or spoon to add scent as an inducement.
-Pickerel are delicious in a chowder. Their unique "Y" bones render filleting virtually impossible. Deal with this by removing the meat from the bones-much more easily- *after* the fish has been cooked.

Best Cape Cod Ponds:

Mashpee-Wakeby Pond, Mashpee
Depot Pond, Eastham
Wequaquet Lake, Barnstable
Great Pond, Eastham
Shallow Pond, Barnstable
Jenkins Pond, Falmouth
(upper) Mill Pond, Brewster
Pilgrim Lake, Orleans
Dennis Pond, Yarmouth
Blueberry Pond, Brewster
Sols Pond, Brewster

America's Most Popular Freshwater Gamefish?

Years ago, kids argued over whether Roy Rogers or Gene Autry was "King of the Cowboys". Today, some of the same kids debate the relative popularity of the black bass versus the trout as "King of America's Freshwater Gamefish". Many of those voting for the bass are motivated by their own sincere belief in the brute strength, rugged beauty, and hardiness of this great gamefish. Some critics maintain that too many of them, however, choose the bass based upon the incredible media hype surrounding bass tournaments. Catch and release notwithstanding, personal glory, money, and machismo, spawned by the industry and testosterone driven anglers popularize the bass through the ubiquitous and obscene tournament circus. To them the bass is king, if not the poor joker.

For others, few fish surpass the trout for beauty and challenge, rallying their supporters. " The trout's fighting spirit and gastronomic preference for insects delight anglers, who have spent centuries trying to outwit this brave fish. Trout are country gents, thriving in cool, clear water with gravel bottoms and plenty of dissolved oxygen." (POND LAKE RIVER SEA, Maryjo Koch) The trout's association with fly fishing spoils it for many anglers because of an image of snottiness projected by some fly fishermen. For most anglers, I am sure, as well as for myself, the fish, any fish, on the end of the line at the moment, gets our vote and settles the debate.

Which is America's most popular freshwater gamefish? (Bait Shack photo) (Capute photo)

Cast 6:

BONUS BRUTES

ATLANTIC SALMON, NORTHERN PIKE

(Limited availability but if you should be so lucky as to hook into one, you'll never forget it.)

ATLANTIC SALMON

"Speed that is known as 'kissing the boys goodbye!'" Describes an Atlantic salmon on the end of a fishing line. Also describes Seabiscuit (one last time) after beating War Admiral in the Santa Anita Handicap. (Bait Shack photo)

Appearance: Long considered the "King of Sportfish", the Atlantic Salmon is the glamour fish of Cape Cod freshwaters; glamorous because an angler would normally have to travel to Canada's Maritime provinces, at great expenditure of time and money just to cast to these fish returning from the North Atlantic to spawn in their birthwaters. Even legendary American fishers like Lee and Joan Wulff and Teddy Baseball spent many fishless days casting to these magical fish. Once believed so thickly found in many of the rivers in the Northeast that you could "walk across the river on their backs". Starting in the 1700s they were deprived of their spawning grounds and thus their reproductive capability by the damming of most of those rivers. The New England states' federally sponsored Atlantic Salmon Restoration project is a long term effort to help the reestablishment of this fish in its native waters. At theU.S. Fish & Wildlife Service's White River National Fish Hatchery in Vermont and at the Roger Reed Salmon Hatchery in Palmer, Massachusetts, fish hatchery employees from the Commonwealth pick up our annual allocation of brood stock salmon between 5-18 pounds, who have bred only once and who will be put out to pasture so to speak at selected ponds across the state, including three waters on Cape Cod. Each year the allocation varies but generally 100 or more are stocked in Cape Cod ponds.

NOTE: These true Atlantic Salmon (salmo salar) are not to be confused with the land-locked salmon (salmo salar sebago) which are stocked in other Baystate lakes, off Cape. The latter, also a joy to catch, are significantly smaller.

Habitat: Spring, fall and winter Atlantic Salmon are lake travelers, circling the edges between shallows and deep dropoffs. They will often chase bait into unlikely shallows, creating bulges in the surface with their 5-20 pound, 3 feet long bodies, raising blood pressure in anglers who sight them on such occasions.

Best Methods: Like trout, salmon feed by cruising and searching.

- **large, live shiners** or mummichogs fished with or without a bobber have been very successful.

-**try spin fishing** or trolling with a silver Wabler, any Mepps spinner, or a classic Mooselook Wobbler.

-**Fly cast** or troll any large, classic salmon single hook or tandem streamer such as the Grey Ghost, Black Ghost, Black Nose Dace, or Franke Shiner.

-Fly cast standard Atlantic salmon flies such as a Rusty Rat, Undertaker, Blue Charm or what Orvis touts as top fly, Ally's Shrimp.

A 17 pound, 7 ounce Atlantic salmon caught on a minnow under a bobber with 4 pound test line while drifting from a jon boat on Peters Pond in February. It towed the boat and took the angler two hours to land it.

World record: 79 pounds, Norway, 1928.

Tips: -If you find yourself fishing any of the Cape's three Atlantic Salmon stocked ponds using an ultra light outfit, say 2-4 pound test, and you intersect one of these brutes, you'll curse yourself all the way to the grave if it breaks you off, which it most likely will, unless you're very skillful and patient. To avoid such a scenario you may want to fish a heavier outfit using at least 6-8 pound test line.

-Those anglers who have caught and eaten them do not rave about the flavor, especially if the fish has been recently stocked from a hatchery and reared on pellet food rather than the natural foods in the lake. Maybe you should pull out the inexpensive, disposable camera you promised always to have with you, snap a few pictures, and release the fish. Another angler catching it will be indebted to you for your act of pure charity/good karma, since the other angler will be unaware of what you will have done, and you will never get "credit", which would taint the act of charity. But you will be one step closer to enlightenment.

Best (the ONLY!) Lakes and Ponds: At this time MDFW stocks only three Cape Cod ponds with surplus broodstock Atlantic Salmon:

Cliff Pond, Brewster
Sheep Pond, Brewster
Peters Pond, Sandwich

While few in number-approximately 20 in each pond-and stocked in only 3 Cape ponds, the Atlantic Salmon is the fish of a lifetime and can be fished for legally only in these and a few other stillwaters across the state. Whether or not you are fortunate enough to hook one, let alone land one, a debt of gratitude is owed our able state employees who have provided us with the opportunity even to try to catch one of these grand fish, a symbol of New England of yore.

Salmon Notes:

-Varied stocking dates:
winter, December-January
spring, April-June
fall, September
-Daily creel limit-2 salmon
-Minimum length- 15 inches
-Virtually any lure, fly, bait, or method used to catch trout will also catch these salmon. That is why if you are trout fishing Peters, Cliff, or Sheep Pond you may get the fishing shock of a lifetime by hooking into a leaping rocket weighing anywhere from 3-20 pounds.

Ponder this:

There has been universal agreement among historians and fisheries biologists regarding alleged "historic runs" of Atlantic salmon on the Connecticut and Merrimack Rivers (like those of the fabled salmon rivers of Maine and the Canadian Maritime Provinces) before they were extirpated by the dams erected in the 1800s. *"You could walk across the river on the backs of the salmon! Indentured servants complained of too much salmon in their diets."* (Similar to the lobster glut complaint familiar to all Cape Codders)

Many of these same biologists will agree that the restoration project has shown very limited success, puzzling all those associated with the project and trying mightily to come up with an explanation.

Recently, a very interesting question has been raised: "Were there really prodigious runs of Atlantic salmon on these rivers in pre colonial and pre industrial revolution eras, as believed?" John McPhee, in *The Founding Fish,* (American shad) makes reference to some fascinating piscatorial detective work. Scientific sleuths digging through native American, colonial, and 19th century middens (food refuse dumps) to ascertain with some certainty the diets of those who lived along the shores of eastern rivers, have turned up almost no Atlantic salmon fish bones among the bones of other fish, game, and raised animals eaten by these folks.

Is the Connecticut and Merrimack Rivers Atlantic Salmon Restoration Project really a *restoration* project? Or is it inadvertently and vainly attempting to *create* a fishery that, as widely held and perhaps without good scientific evidence, never actually existed and is incapable of existing as planned, possibly for as yet unknown biological reasons? Were/are these rivers now below the southernmost ideal breeding grounds of the Atlantic salmon? Don't know, but it will be fascinating to follow this development.

NORTHERN PIKE

Appearance: Generally speaking, members of the same esox genus, the Northern Pike resembles a pickerel on steroids. It is among the largest of all freshwater fish found in the Commonwealth's waters, topped only by the carp, the hippo of our fresh water world. But if the carp is a hippo, the northern pike is a tiger. Its dark green to brown background is mottled with golden morse code dots and dashes from head to tail. They sometimes sport red-orange fins.

Habitat: While they are stocked and angled for in a significant number of lakes in MA, on Cape Cod, the only place to fish for them is **Wequaquet Lake**, in Barnstable.

Pike are the lake's bay fish, where they generally can be found year 'round.In the spring pike prefer the lake's weedy bays, moving farther out into the edges and near drop offs as the weather warms. But they always return to the bays, for camouflage among the weeds improves their hunting prospects among the fish that share this rich environment.

Size: Stocked as 6-12 inch fingerlings they quickly reach the minimum 28" size in 3-5 years. Males do not grow much bigger but females are known to top 4 feet! Pike exceeding 20 pounds have been taken from this lake.

World record: 49 pounds, Lake Tachotogama, Quebec, 1890

State record: 35 pounds. Lake Quacumquasit (South Pond), Brookfield, 1988

Minimum length/creel limit: 28 inches, one fish per day

Best methods: Like bass, pike feed by hiding and pouncing

-Large, live shiners under a bobber.

-Bait cast large lures like Mepps Giant Killer, Tandem Bomber, Long- A Magnum, Eppinger Huskie-Jr., Lindy Giant tandem, Spin Eddy Bait, any giant sized Daredevle Spoon, and Bagley DB-06 (Most of which will have to be purchased through a catalogue due to limited availability on Cape Cod.)

-Fly fish with a Dahlberg Diver or any large, brightly colored salt water streamer such as Lefty's Deceiver or Cowen's baitfish. Tarpon flies like a Greenie Weenie or Purple Demon will also attract them.

Tips:- Northern Pike are so aggressive they can easily be fished out. Be especially aware of this

Angler with a 15 lb Cape Cod Northern Pike. (photo courtesy of Gene Bourque)

catching them in their only Cape Cod lake. Taking a photo and releasing the fish is the only proper thing to do.

-Bait or lure casting for these toothy creatures necessitates a thin wire leader. Don't risk losing a rare hook up. (I have had northerns sever 40 pound test monofilament shock tippet.)

-Fly fishing leaders should have a 12-18 inch tippet of 27 pound test, multi-strand coated wire.

-Northern pike plugs are most effective in the 4-12 inch range.

-A long (6-12") topwater stickbait or propbait can lead to savage, heart pounding surface action.

-If a pike follows your lure to the boat but does not hit, reel in all but about a foot of line, stick the rod tip in the water, and start making a figure 8 through the water. This often will induce a strike. If not, it's sure to make anybody watching laugh like hell.

-Ice fishing is considered the most effective method for catching northern pike. An angler caught and released a 19 pounder at Wequaquet lake in February, 2003, a great winter for Cape Cod ice fishers.

Cast 7:

FISHING CAPE COD WITH GUPPIES

A FISH FOR YOU
There once was a fish. (What more could you wish?)
He lived in the sea. (Where else would he be?)
He was caught on a line. (Whose line if not mine?)
So I brought him to you. (What else should I do?)

My first childhood "fishing" experience with adults occurred in the city, at night, and I was not allowed to fish. My father and Polish émigré grandfather brought me with them on a trip to South Boston's waterfront to fish for silver hake from a floating pier accessed by a gangplank.
While they and other mysterious looking men fished in the dark, I was left to my own devices. Adjusting to nocturnal vision, I roared up and down the slippery gangplank, along the perimeter of the shifting, creaking pier, trying to get closer to those catching fish, getting in the way as they swung their airborne, wriggling, slippery prey at me (so it seemed!) and all the while never once did I get my hands on a fishing pole.
To me, the highlights of the trip were that I found a gold Gruen wrist watch just as it was about to slip off the pier and into the briny deep, and that somehow, I managed to avoid the same fate.
I learned years later that the fishing rods that accompanied my grandfather on the ship from Europe to America were 20' expandable wooden poles-no match for a six year old- and that my father had indeed (I assumed this) kept a watchful eye on me that night and, to prove it, he sported the Gruen for years after.

Action focuses attention.

Despite the hazy afterglow of my fishing baptism, I will not recommend you follow the same formula.

If you have a child you want to introduce to freshwater fishing on Cape Cod, this advice may be of help. You can adapt the advice to fit the level of experience your youngster may already possess. I will assume you don't have a clue. This is first hand experience-not devoid of major blunders in introducing my two daughters and a son to this wonderful pastime. You will also benefit from my improved performance the second time around with my five grandchildren.

There are several considerations in fishing with young children, at least one of which is peculiar to Cape Cod, so let's start there.

CALENDAR/CLOCK

For tranquil fishing, from the beginning of September- mid June, you have the run of the Cape's 900+ ponds.

However, whether vacationing or living here but bound by school and job, after schools close through July and August, it's a totally different scenario. The height of the season finds most lakes clogged with squealing, splashing, bathers. The fish mostly give them a wide berth. If you were to visit a lake in the middle of the day, it would only be after negotiating the family car through the thronged roads and when you finally did arrive, may not find a parking space or, if you did, that a parking sticker is required.

So how *do* you get your kids fishing during the mad cap summer scrimmage?

Dawn or Dusk

Go early-rising before dawn, when most vacationers are asleep. Children enjoy the excitement of being awakened in the dark, rubbing the sleep from their eyes, dressing, clicking the seat belt, and downing the breakfast you prepared the night before. At dawn, the lake will be yours, serene and in its unfolding palette of splendor for 2-3 hours, more than enough, yet leaving you the shank of the day for other activities.

If a dawn trip strikes fear in your heart, head out at 5-6 p.m. when the bathers are baked, cranky, hungry and emigrating, leaving the place for you and the fish.

CLOUDY OR RAINY

These conditions drive bathers from the beaches to the town centers, malls, bowling

Rain doesn't bother the fish.

alleys and T shirt emporiums, leaving the waterways to eager anglers.

LITTLE LEGS, SHORT ATTENTION SPANS, AND "ONE MORE CAST!"

The most crucial factor in fishing with **children is paying attention to where they are developmentally.** They take two strides to your one, putting out twice the effort you do to cover the same ground. Their attention spans are proportionate to their size – relatively short. To keep them engaged, having fun, and looking forward to another fishing excursion, both you and the fish must be active. Catching-as opposed to just fishing-is critical. As a little kid, if she did not chain catch fish, my older daughter, Robin, concocted "fish supreme", a recipe of sand and fish slime stirred with a stick in a beach front hole. This worked to my advantage, providing time to find her younger brother , Doug, who had disappeared into the woods while I was baiting Robin's hook, at the same time carrying my younger daughter Jennifer on my shoulders because she was too young to have any semblance of an attention span for fishing. It also enabled me to look over at Doug's and my bobbers to see if the fish were nibbling. They were. They always do after you walk away from them. What's wrong with this picture?

To keep kids interested-and proud!- catching is important.

- **Guide only one child at a time** on a fishing trip, especially an inaugural one. Both of you will benefit from the focusing and attention to the details of the fishing ritual: baiting the hook, casting, reeling in slack, watching the bobber, setting the hook, bringing in the catch or rebaiting a stripped hook, disconnecting a fish from the hook, releasing the fish or putting it on the stringer, wiping your hands, and threading on another worm to begin the sequence anew. And you're doing this at the same time you're wiping a little nose, opening snacks, answering myriad questions, pointing out flora and fauna, and scanning for a nearby port- a- potty. Imagine doing this with more than one child.

-Child and fish will set the schedule. When the child asks if you know the recipe for fish supreme, take that as a cue to wrap up the trip.

My granddaughter, Chandler, quit after her first yellow perch. Releasing it, the fish's tail splashed water on her face. "Let's go home Poppa!" "Wait Chandler. Let Poppa take just one cast." "No Poppa, let's go home." Chandler, the youngest , with two older brothers, has learned to be assertive. Of course we went home.

At the other extreme, my nine year old grandson, Nate, who learned to handle a fishing outfit before he could feed himself and who would happily fish in a rain puddle, never wants to quit. There are trips with Nate when Poppa has to be assertive.

-Never fish at the same time you're fishing with a child. It's tempting but it just doesn't work; the child will lose out on the experience, subverting the objective.

- Capping off an introductory fishing excursion with a side trip for a treat-ice cream, brownie, any taboo goody will suffice- is a joyful way to complete the bonding, leaving a good taste, so to speak, in the child's memory.

Pumpkinseed and worms—fireworks for kids!

EQUIPMENT

Rods & Reels

Kid fishing dictates simple equipment. Four of my five grandchildren have two fishing outfits: an old fashioned bamboo pole rig and a close- faced spinning reel and rod. The first is durable, inexpensive, and simple-just flip it in the water. The second enables longer casts, and is easier for little hands and developing eye-hand coordination: press a button then release as the rod moves forward. Avoid open- faced spinning reels requiring more coordination and skill. Avoid cartoon character outfits; they are more toys than tools, more handicap than help. Nate, my fifth grandchild, shudders at the thought of a close-faced outfit-"They're for babies!"- long ago having graduated to more sophisticated gear.

Terminal Tackle

This refers to what is attached at the end of the line, critical, since its purpose is to connect fisher to fish. Only two items are necessary: hook, bobber. The bobber, affixed 18-24" above the hook, is the object of the child's focus. When it bobs or disappears all hell breaks loose. That's when you start yelling "Watch your bobber! Where did it go? Set the hook!" The bobber is key- the child's visual cue to action, necessary to keep a successful trip from morphing into fish supreme. Bring lots of bobbers. Lakeside trees are festooned with miscast bobbers.

Sources

Equipment can be purchased at Cape bait and tackle stores which will help in the selection of hook sizes, bobbers, line strength, and bait. Don't buy anything but worms for bait. "Dillies", worms smaller than anaconda- sized nightcrawlers, are perfect. They also keep indefinitely in the refrigerator. Covered, of course.

THE FISH

Set to music, vivacious, graceful, finely hued and balletic trout of colder freshwaters are Vivaldi's *Four Seasons*. But for ease of catching, beauty, fast action, and flavor, nothing is more melodious and ubiquitous for children than **SUNFISH**, the *Joy to the World* of warmwaters.They include pumpkinseeds, bluegills, yellow perch, and to a lesser extent, white perch and black crappie. Their varied shapes and vivid colors dazzle kids. Their haunts also produce largemouth bass, *King of the Road*, and pickerel, *Mack the Knife*. Careful of those teeth!

Forget trout; the action is simply not fast enough. Sunfish are abundant and eager eaters who create fishy fireworks-just what kids need to maintain their attention.

A TACKLE BOX FULL OF ADVICE

-License: Required at age 16.You also should have one.Questions? Call (508)792-7270 or www.masswildlife.org

-Comfort: -Dawn and dusk are buggy. Use kid safe repellent. Try NATRAPEL Sunscreen and Insect Repellent SPF 30, DEET Free www.natrapel.com Tick check before baths.

-Hooks: Use single, long shaft hooks, not treble hooks. Plier smash barbs on hooks to make fish release easier and to save a doctor trip if someone is impaled.

-Safety: In boats use a fitted, Type ll Personal Flotation Device on the child and yourself. Questions? Boating Safety Hotline 1-800-368-5647

-Cape Lakes: Buy a Butterworth Cape Cod & Islands Atlas & Guide Book. It contains nearly 100 lake maps with locations, size, and types of fish.
(508) 432-8200

-Keep or Release? Barb-crushed hooks enhance fish release. Before letting a child keep a fish to bring home, it usually works to ask first if she/he will eat it. If not, let the child release it. If keeping, bring a stringer. Fried sunfish are delectable.

-Buying Equipment: Try Cape bait and tackle stores,providing free local information. Yellow pages. Catalogues:

CABELA'S 1-800-237-4444 www.cabelas.com. Also BASS PRO SHOPS 1-800-227-7776 www.basspro.com

-Values/Ethics: Teach kids best by modeling behavior rather than preaching: all life is precious and should be treated with respect; don't leave trash and pick up any you see; don't crowd other anglers; avoid behavior that will spoil the serenity of your surroundings; model by your own behavior that fishing enjoyment is personal, not about consumerism, competing, winning prizes, but that you fish because fish live in beautiful, restorative places; articulate that we are fortunate to be able to participate in such a wonderful natural activity.

(Adapted from FISHING WITH GUPPIES, by Peter Budryk, originally published in the June, 2002 ,issue of Cape Cod Magazine. Included here with permission of Rabideaux Publishing.)

Kids catching their first fish will remember the experience (and YOU!) for the rest of their lives.

Cast 8:

FINDING TROUT & OTHER FISH IN CAPE COD LAKES AND PONDS

WHAT TO LOOK FOR
WHAT TO DO

> *"Fish! They manage to be so water-colored. Theirs is not the color of the bottom, but the color of the light itself, the light dissolved like a powder in the water. They disappear and reappear as if by spontaneous generation: sleight of fish."*
>
> ANNIE DILLARD (1974)

HEAVE & HOPE, OR...

A pond or lake can present an inscrutable face to an angler. How do you read a body of water that appears to offer a blank expression, giving no hint of its subsurface makeup? You know it holds fish, but where are they? Are they shallow or deep? Do you just pick out any spot, heave your offering, wait, and hope some fish will notice? Most anglers do just that: pick out a location that looks "fishy" and proceed to fish; sometimes they find more fish than at other times, and perhaps too often, on even other occasions, no fish at all.

As puzzling as a pond or lake may seem, especially one being fished for the first time, the angler can increase success by becoming a student of stillwaters. Approaching a body of water with some general knowledge of lake dynamics and structure as well as fish behavior, can help the angler solve the puzzles of open stillwater fishing.

First, consider that all fish have several basic needs: the need to eat, the need to escape from predators, the need to feel comfortable in its environment, and the need to reproduce, Each of these needs drives the fish to move about in a lake according to some patterns that if understood by the angler, can increase catches. It should quickly be pointed out, however, that no amount of knowledge is a guarantee for angling success. Obviously, fisheries biologists and lake scientists do not always catch their limits. However, this is no argument to fish lakes and ponds totally ignorant of at least some information that can put you into fish. Following is the most comprehensive list ever published of what to look for and what to do when fishing a lake or pond. As you learn and use them you will become more confident in your fishing and will discover other insights yourself that will increase your store of knowledge and add more enjoyment to your fishing.

RULES OF THUMB: Generally, trout fishing conditions improve with preferred water temperatures, a steady or rising barometer, overcast skies, and a surface ruffle. Conditions become less ideal for trout at the same time they become more suitable for bass and sunfish- as waters warm, the barometer falls, the sun

shines, and the lake is calm. The rule of thumb in color selection for lures and flies on overcast days is to use duller metals -- copper, colored, hammered spoons and dark colored- black, brown- flies which are more visible to fish under these conditions.

SURFACE ACTIVITY: Observe the water's surface for signs of trout activity. If you can see where the fish are, you do not have to guess. This is the single most effective way to locate trout in a lake or a pond. Bring along a pair of binoculars to assist you in scanning the surface. In fact, you may only see adult insect activity at the surface, while the trout are feeding on the swimming and pre-emergent insect forms beneath the surface. If you sight a cruising trout, anticipate the path of this surface feeding and cast ahead of it rather than right at it which usually spooks the fish. If bass are your quarry, look for splashing bass chasing bait in the shallow, weedy areas of the pond. Spend some time observing before you fish.

ANGLER ACTIVITY: The second best tip off can be the location of anglers along the shoreline or in boats. The key is activity: Are their rods bent? Are they moving about in the special hurried way that tells you something is happening? Or are they just sitting or standing along the shoreline, not even holding their rods? Are their boats moving all the time and not stopping to fight fish? Again, a pair of binoculars can provide you with the answers to these questions. If you do get tipped off to fish in this way, be courteous. Don't just move right next to the other anglers. Provide them some space to continue enjoying their fishing without feeling that some unthinking vulture has just swooped down on their lake. At times, circumstances may tell you there is no way you can get into their action without spoiling it

Chuck, native Bay Stater, now a Californian, returns to a Cape Cod lake heavily stocked with childhood memories and hoists a healthy smallmouth bass.

for them. When that is the case, pass it up and look for alternatives. They will appreciate this consideration just as you will when positions are reversed. Even in these cases, observe how they're fishing-- bait, depth, retrieve, etc.-- and you may learn something that will get you into fish at another spot on the lake. It's pleasant to interact with other anglers at times, but keep in mind that while not always possible on some Cape Cod lakes and ponds, most anglers are seeking a degree of solitude and tranquility rather than a crowded and possibly irritating confrontation with a thoughtless person.

Trophy Cape Cod trout caught and released. (Courtesy of Jeff Capute)

DRAIN THE LAKE: Unless you have a bottom contour map (not available for all of Cape Cod's trout ponds and lakes), how will you know how it is shaped beneath the surface, telling you where trout are likely to be lurking? Shoreline areas are distinctive and fairly easily read: gradually sloping areas usually continue that way into the water and steep, sharply falling shoreline areas do likewise. By observing the outline of the lake and noting elevations and other features along the shoreline that very likely continue their tendencies right into the water, you can use your imagination to help you "drain the lake" and guess at what the shape is like in many spots. Calm, sunny days are best for this. I never pass up the chance to look at lakes when on an airplane which provides another perspective on lake depths.

INLETS from streams are conveyor belts into the (handful of Cape Cod waters) that have them especially after rains, bringing an assortment of foods to waiting fish. In spring, spawning rainbows congregate near inlets as will brook and brown trout in the fall. Try salmon eggs, since trout follow spawning fish to feed on their eggs. During the heat of the summer, trout will often congregate off the mouths of inlets to take advantage of the cooler moving and more highly oxygenated waters.

CLIFFS OR STEEP HILLS at the shoreline usually mean deep water and shade close to shore. These areas provide insects that get blown or fall off the walls and into the water to opportunistic fish who cruise these areas or lie in the depths for comfort and safety.

WEEDS provide food and cover for insects, which are fed upon by baitfish, panfish, bass, and trout. The gamefish also pursue the bait and panfish. Weedy areas are the most likely places to find all gamefish at dawn and dusk and on overcast days in the spring and fall. Sharp dropoffs near weed beds provide easy escape and cooler waters for shuttling gamefish. Fish the open channels between emergent growth.

BAYS provide protection from the destructive forces of wind enabling more plants to grow and hence, more fish food.

SHOALS, like submerged islands, are bottom areas or reefs that swell up just beneath the surface of the lake. Their shallows harbor insects and bait fish while their nearby depths provide escape and comfort for gamefish.

WATER COLOR: light shades indicate shallow and dark shades indicate deep water on lakes and ponds. The dark shade can show you the location of deep underwater channels, dropoffs, and deep holes that offer cooler water, food and lower light for gamefish, trout in particular who will especially seek these areas on warm, sunny, calm days. When light conditions do not cooperate, try Thoreau's method of locating the deepest spot in the lake at the intersection of imaginary lines connecting a lake's longest and widest parts. The light shades can point the way to shoals and sandy bottoms which gamefish always prefer over muddy bottoms, and which trout will even use for spawning if the lake has no inlets. Quality polarized sunglasses are invaluable in reading lakes. In some countries, searching for fish in this way is called "polaroiding". Here we call it sight fishing.

POINTS OF LAND which extend into the lakes create an obstacle which cruising fish must go around , thus bringing them closer to shore and within casting range.

ISLANDS, with boulder strewn bottoms leading to sharp drop offs, provide food, comfort, and easy escape for feeding gamefish.

WIND: even a slight breeze ruffling the surface of a lake provides better conditions for all gamefish than a perfectly calm surface because they feel less vulnerable moving about foraging for food under the cover of the surface water movement.

CALM LANES: on breezy days they often provide slicks of flat water that hold insects trapped by winds. Gamefish cruise these areas for food.

FOAM LINES are created by the merging of winds from different directions. Insects get trapped in the foam, attracting fish to them. Look for them after a windy period. Often they will be offshore since the shoreline acts as a bufffer when the wind is blowing in and creates an underwater current literally bouncing off and moving away from the shoreline.

"Most lakes have a holdover of trout. How to get them is another story. In the spring, worms, corn, minnows. As the waters warm nymphs are best. A rule of thumb is 12-14 size, dark in the early season- going smaller and lighter in color later is the season. Don't forget ants, beetle, grasshopper imitations are sometimes deadly."

- Ken Hancock

WINDWARD SHORES are those that blow the wind directly in the face of the shore angler. Gamefish, trout, in particular, will often face into the wind offshore and feed on insects and disoriented baitfish that are driven to them near the surface. After a continuing wind, the force of wave action bouncing back off the shoreline will create an underwater action that then brings the bait out to deeper water in the opposite direction of the blowing wind. At times, a strong wind blowing parallel to a shallow sandy shoreline area dredges up insects and attracts fish. Look closely in these areas for porpoising trout. Although it can be uncomfortable, a windy day often is more productive than at most other times. (see the section on plastic bubble fishing)

LEEWARD SHORES are those on which the wind direction is from the back of the shoreline angler. Even on windy days, most lakes will provide a leeward or protected area of the shoreline that serves as a safe harbor for baitfish and which provides the necessary conditions for an insect hatch, both of which will attract trout and bass. If you don't like fishing into the wind, seek out these areas.

SHORELINE VEGETATION harbors insects that fall or are blown into the lake for trout and bass that patrol these areas. Use waders or a boat and cast close to the vegetation whether it grows thickly right into the water or if it is in the form of shoreline trees that grow out over the water. On sunny days, shady areas are most likely to hold bass and trout.

NORTHWEST CORNERS of lakes receive sunlight for the longest part of the day and as a result warm up earliest in the spring. Winter weary fish can be found foraging in these areas during early spring periods.

Light, Gravitational Pull, or Both?

Clear Water Conditions

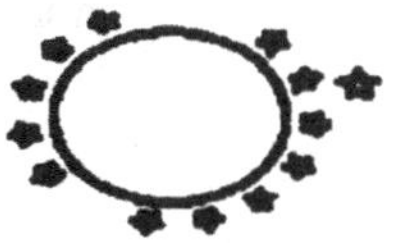

	Full Moon	New Moon
Daytime:	Best	Poorest
Night:	Poorest	Best

Unclear Water Conditions

	Full Moon	New Moon
Daytime:	Best	Poorest
Night:	Poorest	Best

OVERCAST DAYS are usually more productive because the fish feel more secure in moving about a lake than when the sun is shining, the depths are clearer, and their locations are thus more evident to predators. On these days trout can usually be caught near the surface as well as at other depths, especially if the water temperature is within their comfort zone.

> *"There is nothing more frustrating than seeing trout being taken by anglers near you and find that your efforts are not rewarding. There are no doubt hundreds of secrets in catching trout but we have found these following secrets as some of the more successful."*
>
> - Jack Meehl, Sr.

SUNNY DAYS are generally not as productive as overcast days, especially for trout, which nevertheless can still be caught. Studies have shown that on a clear, calm lake on a hot day, the sun's reflection off the silvery scales of a shiner is visible to trout and bass for distances of 25 feet or more. Use silver colored, reflective, or brightly colored spoons, spinners lures and flies to capitalize.

MAJOR TROUT FOOD SOURCES for your consideration in bait, fly, and lure selection, I offer one set of opinions listed in descending order:

1. midges, chironomids, mosquitos

2. forage fishes, smelt, alewives, shiners, fry of other fish
3. scuds (shrimplike creatures), crayfish
4. dragonflies and damsel flies
5. leeches
6. mayflies
7. caddisflies
8. terrestrials: ants,bees, grasshoppers, moths,
9. eggs: of all fish, including their own species
10. waterboatmen
11. snails (tough to imitate or get on hook)

Check this list out against your own experience. Analyze the stomach contents of any trout you keep (or use a stomach pump) noting the most common foods found at different lakes throughout the various months. This can help you anticipate bait, lure, and fly selection on your fishing trips. Of course, this requires conscientious record-keeping.

TROUT CATCHING SECRETS

-As with most skills one has to have the PROPER TOOLS to work with, so get quality fishing equipment and you'll fish better.

-Generally speaking, the LIGHTER THE LINE the more strikes. Lighter lines make for more natural presentations and movements overcoming wariness and leading to more strikes.
-One of the mysteries of trout fishing is that they take one thing today and not tomorrow. The willingness to SWITCH BAITS, LURES, FLIES and the concentration to vary retrieve speeds are very important.

-Early in the season trout are BAIT minded so garden worms, helgramites, crayfish, caddis nymphs, minnows, perch bugs, cheese balls, and salmon eggs are by far the most productive. At times you can turn fish on by throwing out a handful of salmon eggs or corn.

-At night big brown trout like BIG BAIT.

-Trout are sensitive to noise and shadows which signify danger. Be QUIET on your approach. Don't clank tackle boxes.

-Trout do most of their active feeding in the EARLY MORNING AND IN THE EVENING into nighttime. These hours most people are not at the lakes. For the 10% of the anglers who are there at the active feeding times this makes all the difference.

-For you skeptics who are still wondering about the PHASES OF THE MOON in regard to trout fishing, you'd better check it out and start using this information.

SPRING AND FALL STREAMER TROLLING

Streamer trolling is an old and revered trout-catching method said to have originated in New England. While I have trolled streamers with fly-fishing gear for a long time, with little luck, I discovered a streamer trolling method that has proved highly productive. The method is simple and somewhat unorthodox. Its simplicity rests in slowly trolling (#1 setting on an electric trolling motor) a streamer on relatively light spinning gear, using from 2 to 6-pound test untinted monofilament, from 75 to 100 feet

behind the boat. Its unorthodoxy lies in the use of a small, brass snap swivel to attach the streamer to the line. This is somewhat unusual because most anglers who fish with flies have been taught to believe that the juncture between fly and line should be as clean and uncluttered as possible to increase the natural appearance of the streamer that is imitating a living organism, usually a bait fish. When was the last time you saw a swivel-nosed shiner? No matter, the method works. I was introduced to it by a lake angler who showed me a stringer of rainbows and then proceeded to explain how he caught them, indicating that he produces his limit this way with regularity. He explained that these factors are critical: the line must be untinted or the trout won't be as cooperative; the lighter the pound-test of the line, the more action you'll get; the brass swivel either adds a sparkle or an action or both that the trout find attractive; 75 feet appears to be the optimum amount of line to have out. The streamer he showed me was a size 12 Supervisor, really chewed up.

The next time I was on a pond, I dug out my brass swivels and tried Andy's method. It was the day after Thanksgiving, sunny and unseasonably mild. I would have only three hours to prove itseffectiveness since I wanted to be back home in time to watch the Boston College - Miami football game. Because I didn't have a Supervisor, I started trolling a light green Matuka at approximately 11:30 am. By 12:50 pm, I had caught six rainbow trout. At the end of the day, I didn't know whether I was more excited about the success of this method or about my alma mater, Boston College, beating Miami with no time left on that unbelievable 65-yard Doug Flutie to Gerard Phelan touchdown pass. Either way, it made for a very

Native American Full Moons

January - Full Wolf Moon	July - Full Buck Moon
February - Full Snow Moon	August - Full Sturgeon Moon
March - Full Worm Moon	September -Full Harvest Moon
April - Full Pink Moon	October - Full Hunter's Moon
May - Full Flower Moon	November - Full Beaver Moon
June - Full Strawberry Moon	December - Full Cold Moon

Plastic bubble rigged with a Muddler Minnow.

enjoyable day. Since then, using many different streamers - usually light-colored on bright days and dark-colored on overcast days - this method has consistently produced at least several trout for me. If you're fortunate enough to have access to a boat (slow rowing is good exercise and eliminates the need for a motor), I strongly recommend it as a very productive trout catching method.

"SPIN" SOME FLY FISHING MAGIC: PLASTIC BUBBLES- Don't Leave Home Without Them !

You need not be a fly fisher to catch trout, pan-fish, or bass on flies. As a matter of fact, other than a few flies, you don't need any other fly fishing equipment.

When the fish seem to be feeding on insects and your bait or lures are not producing, that may be the time to put a plastic bubble on your spinning outfit, attach a leader and fly, and see if your luck changes.

The technique is fairly simple. Plastic bubbles come in various sizes with different devices to affix them to the spinning line. Experimentation has convinced me that two types are best: 1- the oval bubble with the interior rubber or plastic tube through which you insert the line, pull 6-8 feet through and, holding the tube terminals at both the top and bottom of the bubble, twist it so it ensnares the line inside the bubble, and tie on a fly; 2- the oval bubble with the peg that fits into the center shaft requires threading the line first through the thin end and then out the stout end of the peg, a sequence which- **in thin, out stout**- if not followed will not work properly; attach a small barrel swivel that will serve as a stop at the bottom of the bubble and then attach 6-8 or more feet of leader to the other end of the swivel and tie on a fly. Both types of bubbles need to be filled with water to serve as a weight for casting.

Now you are ready to fish. Allow the bubble to hang at least 18" from the tip of the rod. Keeping the long leader and fly even with or behind the side of your body, make a side angle cast. Slowly reel in the slack line, but initially allow at least ten seconds for the bubble to sink, bringing the fly with it. A *slowwww* retrieve is important for several reasons. The first is that the insect imitated by the fly would naturally move quite slowly through the water. Another reason is that anything but a very slow retrieve will force the bubble to the surface, perhaps above the depth at which the fish are feeding.

If the fish are feeding on the surface and you want to try a dry fly, e.g. size 14 Black Gnat, simply leave some air in the bubble. This will furnish sufficient water to provide the weight necessary to cast while the air will float the bubble and keep the fly on the surface.
When dry fly fishing, avoid casting directly on top of the surfacing fish or you will put them down with this less than graceful rig. Either cast beyond or ahead of the fish, especially if you can determine the path of their swimming. Reel in slack and slowly make contact with the bubble just enough to straighten the leader. Now, let the fly rest for at least ten seconds, staying alert for a hit. If nothing happens, move the fly-not more than a twitch-followed by another ten second delay. Remember, you're imitating a surface insect, not a power boat. Then, keep your eye on the fly. With the weight of the bubble so close to the fly, a slight lift of the rod is all that is required to set the hook.

If you try a plastic bubble, remember these key points:

- A longer, stiffer rod improves casting and leader handling.
- A longer and finer leader- 2 to 4 pound test- results in more hits.
- Keep the leader as far away from you as possible to avoid hooking yourself.
- Wet flies-all air out of bubble, just water; countdown for prospecting at various depths; reel very slowly.
- Dry flies- don't splash down on feeding fish; straighten leader connection; delicately twitch fly; carry some dry fly floatant to freshen drowned or trout slimed flies.
- Experiment with different flies of various sizes if you are unable to detect and match the insects on which the fish appear to be feeding.
- Wet or dry? –remember that for every fish you see feeding on the surface, there are many more you cannot see feeding beneath the surface.

In addition to providing the lure or bait-spinning angler with the opportunity to fish flies, the plastic bubble often times can put the spinning angler over fish that cannot be reached by conventional fly fishing because of obstructions, distance, or wind conditions. In fact, bubble fishing with wet flies into the wind- typical spring and fall conditions- can be very productive.
The plastic bubble has been around since the dawn of plastics, but very few anglers are willing to give it serious consideration. Those who do broaden their arsenal of effective fish catching techniques and enliven those dead, inactive hours when bait fishing is just sitting and letting ugly thoughts creep into your head.
Give it a try. At first you might find it awkward and maybe even a little frustrating, but if you give the little plastic bubble a fair chance , you will find it well worth the small investment.

Cast 9:

HOW TO CATCH TROPHY TROUT

"Few freshwater fish can match the trout for natural beauty and grace, or for fighting power when hooked."

POND LAKE RIVER SEA BY MARYJO KOCH

The world record brown trout, 40 pounds, 4 ounces, was caught on a 1/32 ounce marabou nymph. So much for big lure/bait = big fish. But this is yet another facet of fishing that makes it a fascinating pastime and keeps you humble. No sooner do you fool yourself into believing that you have them figured out then they spit your theory back into your face.

Another spectacular trout landed and then released in a Cape Cod pond. (Capute photo)

> *"Innocence is a wild trout. But we humans, being complicated, pursue innocence in complicated ways."*
>
> DATUS C. PROPER, 1982

Nevertheless, while a foolproof trophy trout catching method awaits invention, there are some ways that will improve the odds of your catching trophy trout.

-MINDSET: Believe that every Cape Cod lake and pond holds a number of very large trout.

-LOCATION: The large trout stay in the deep water, except early in the season, after ice out.

-BEHAVIOR: Once trout exceed 15 inches, their instinctive predation pattern is to seek maximum protein input with minimum energy output. This isn't rocket science- it's also how we humans get to be "trophy" size- by making more deposits than we make withdrawals. After

following spawning baitfish into the shallows after ice out, they gradually set up in the deeper holes of a lake, especially during bright, sunny days. Here, they cruise, search, and feed on schools of baitfish like smelt and herring (baby or peanut bunker), plump servings of protein rich grub.

-DO NOT: bother trying to fool big trout with dainty fare.

-DO: look at their menu and feed them what they want.

-HOW? Try to match live bait to the lake's natural forage fish. If it's herring in Gull Pond, use herring. If it's golden shiners in Little Cliff Pond, use golden shiners. You can hand net juvenile, but check with each town's herring warden for limits–usually 15. Golden shiners can be caught when they are most active at dawn or dusk on tiny flies-mosquito or gnat patterns-or on tiny hooks baited with a bit of worm or a small bread pellet.

LARGEST RAINBOW TROUT

The "Kamloops", Native American for "meeting of the waters", are trout originally native to the meeting place of the North and South Thompson Rivers connecting Kamloops Lake in British Columbia. In Jewel Lake, B.C. and Lake Pend Oreille, Idaho, specimens have been caught weighting 32, 37, & 52 1/2 pounds. Smaller growing strains than the enormous Gerrard strain have been stocked in various New England waters. You will recognize a Kamloops on the end of your line if it is airborne more than it is in the water.

-METHOD: Gently impale the bait through the lip on a size 10 hook to keep them lively as long as possible. The combination of the familiar food source and its panic vibrations will invariably be sensed by big trout through their lateral lines-acutely sensitive motion detectors. This is like ringing the dinner bell around hungry NFL linemen.

-EQUIPMENT: This is the key. Use the lightest line possible in order to minimize detection by these big, wary, line shy fish.This means, as conditions permit, 2 or 4 pound test line. Use the 2 pound test in the clearest water or the 4 pound test if the water has been roiled by rain. Some expert anglers attest that 75% of their big trout strikes occur on the 2 pound line. Granted, they and you will lose some fish but this technique will get you connected to trophy sized trout far more often than anglers using other methods.

Don't bother trying to fool big trout with dainty fare.

Cast 10:

HOW TO CATCH TROPHY BASS

ESTIMATING WEIGHT OF A TROPHY BASS

If you want to release a trophy bass, but don't have an accurate scale, use this formula to give you a close approximation of its weight: **Length x Length x Girth ÷ 1200 = Weight**

Example: for a 25" fish with a 20" girth: $\frac{25 \times 25 \times 20}{1200}$ = **10.42 pounds**

FROM ADVANCED BASS FISHING, DICK STERNBERG

Much of bass behavior and feeding is related to its spawning cycle: the pre-spawn period, the spawning phase, and the post-spawn period.

PRE-SPAWN

All bass do not spawn at the same time. It takes place gradually and depends on weather and the availability of beds in the shallows. In Cape Cod lakes and ponds, late in the spring, in anticipation of the spawning ritual, bass "stage" in depths near flats and gradually move from the depths and begin seeking shallow water, 7-10 feet from shore, preferably with a sand or gravel bottom, from 1-3 feet deep. The male bass sweeps out a nest with its tail and then tries to induce a female to use it. The conditions that exist for bass several weeks before spawning can make for productive fishing. The harshness of winter is well behind, the warmer weather has activated forage fish, the bass are especially aggressive as they move onto the flats, and both the male and female bass are in the best physical shape of the year.

Paul DuClos with 18 pound California largemouth bass. (DuClos photo)

Spinner baits, crankbaits, and jigs will all produce if presented properly. For pre-spawn bass this means slowing down the speed of your offerings;

SPAWNING PHASE

On Cape Cod stillwaters, bass start to spawn when water temperatures reach 62-65 degrees F. This can be from May to June, depending on the weather vagaries of each spring. You'll know they're spawning because the nests are in the shallows and you'll see the bass on and around them. The male bass guards the eggs and fry, eating very little himself as he chases egg and fry stealing sunfish that maraud individually or tactically with others, much like hyenas harrassing lions on a kill. Often the schooling fry hang around the nest until about one inch in length. It has been observed that, at that stage, the once protective male attacks the fry, devouring as many as a third of them and scattering the rest. It may be nature's way of instilling a flight reaction in the fry when a larger fish appears. It is estimated that a mere one percent of the eggs survive and develop into catchable sized fish. Given the pressures on bass while in the spawning phase, it raises a question of ethics to take advantage of their vulnerability by trying to catch them during this resource critical period. It is in the best interest of the bass in Cape Cod ponds and lakes, and hence for anglers, to refrain from fishing for them during the spawning period.

POST-SPAWN PERIOD

Both the male's and female's energies are depleted after the spawning ritual. They will move to deeper water and are not very likely to forage or chase anglers" offerings for as much as several weeks after. This transition may be

Another swag- bellied bruiser from a Cape Cod pond. (Bait Shack photo)

the most difficult time of the year to catch large bass, especially females. When the bass's hunger reflex returns, the post-spawn catching shifts into high gear. When this happens *"The lure's edibility takes on paramount importance. It must smell, feel and look alive in its movements to attract post-spawn bass. The spawn is over and the bass" senses are primed for foraging and getting on with their growth."* (MASTERING LARGEMOUTH BASS, Larry Larsen, North American Fishing Club Library)

METHODS

Pre-spawn:

- Crankbaits, spinnerbaits and jigs fished slowly are most productive.
- Crankbaits:Try Poe's RC-1, Size 5 Shad Rap, Bomber 7A, Norman DD22 and variations of such lures depending on the depth bass are holding.
- Spinnerbaits: try Mann"s Hank Parker Classic, Haddock Tandem, Haddock Single, Hildebrandt Tin Roller, Lunker Lure Triple Rattleback with big blades for deep water and smaller blades for shallower water.

Spawning Phase:

- Fish for other species. Cape Cod"s trout fishing often peaks in late May to mid June.

Post-spawn:

- Try top water lures on cloudy days and early and late in the day, fished slowly. Cast: buzzbaits such as a Blue Fox Roland Martin Buzzer, Bulldog Four-blade Buzzbait; Frog imitations like Renosky

Lunker smallmouth bass caught and released. (Capute photo)

Natural Frog, rebel Crankin" Frog, Plummer Superfrog; Propbaits such as Gilmore Jumper, Dalton Special, Heddon Tiny Torpedo; Classic topwater lures-Arbogast Jitterbug, Hula Popper, Crazy Crawler-darker colors late and at night.

OLD RELIABLES-LIVE BAIT

- Big, trophy sized Cape Cod bass just love large baits: minnows, mummichogs, alewives (especially in the fall when large schools are circling the shores searching for an exit to the Atlantic); golden shiners (You"ll have to catch your own; read how in section on trophy trout); leeches, night crawlers, and crayfish, which are like candy to large smallmouth bass. (Again, you"ll likely have to catch your own leeches and crayfish under shoreline rocks.)

> *"A full moon and a big spangle of stars make a romantic setting, but bass like darkness better... The best fishing usually starts after midnight."*
>
> H.G. TAPPLY, *The Sportsman's Notebook*

A picture perfect Cape Cod largemouth bass that posed and went right back into the water. (Capute photo)

Cast 11:

ICE FISHING

COLDEST DAY ON RECORD IN MASSACHUSETTS
On January 22, 1984, the town of Chester recorded a temperature of –40 degrees F. No doubt there were avid MA ice fishermen who didn't notice the cold.

COLDEST DAY ON RECORD ON CAPE COD
On February 9, 1934, the town of Hyannis recorded a temperature of –12 degrees F.

The ponds and lakes of Cape Cod, unlike most of the stillwaters in the rest of the Commonwealth, do not always freeze over during an average winter. The salty influence of the Cape's weather patterns produces milder winters. This difference cuts two ways:1- the less severe winters mean bigger fish because it results in a longer feeding and, therefore, growing season for the Cape's freshwater fish; 2- for those who enjoy ice fishing on the Cape, it can be a long time between opportunities, since the ice that may form on the lakes and ponds is most often not thick enough for safe fishing out on the ice. Of course, shore bound fishing, when the lake is not supportive of ice fishing, can be productive.

"Oh boy! It's finally thick enough."

In those rare Cape winters when the lakes freeze deeply enough to be safe for ice fishing (see the Cape Cod weather box), the intersection of large, hungry fish and the knowledgeable ice angler results in spectacular catches. Unusually long and cold winters like 2002-2003 & 2003-2004 are memorable for the fanatical Cape Cod ice fisherman who uses any rationale to get out as often as possible, not quite to make hay while the sun shines, but the opposite, whatever that is-catch fish while the ice holds?

- Smaller, shallower lakes/ponds freeze and thaw sooner than larger, deeper stillwaters.

CAPE COD WEATHER: AVERAGES, RECORDS, PRECIPITATION

Month	Normal* Hi/Low Temp F	Record High	Record Low	Precip.
January	37/21	65 Jan.14, "32	-8 Jan. 31,"61	4.06 "
February	38/23	64 Feb. 28, "76	-12 Feb.9,"34	3.29
March	44/29	78 March 14,"90	-3 March 19,"67	3.94
April	52/38	87 Apr. 29,"90	9 Apr.5,"54	3.76
May	62/55	91 May 23,"64	24 May 8,"67	3.23
June	72/57	94 June 26,"49	31 June 4,"57	3.23
July	78/63	100 July 5,"99	42 July 7,"65	2.81
August	77/62	100 Aug. 28,"48	34 Aug.31,"65	3.50
September	70/65	95 Sept.2,"53	26 Sept.29,"57	3.33
October	60/45	83 Oct.6,"46	9 Oct.31,"66	3.91
November	51/37	74 Nov.4,"90	7 Nov.17,"67	3.87
December	42/27	65 Dec.5, 2001	-10 Dec. 25,"83	4.12

• ***Normal is an average of a recent 30-year period. Data based on Hyannis climatology***

Source: Courtesy of Dr. Joseph P. Sobel, Director of Forensic Services, AccuWeather, Inc. State College, PA World's largest commercial weather service.

Nothing stops every angler from fishing. (The Bait Shack photo)

- If in doubt, do not step out onto the ice. This is truly a matter of life or death.
- A 2 inch minimum of ice is necessary to support one person of average weight.
- Ice can be thicker or thinner near shore than in the middle; check carefully as you go.
- "Black ice" is formed from deep cold snaps and is quite strong.

- Ice forming during snow falls or a series of freezes and thaws will be weaker than black ice.
- Ice near springs and inflows from streams will be dangerously thin even if ice on the rest of lake is safe.
- Remember: **If in doubt, don't step out!**

Trophy lagemouth bass landed through the ice (Capute photo)

In February of 2003,I had an experience in Goose Hummock Bait and Tackle that demonstrated to me just how much Cape Cod anglers love their ice fishing and manage to align their priorities to exploit it when the conditions are right. The winter of 2002-2003 was one of the coldest in many years. Lakes and ponds froze solid and deep from shore to shore.

On this particular February work day the temperature was 19 degrees F, with a wind chill of –5 degrees F. On my way into the shop I held a door open for several exiting customers, each holding a freshly filled bucket of shiners and I observed 4 to 5 others inside quickly choosing items at the ice fishing display. Walking in, I was greeted by the smiling countenance of manager Mark Palmer.

A study in extremes of weather and "finaticism" on a Cape Cod pond.

"Hi Mark," I greeted him, *"Is it my imagination or are there a lot of guys out ice fishing?"*

Mark, with a dead pan expression on his face replied, *"Hell yes! It's way too cold to work!"*

Look at the photos in this book of some of the

catches of trophy fish pulled up through the holes in the ice (and then put back in) by those who know how to do it and you cannot help but be impressed.

Quickly back into the lake to fight another day. (Capute photo)

If you are one of the ice fishing fanatics, you already know the clothing, gear, bait, food and drink, and special equipment drill necessary for a safe, comfortable and productive trip. If not, and you want to try it, hook up with a fanatic who can shorten your learning curve and, in the process, perhaps save you from frostbite or worse. At the very least, call or stop in at one of the Cape Cod bait and tackle stores. There, you will be able to get what you need and, most importantly, be provided with up to date reports on ice conditions which will dictate whether or not you should even be out on the ice.

> *"The fanatics will be out there in Arctic conditions, but that's not true of all ice fishermen. Sometimes, like this past winter (2002-2003),even with plenty of safe ice on ponds, business suffers. If it gets too cold, fishermen don't have proper clothing or the will to stand out drilling on two feet of ice with the wind chill below zero and a gale blowing. Most ice fishermen want optimal conditions: no more than six inches of ice, 30 degrees F, sun, and no wind."*
>
> DON STROMYER, PROPRIETOR OF RED TOP SPORTING GOODS, INC. BUZZARDS BAY, CAPE COD.

"Is there anything we forgot to bring?"

Cape Cod Maps

TOWNS
PONDS & LAKES IN EACH TOWN
FISHING TIPS FROM EXPERTS PANEL
ACCESS
BOATING INFORMATION

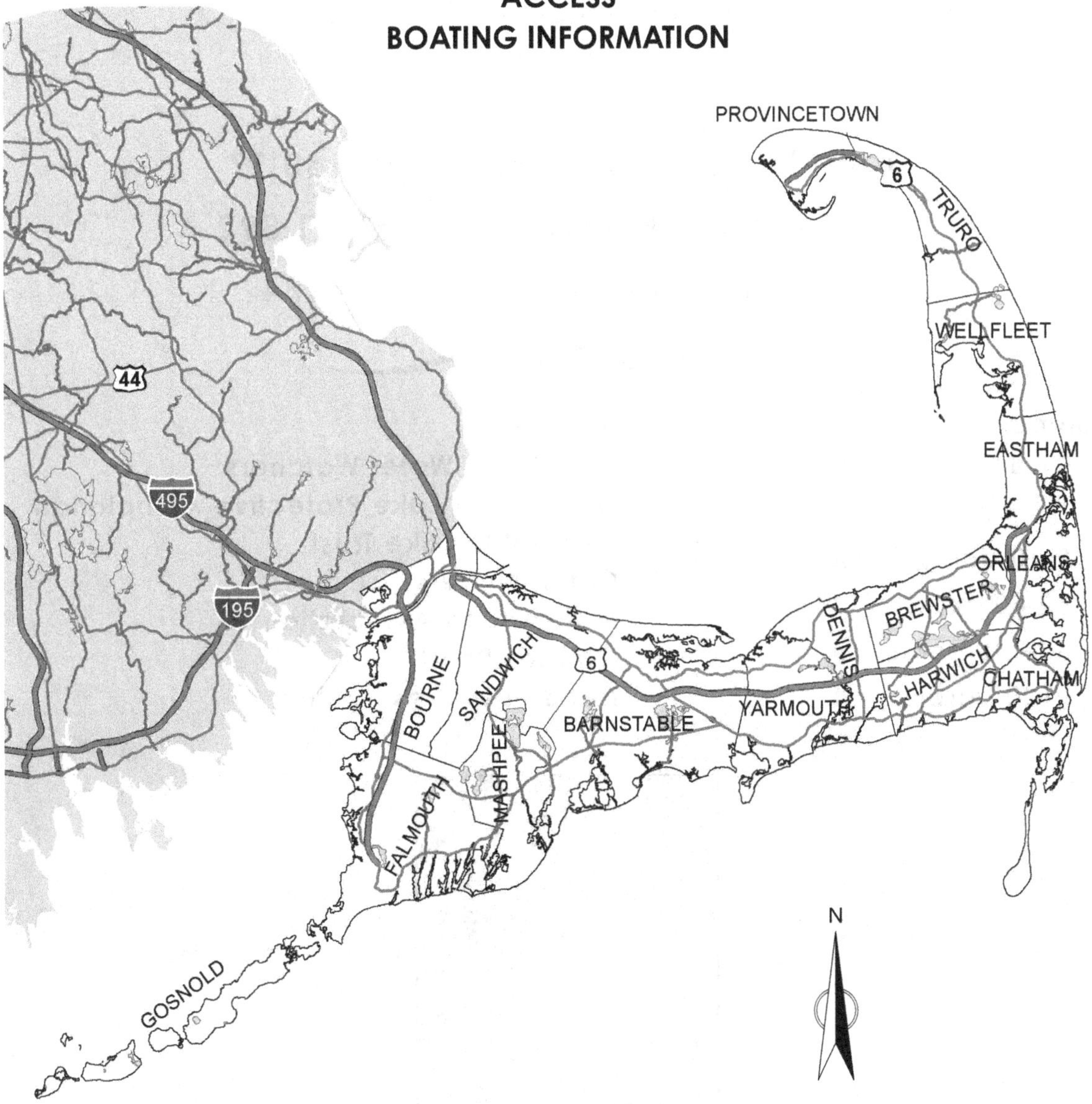

PROVINCETOWN
6
TRURO
WELLFLEET
EASTHAM
ORLEANS
BREWSTER
DENNIS
HARWICH
CHATHAM
YARMOUTH
BARNSTABLE
6
SANDWICH
BOURNE
MASHPEE
FALMOUTH
GOSNOLD
44
495
195
N

Cast 12:

BARNSTABLE

PONDS & LAKES

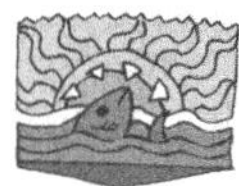

Total Land Area (sq. miles) **60.17**

Total Area of Ponds (acres) **1,892**

Total numbers of Ponds 184

Number of Ponds by size:

<1 acres:	92
1-5 acres:	43
5-10 acres:	22
20-50 acres:	3
50-100 acres:	6
>100 acres:	4

Pond groups:

- Barnstable Water Watchers
- Wequaquet Lake Protective Association
- Barnstable Lake Trust
- Cotuit Waders
- Indian Pond Association
- Garretts Pond
- Three Bays Preservation

Happy young angler mugs it up for the camera before releasing a hefty largemouth bass.

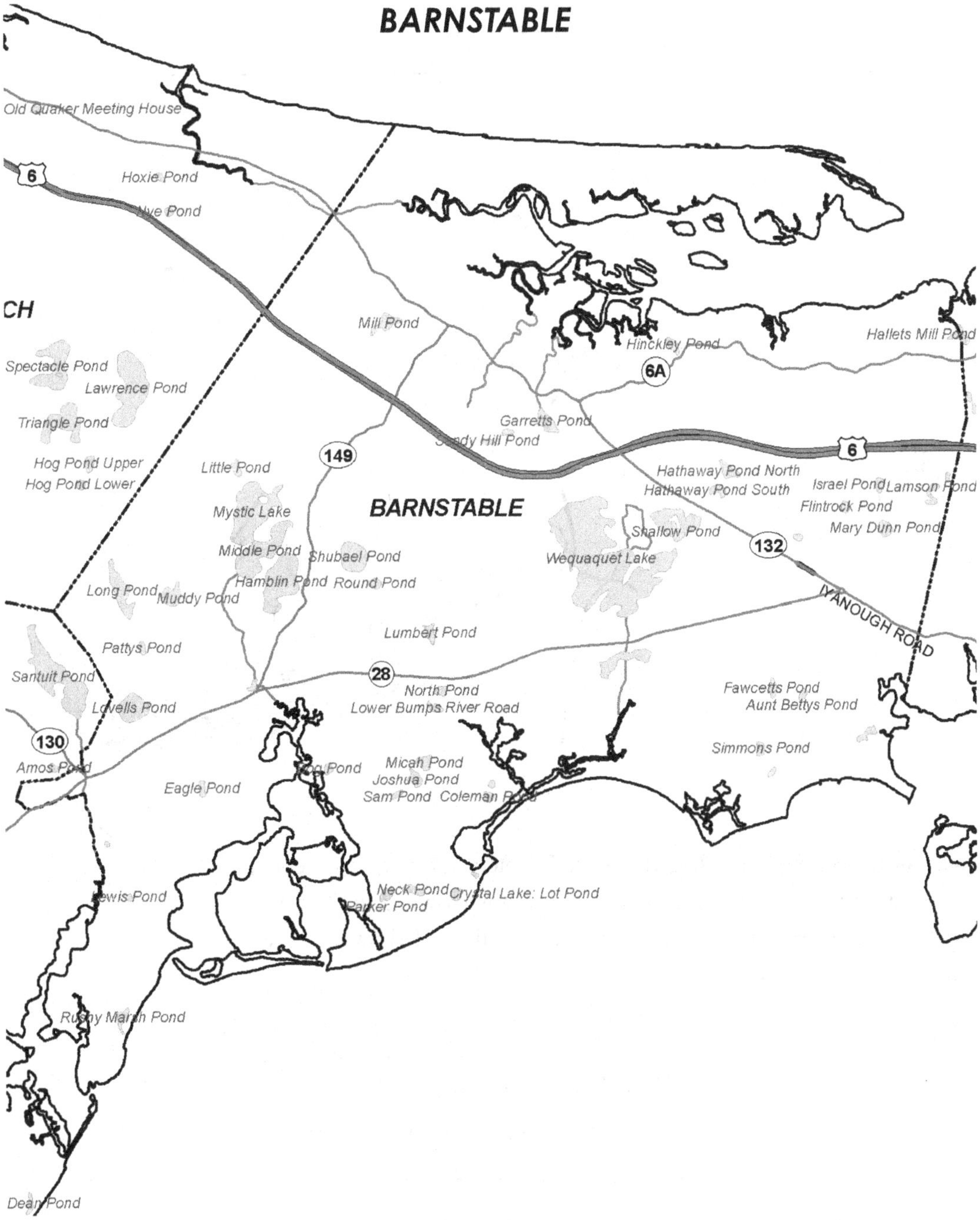

BARNSTABLE

Old Quaker Meeting House
6
Hoxie Pond
Nye Pond
CH
Mill Pond
Hinckley Pond
Hallets Mill Pond
6A
Spectacle Pond
Lawrence Pond
Triangle Pond
Garretts Pond
Sandy Hill Pond
6
Hog Pond Upper
Hog Pond Lower
Little Pond
149
Hathaway Pond North
Hathaway Pond South
Israel Pond
Lamson Pond
Flintrock Pond
Mystic Lake
BARNSTABLE
Mary Dunn Pond
Shallow Pond
132
Middle Pond
Shubael Pond
Wequaquet Lake
Hamblin Pond
Round Pond
Long Pond
Muddy Pond
IYANOUGH ROAD
Lumbert Pond
Pattys Pond
Santuit Pond
28
North Pond
Fawcetts Pond
Aunt Bettys Pond
Lovells Pond
Lower Bumps River Road
130
Simmons Pond
Amos Pond
Bog Pond
Micah Pond
Joshua Pond
Eagle Pond
Sam Pond
Coleman Pond
Neck Pond
Crystal Lake: Lot Pond
Lewis Pond
Parker Pond
Rushy Marsh Pond
Dean Pond

GARRETTS POND

Barnstable

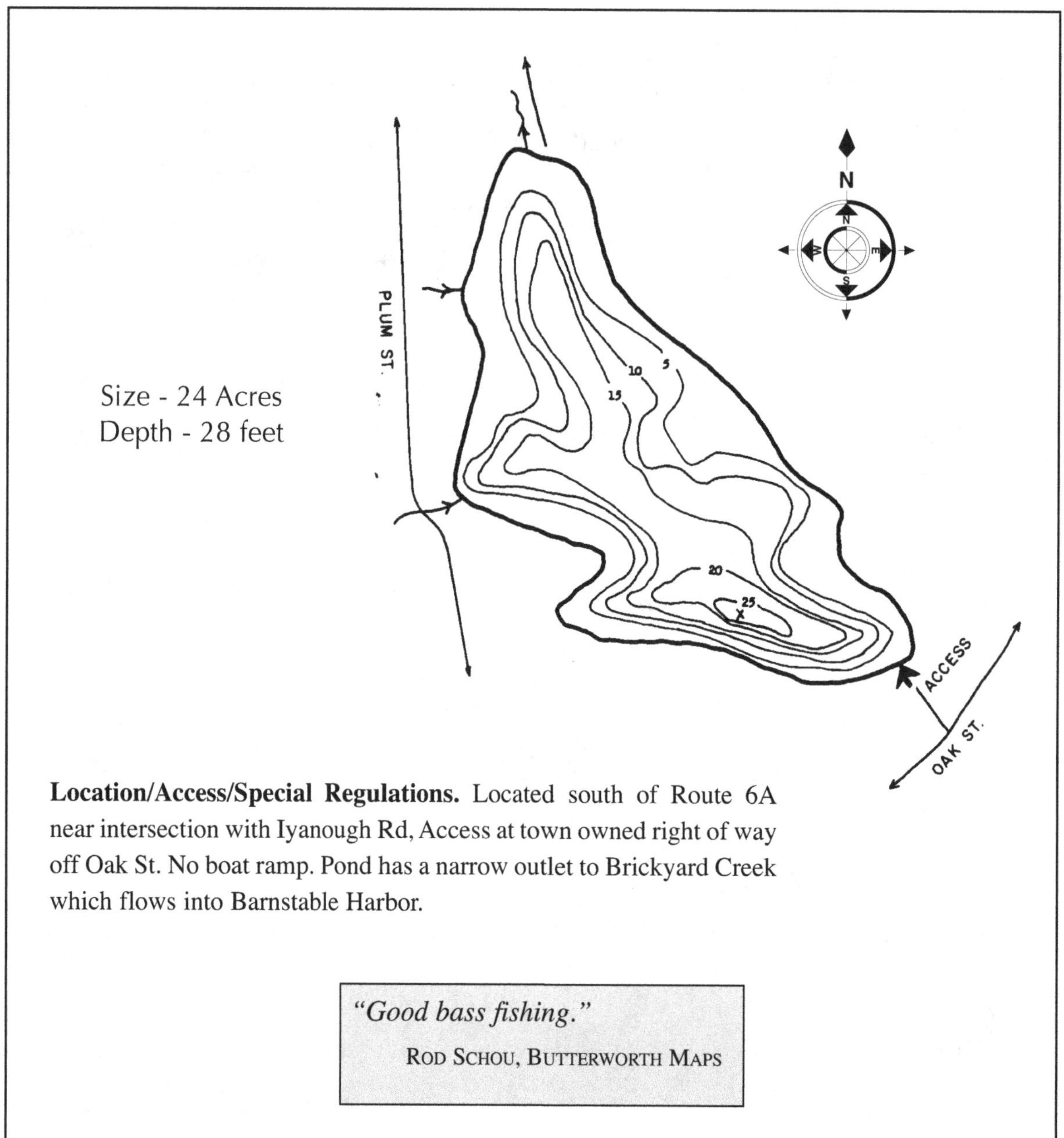

Location/Access/Special Regulations. Located south of Route 6A near intersection with Iyanough Rd, Access at town owned right of way off Oak St. No boat ramp. Pond has a narrow outlet to Brickyard Creek which flows into Barnstable Harbor.

> *"Good bass fishing."*
>
> Rod Schou, Butterworth Maps

HAMBLIN POND

BARNSTABLE

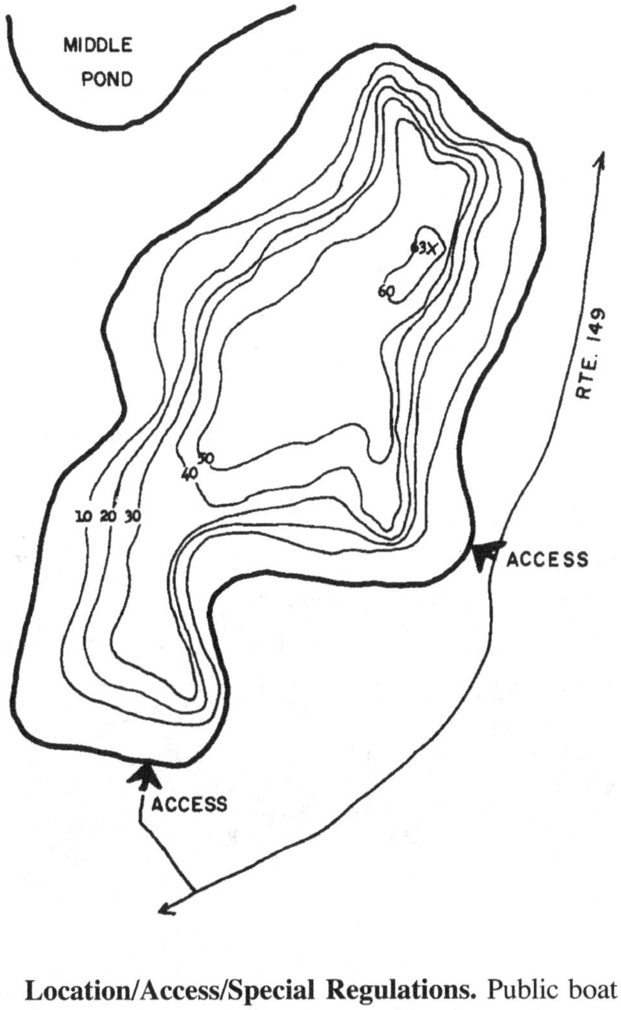
MIDDLE
POND
N
63X
60
50
40
10 20 30
RTE. 149
ACCESS
ACCESS

Size - 114 Acres
Depth - 63 feet

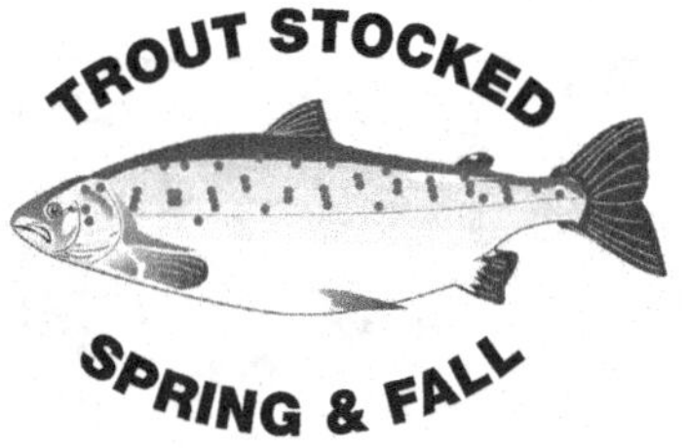
TROUT STOCKED
SPRING & FALL

Location/Access/Special Regulations. Public boat ramp, gravel. Ten HP limit on outboard motors. Located off Route 149, street adjacent to cemetery. Source of water for abutting cranberry bog. Second access on eastern shore beyond Burgess House.

HAMBLIN POND - TIPS FROM EXPERTS

"One of the Cape's best ponds for smallmouth bass and trout. Grass shrimp will take small-mouths and trout through about the middle of June. Bounce 'em slowly along the bottom."

PETER MIRICK, EDITOR, MASSACHUSETTS WILDLIFE

"A very good pond for trout. Try power bait."

JEFF CAPUTE, AWARD WINNING ANGLER

"The best trout pond in town. #1 fly fishing spot Good hatches. Good wading. Fly fisherman's gathering spot."

GENE BOURQUE, EDITOR, ON THE WATER.

"Probably one of the most beautiful and easily accessible ponds around. Fly fish drop offs with sinking line, bead head nymphs."

ROBERT JESSUP, THE SPORTING LIFE

"The pond god gave me a birthday gift at dawn on October 30 one year when I caught my largest Cape Cod rainbow trout-20 inches- on a grey Wooly Worm pulled slowly in 3'strips on a floating line. Beautiful sunrise! Gorgeous fish! Memorable day!"

PETER BUDRYK, A FISHERMAN

Kevin Moak of Arlington, Va., cast his line into Hathaway's Pond, while fly fishing with has father Stan Moak from Brewster, (not in photo). (Kevin Mingora/Cape Cod Times)

HATHAWAY POND, NORTH

BARNSTABLE

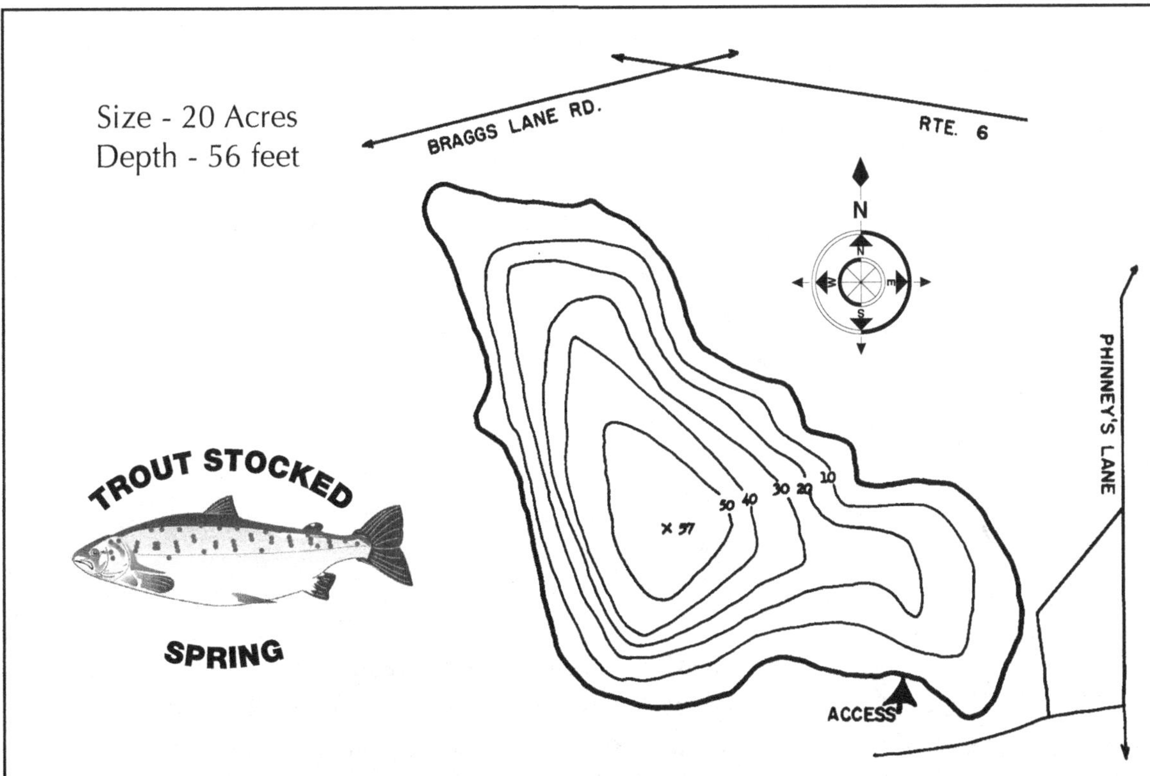

Location/Access/Special Regulations. South of Route 6 between Exits 6 and 7. Access via Iyanough Rd. (Exit 6) to Phinney's Lane, north. Reclaimed. Boat ramp. Electric motors only. Surrounded by conservation land. Hiking trails.

> *"Good for brook trout and smallmouth bass. Also has yellow perch."*
>
> STEVE HURLEY, MDFW
>
> *"Best for trout, but also is an excellent smallmouth pond. Sometimes in the spring a Hornberg is the fly of choice, Quill Gordon is also good. Spring stocked trout carry over."*
>
> STAN MOAK, TROUT UNLIMITED

LONG POND (CENTERVILLE)

BARNSTABLE

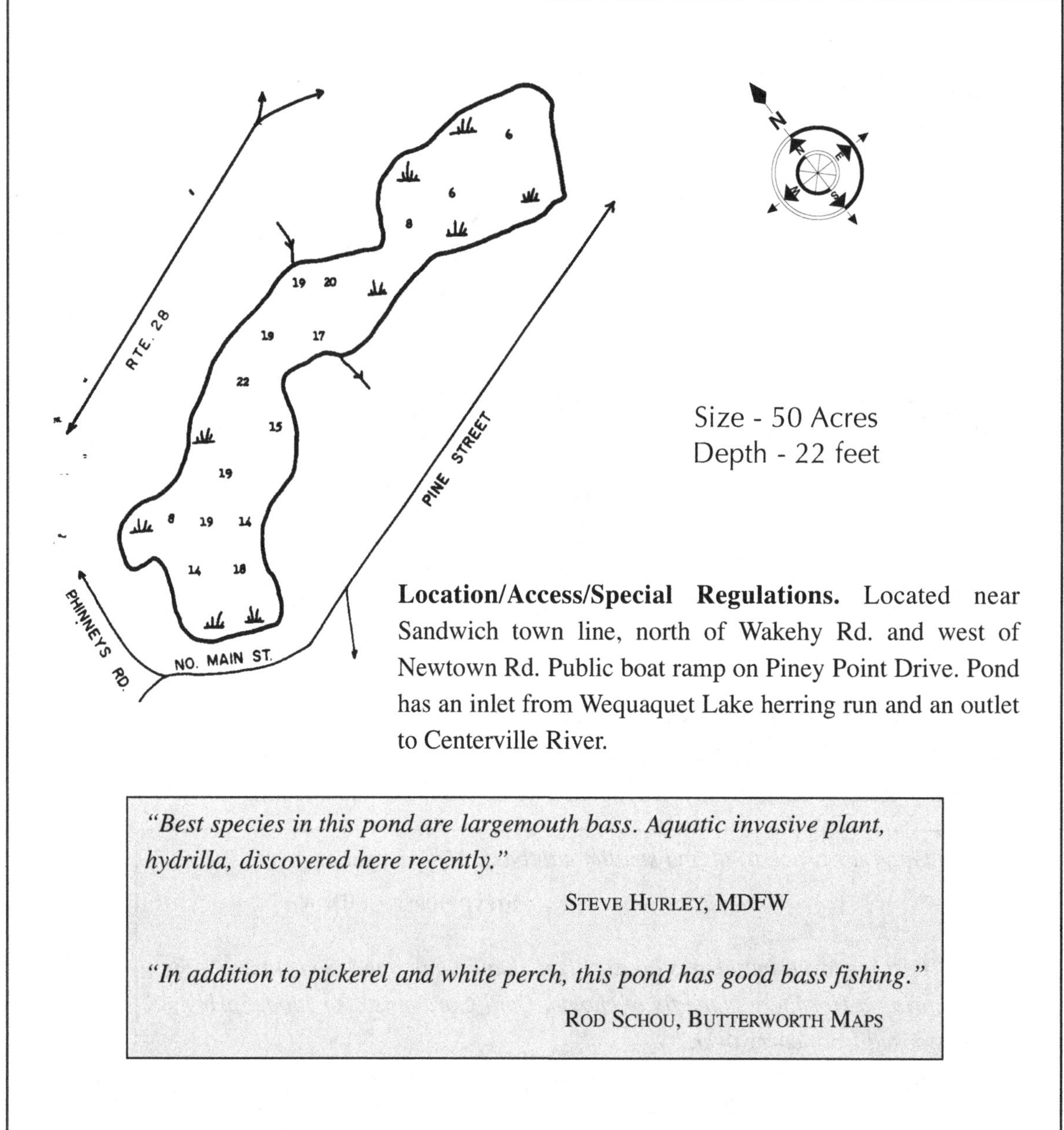

Size - 50 Acres
Depth - 22 feet

Location/Access/Special Regulations. Located near Sandwich town line, north of Wakehy Rd. and west of Newtown Rd. Public boat ramp on Piney Point Drive. Pond has an inlet from Wequaquet Lake herring run and an outlet to Centerville River.

> *"Best species in this pond are largemouth bass. Aquatic invasive plant, hydrilla, discovered here recently."*
>
> STEVE HURLEY, MDFW
>
> *"In addition to pickerel and white perch, this pond has good bass fishing."*
>
> ROD SCHOU, BUTTERWORTH MAPS

LONG POND, NORTH (NEWTOWN)

BARNSTABLE

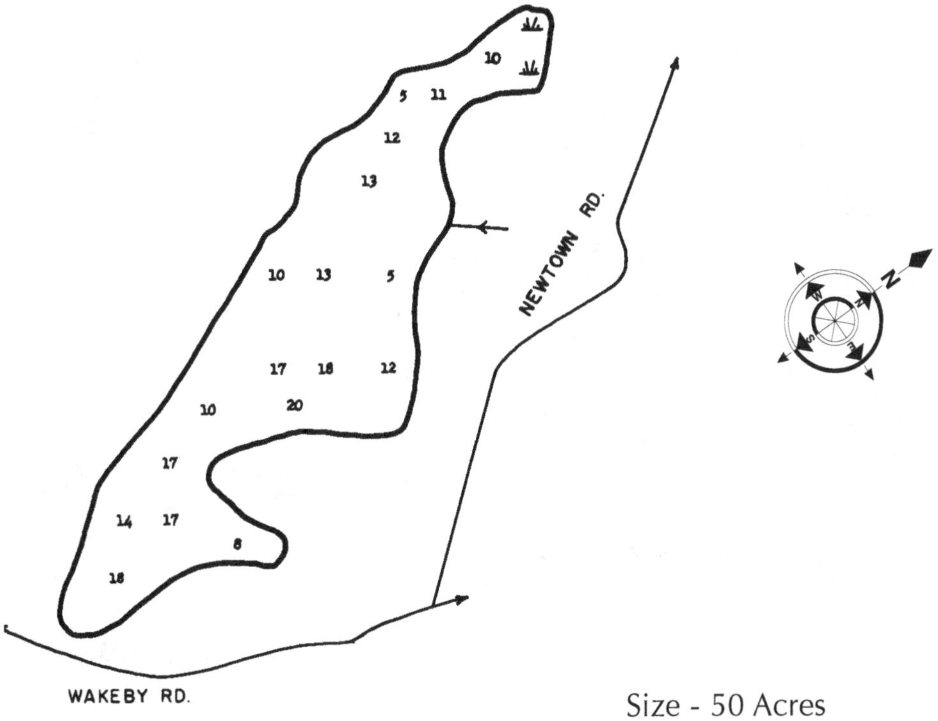

Size - 50 Acres
Depth - 15 feet

Location/Access/Special Regulations. Informal access.

> *"Has bass, pickerel, and white perch, but is not readily accessible."*
>
> ROD SCHOU, BUTTERWORTH MAPS

LOVELLS POND

BARNSTABLE

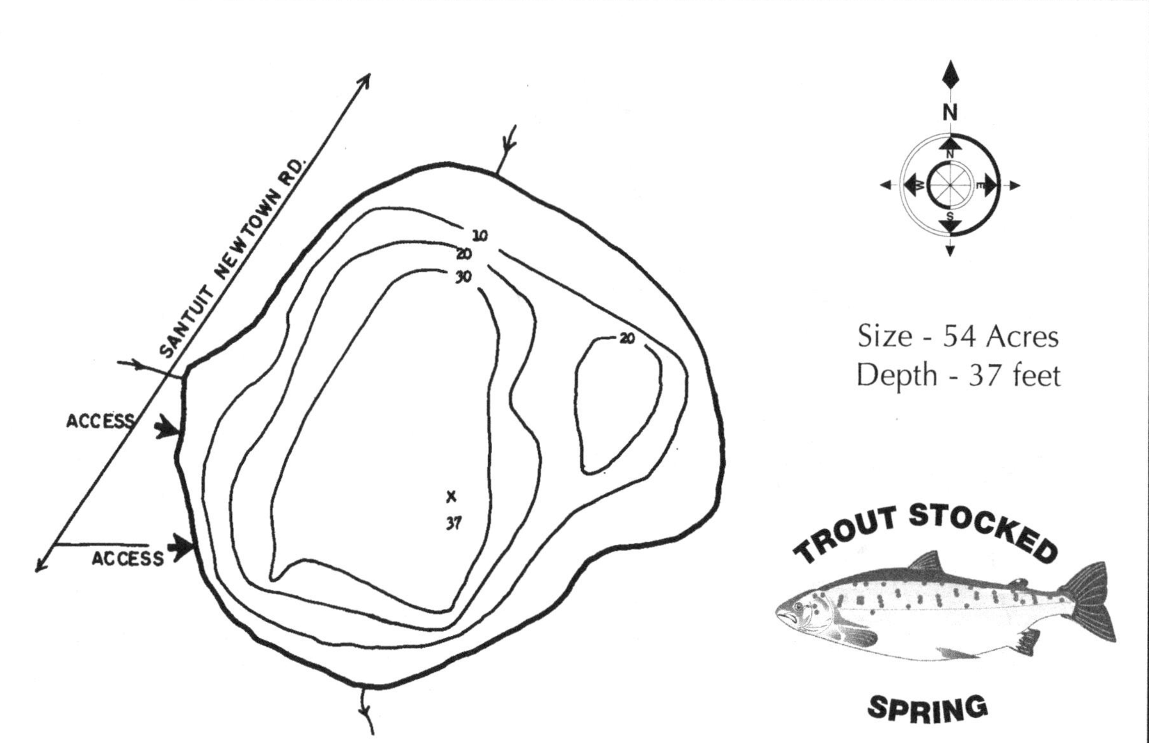

Location/Access/Special Regulations. Located in village of Cotuit, north of Route 28 and east of Newtown Road. Public boat ramp, car top. Access by boat ramp off Newtown Road and a small beach on south shore. 10 HP limit. Small brook inlet from cranberry bog. Discharges water to Little River via pipe.

> *"Average trout and largemouth bass fishing. Also has yellow perch, pickerel, and pumkinseed."*
>
> STEVE HURLEY, MDFW

MIDDLE POND

BARNSTABLE

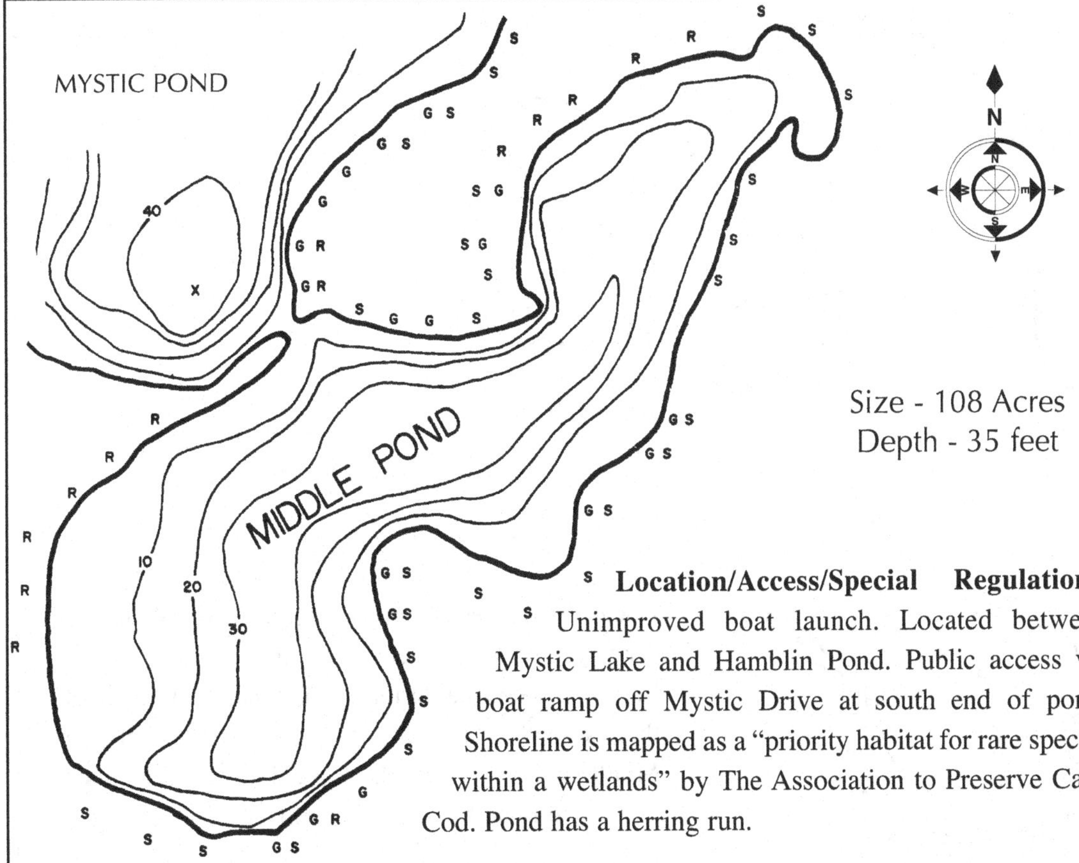

MYSTIC POND

MIDDLE POND

Size - 108 Acres
Depth - 35 feet

Location/Access/Special Regulations. Unimproved boat launch. Located between Mystic Lake and Hamblin Pond. Public access via boat ramp off Mystic Drive at south end of pond. Shoreline is mapped as a "priority habitat for rare species within a wetlands" by The Association to Preserve Cape Cod. Pond has a herring run.

"A good pond for both yellow and white perch. Drift a worm/spinner combination in late April-early June. Can produce great quantities of 8-11 inch yellow perch, whites a little bigger."

PETER MIRICK, EDITOR, MASSACHUSETTS WILDLIFE

"Can be good for smallmouth bass."

Steve Hurley, MDFW

MYSTIC LAKE

BARNSTABLE

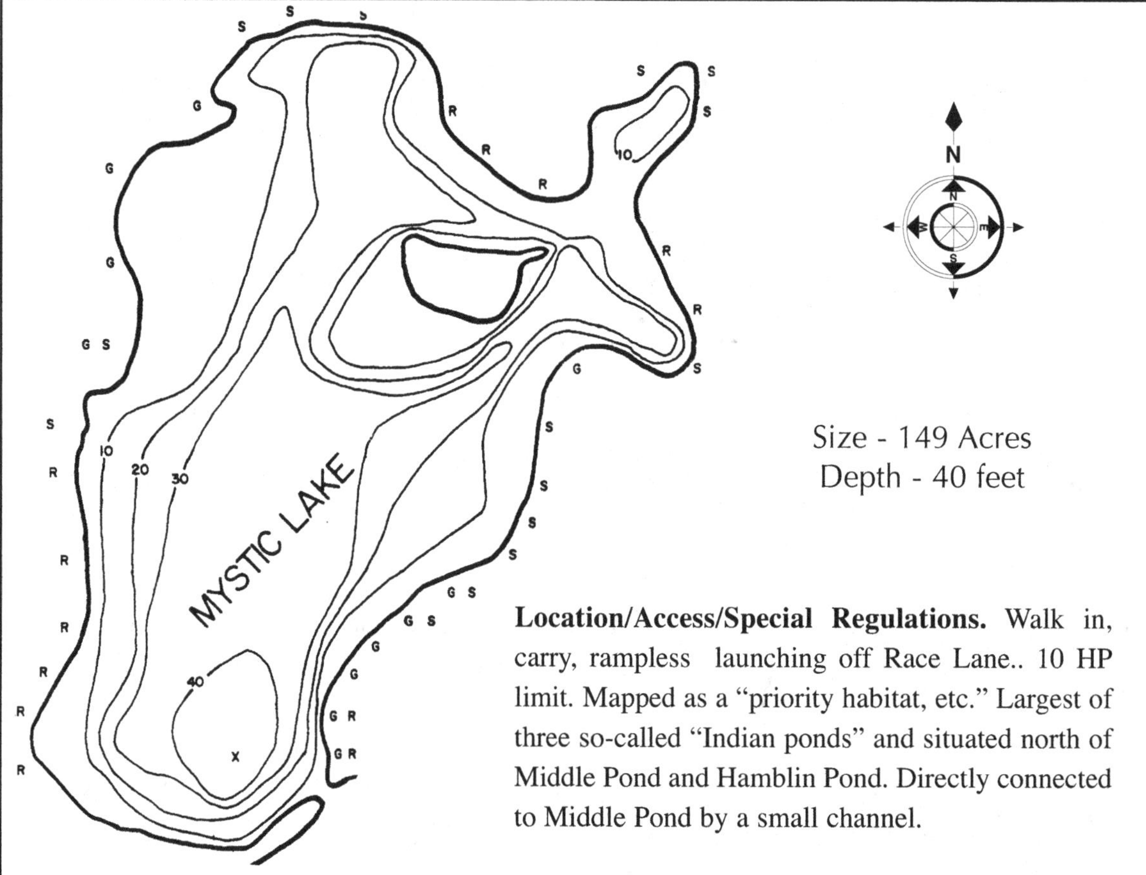

Size - 149 Acres
Depth - 40 feet

Location/Access/Special Regulations. Walk in, carry, rampless launching off Race Lane.. 10 HP limit. Mapped as a "priority habitat, etc." Largest of three so-called "Indian ponds" and situated north of Middle Pond and Hamblin Pond. Directly connected to Middle Pond by a small channel.

"A beautiful smallmouth lake. Use a canoe or kayak to creep up on fish. Most methods work-small spinner baits, grubs, tiny tubes jigged off structure will produce explosive strikes."

ROBERT JESSUP, THE SPORTING LIFE

"The best lake in Barnstable for yellow and white perch. A favorite to fish for yellow perch with a small metal spoon, single hook, baited with a worm."

PETER MIRICK, EDITOR, MASSACHUSETTS WILDLIFE

SHALLOW POND

BARNSTABLE

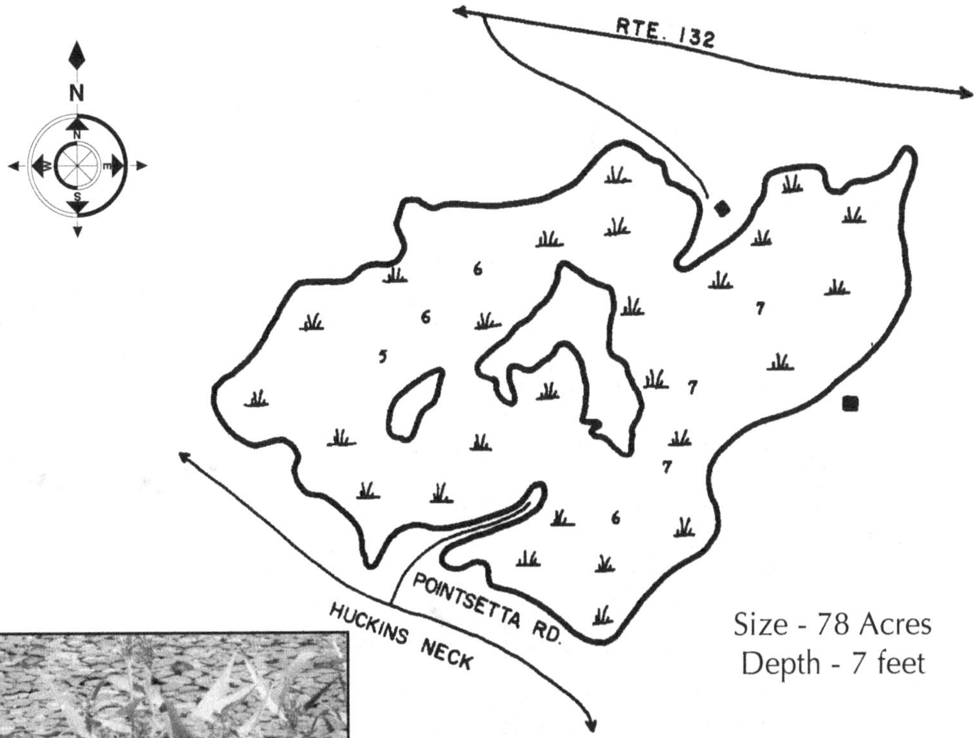
RTE. 132
N
6
6
5
7
7
7
6
POINTSETTA RD.
HUCKINS NECK

Size - 78 Acres
Depth - 7 feet

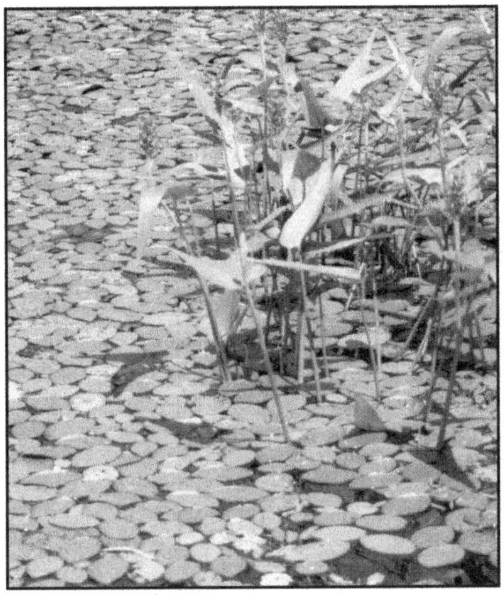
Pickerel weed.

Access: From road off Route 132 north of pond.

"A fair pond for pickerel."

STEVE HURLEY, MDFW

"Lots of pickerel!"

ROD SCHOU, BUTTERWORTH MAPS

SHUBAEL POND

Barnstable

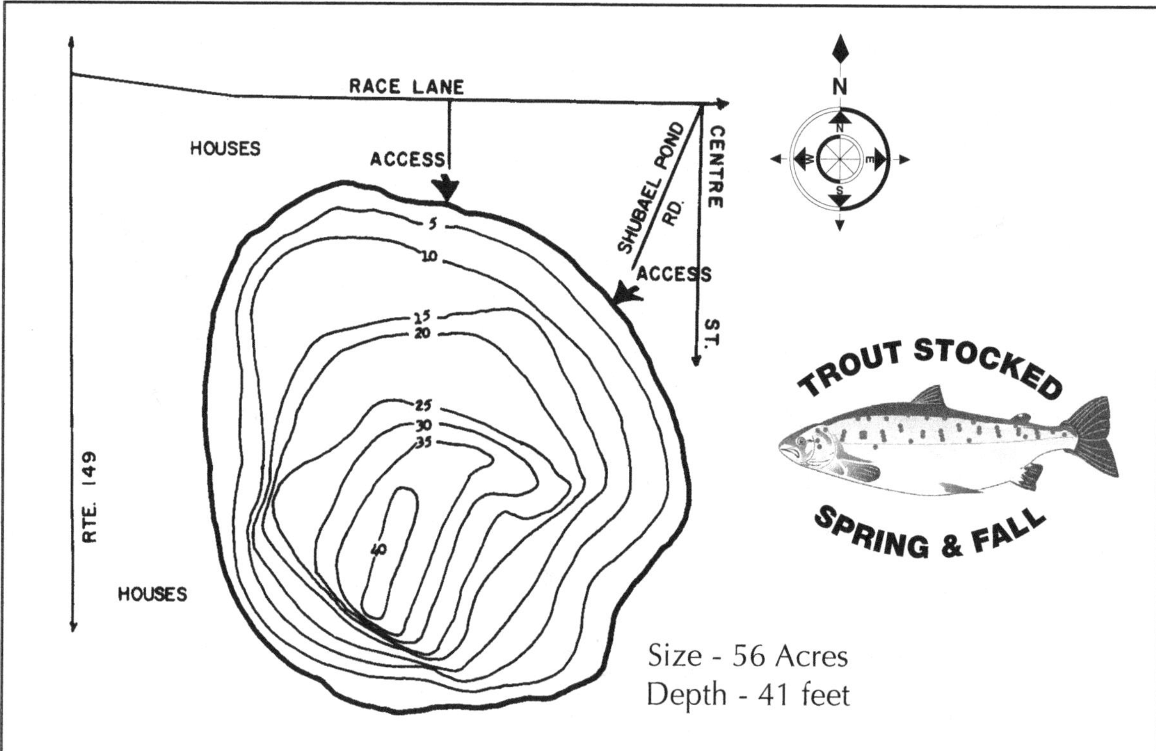

Location/Access/Special Regulations. Located in village of Marstons Mills. Public access via gravel boat ramp off Shubael Pond Drive and Willimantic Drive. Shoreline is highly developed with homes. Pond is extensively used for fishing, boating, and swimming.

> *"A good trout, largemouth bass and smallmouth bass pond."*
>
> Steve Hurley, MDFW
>
> *"It's supposed to be good, but I've never had much luck here."*
>
> Stan Moak, TROUT UNLIMITED

WEQUAQUET LAKE

BARNSTABLE

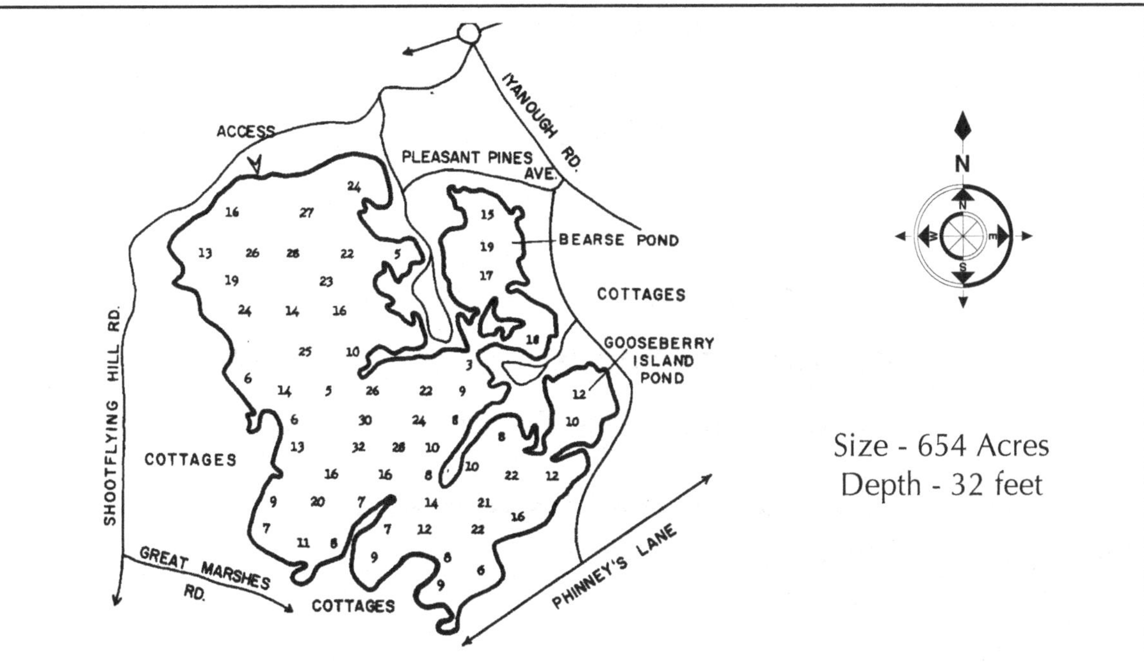

Size - 654 Acres
Depth - 32 feet

Location/Access/Special Regulations. Third largest lake on Cape Cod. Centrally located west of Route 132 and south of Route 6. Public boat ramp located off Shootflying Hill Road. Supplies surface water to a dam controlled herring run leading into Long Pond during average to high water conditions.

"The only known lake on Cape Cod with a population of northern pike."

STEVE HURLEY, MDFW

"Actually my #1 lake. Very good bass and pickerel fishing. A few monster northern pike.

ROD SCHOU, BUTTERWORTH MAPS

"For pike try Mepps Giant Killer, big live shiners. Go for yellow perch with worms or small shiners, worm baited jigs."

PETER MIRICK, EDITOR,
MASSACHUSETTS WILDLIFE

" A good largemouth bass lake. Try spinner baits and rubber worms."

JEFF CAPUTE, AWARD WINNING FISHERMAN

Cast 13:

BOURNE

Ponds & Lakes

Total Land Area (sq. miles) **41.02**

Total Area of Ponds (acres) **247**

Total numbers of Ponds **73**

Number of Ponds by size:

<1 acres:	38
1-5 acres:	19
5-10 acres:	9
10-20 acres:	5
20-50 acres:	2
50-100 acres:	
>100 acres:	

Pond groups:
Coalition for Buzzards Bay

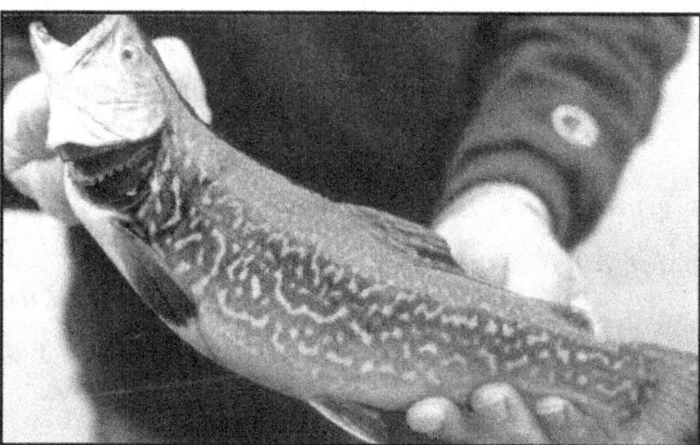

Well marked Cape Cod Tiger Trout.

BOURNE

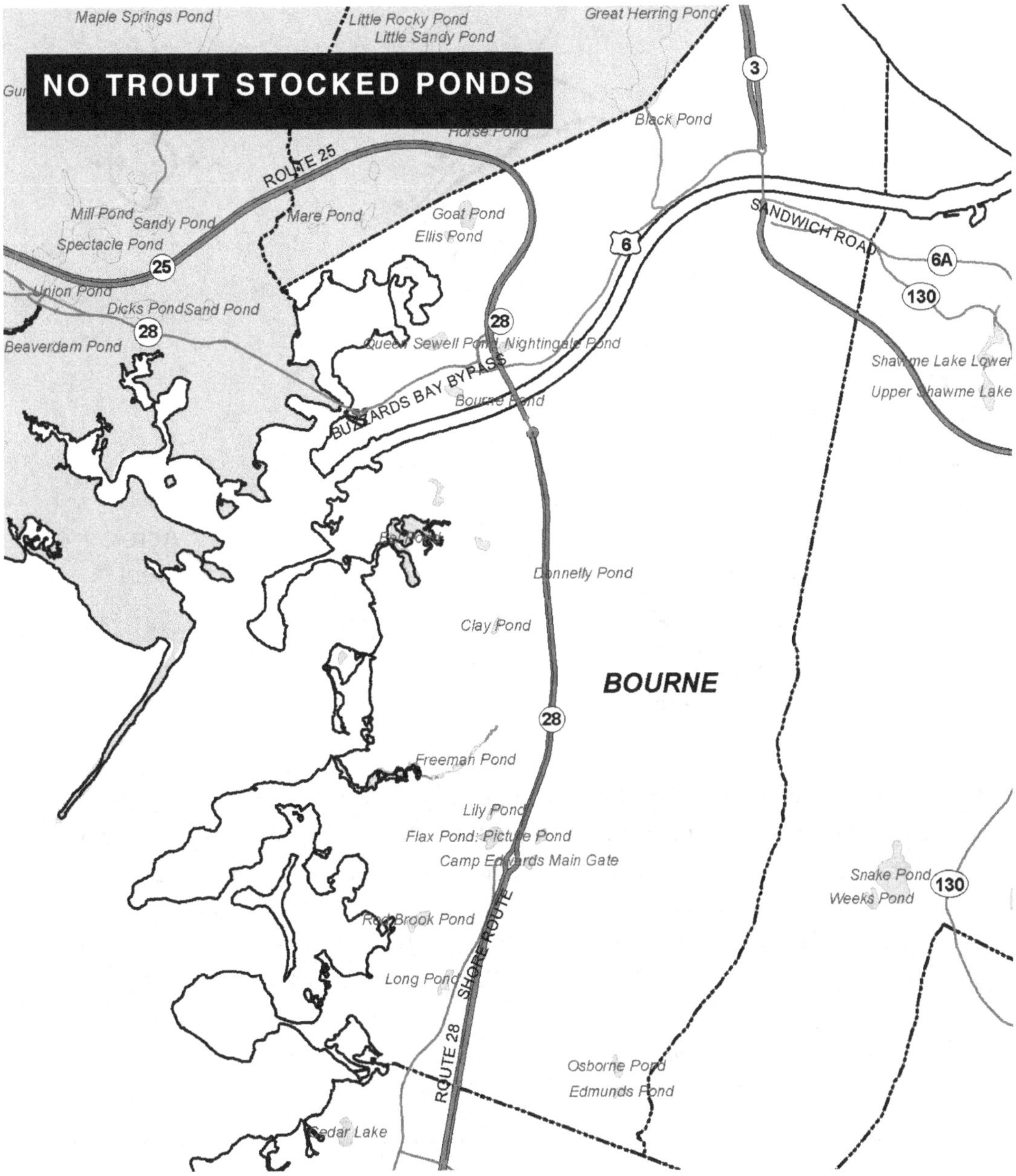

NO TROUT STOCKED PONDS

Maple Springs Pond
Little Rocky Pond
Little Sandy Pond
Great Herring Pond
Black Pond
ROUTE 25
Mill Pond
Sandy Pond
Spectacle Pond
Mare Pond
Goat Pond
Ellis Pond
SANDWICH ROAD
Dicks Pond
Sand Pond
Beaverdam Pond
Nightingale Pond
BUZZARDS BAY BYPASS
Donnelly Pond
Clay Pond
BOURNE
Freeman Pond
Camp Edwards Main Gate
Snake Pond
Weeks Pond
Long Pond
SHORE ROUTE
ROUTE 28
Osborne Pond
Edmunds Pond

FLAX POND

Bourne (Also known as Picture Lake)

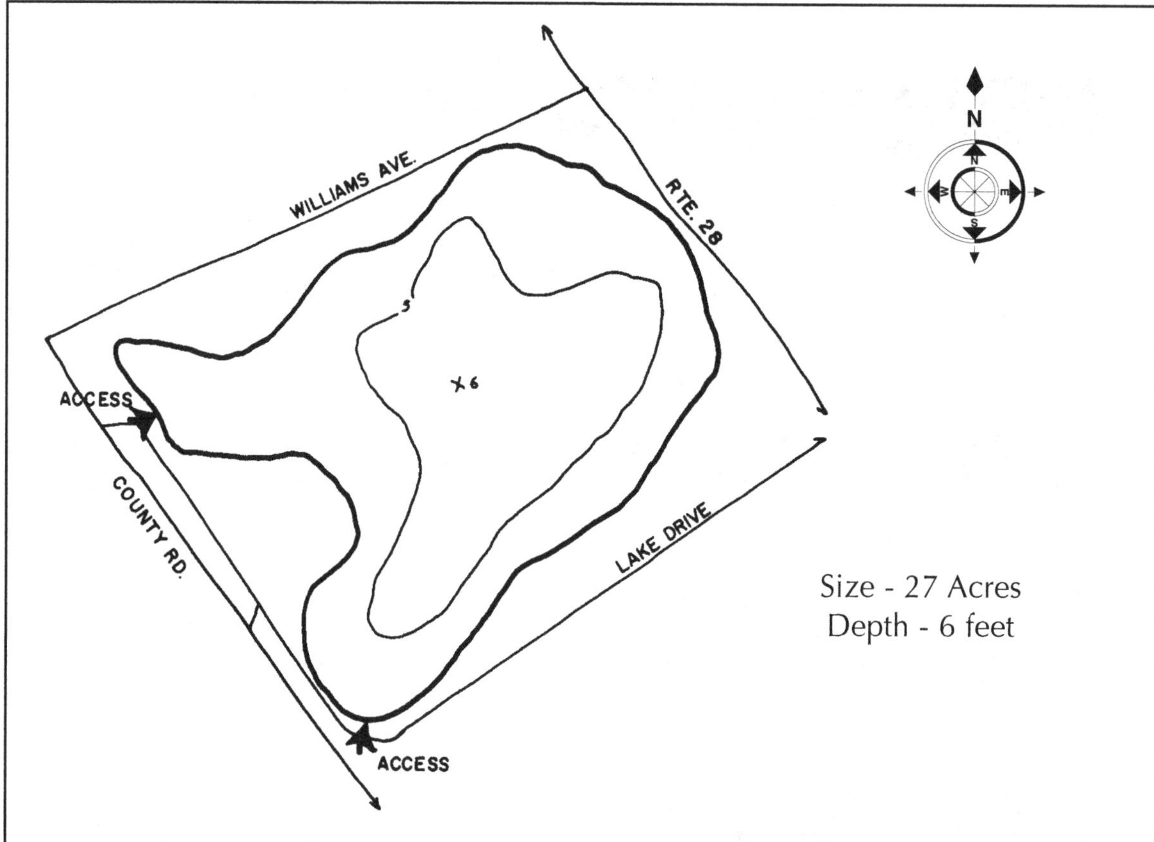

Location/Access/Special Regulations. Located west of Route 28, General MacArthur Boulevard and the Otis Air Force Base Rotary. Public access from two points on west shore, off County Road through a town park and a beach area.

> *"Good largemouth bass fishing. Best bets are spinnerbaits or shiners."*
> Steve Hurley, MDFW
>
> *"This pond has good bass fishing and pickerel. Access is easy."*
> Rod Schou, Butterworth Maps

The Innermost Waters.

The outermost Atlantic and the innermost Scargo Lake as viewed from Scargo Hill Tower.

Cast 14:

BREWSTER

Ponds & Lakes

Total Land Area (sq. miles)	**22.5**
Total Area of Ponds (acres)	**2,028**
Total numbers of Ponds	**76**

Number of Ponds by size:

<1 acres:	**23**
1-5 acres:	**25**
5-10 acres:	**6**
10-20 acres:	**5**
20-50 acres:	**10**
50-100 acres:	**2**
>100 acres:	**5**

Pond groups:

- **Brewster Pond Monitoring group**
- **Canoe Pond Association**
- **Long pond Watershed Association**

BREWSTER

Little Cliff Pond in Brewster

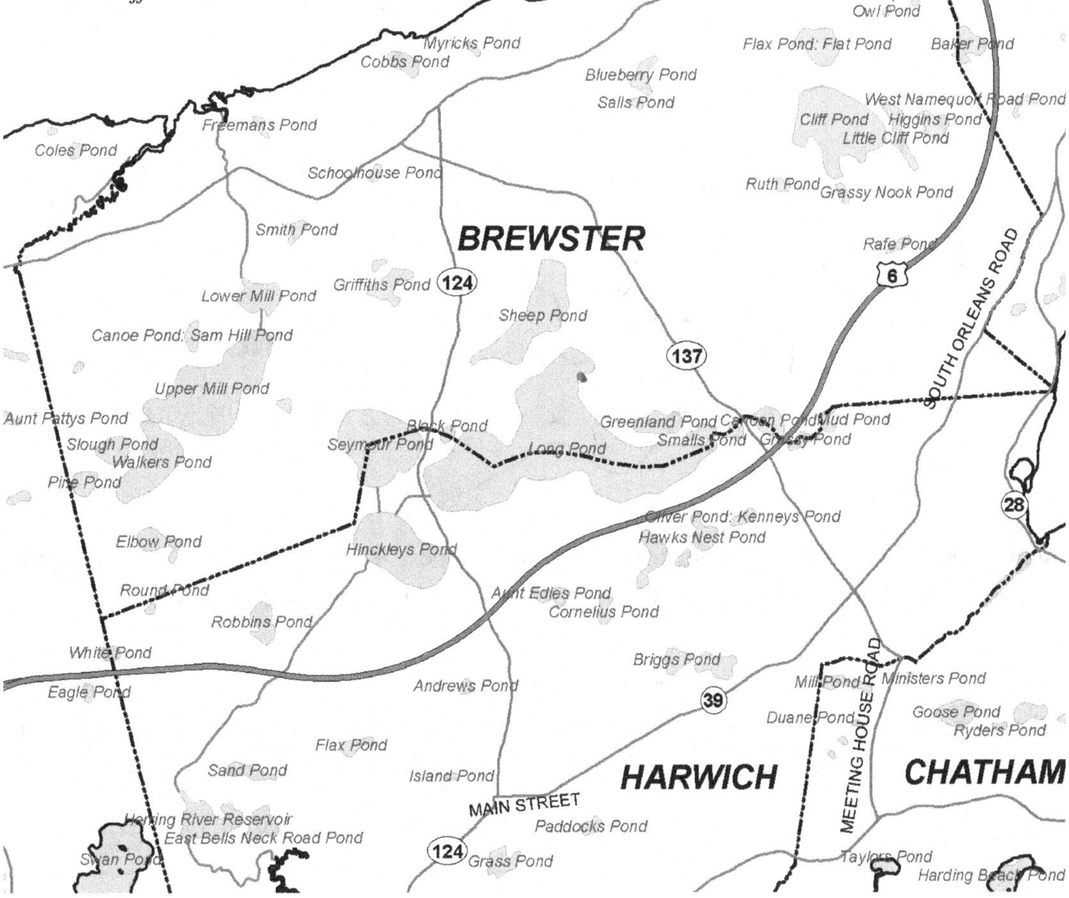

BREWSTER
ORLE
HARWICH
CHATHAM
6A
6
124
137
28
39
SOUTH ORLEANS ROAD
MEETING HOUSE ROAD
MAIN STREET
Cedar Pond
Boland Pond
Vespers Pond
Owl Pond
Flax Pond: Flat Pond
Baker Pond
Myricks Pond
Cobbs Pond
Blueberry Pond
Salls Pond
West Namequoit Road Pond
Cliff Pond
Higgins Pond
Little Cliff Pond
Freemans Pond
Coles Pond
Schoolhouse Pond
Ruth Pond
Grassy Nook Pond
Smith Pond
Rafe Pond
Griffiths Pond
Lower Mill Pond
Sheep Pond
Canoe Pond: Sam Hill Pond
Upper Mill Pond
Aunt Pattys Pond
Slough Pond
Walkers Pond
Pine Pond
Black Pond
Seymour Pond
Long Pond
Greenland Pond
Cahoon Pond
Mud Pond
Smalls Pond
Grassy Pond
Elbow Pond
Hinckleys Pond
Oliver Pond: Kenneys Pond
Hawks Nest Pond
Round Pond
Robbins Pond
Aunt Edies Pond
Cornelius Pond
White Pond
Eagle Pond
Andrews Pond
Briggs Pond
Mill Pond
Ministers Pond
Duane Pond
Goose Pond
Ryders Pond
Flax Pond
Sand Pond
Island Pond
Herring River Reservoir
East Bells Neck Road Pond
Swan Pond
Paddocks Pond
Grass Pond
Taylors Pond
Harding Beach Pond

CLIFF POND

BREWSTER

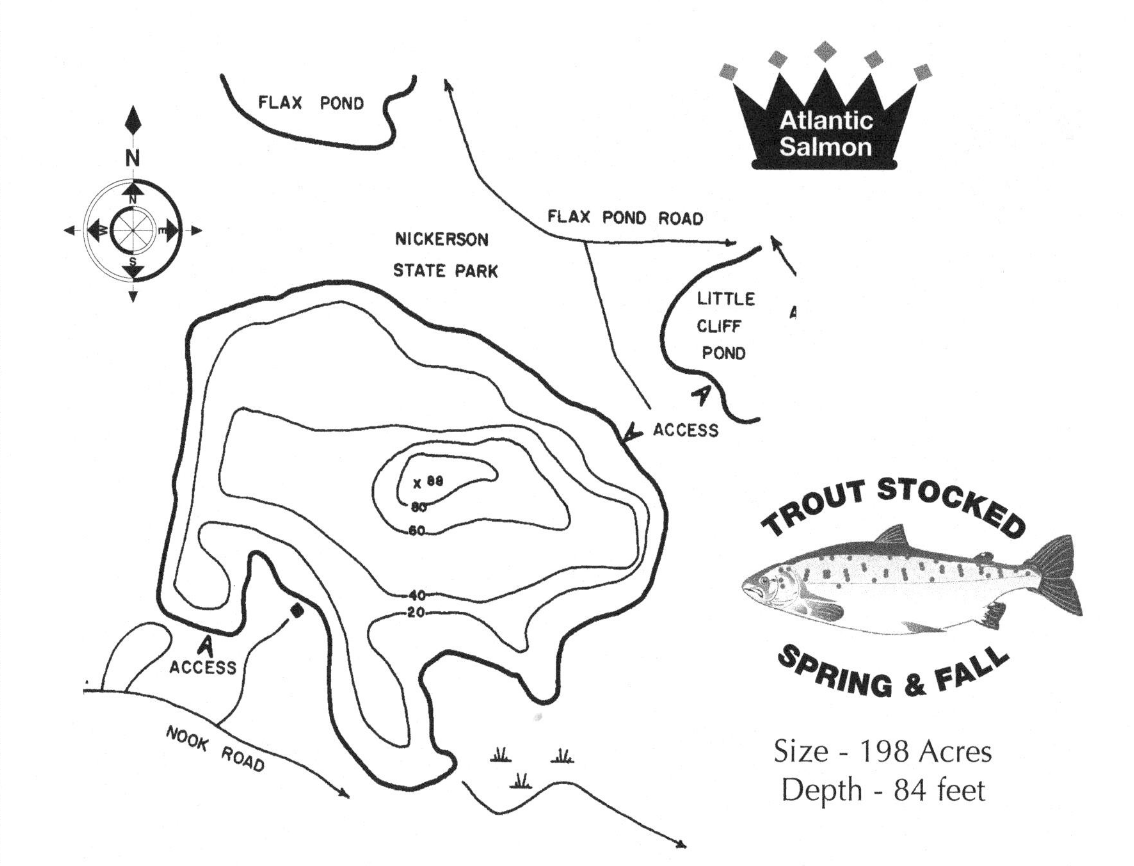

Location/Access/Special Regulations. Second deepest Cape Cod lake. Located on Nickerson State Park, off Route 6A. Concrete boat ramp on south shore access.

> *"Can't beat this one! Early on, drift a worm/spinner rig, or lightly weighted powerbait (multi-color works best here) best fly is a Grey Ghost streamer with a little red added."*
>
> PETER MIRICK, EDITOR, MASSACHUSETTS WILDLIFE

CLIFF POND - TIPS FROM EXPERTS

"This is an excellent trout pond."

ROD SCHOU, BUTTERWORTH MAPS

"Cliff is the best pond on the Cape for yellow perch, smallmouth bass,trout, and Atlantic salmon. I have caught some very large bass in this pond on a gold Thomas Cyclone. I have found this to be the best all around lure for this pond. In gold it's also good for yellow perch. Trout will hit gold, silver, or red.. For Atlantic salmon I use a Super Duper or a Krokodile in silver, red, or gold. The last Atlantic salmon I landed, a 28 inch fish, hit a silver Krokodile."

ELLA SCHULTZ, EXPERIENCED CAPE COD ANGLER

"One of the three best lakes on the Cape. You name it, it's here. Stocked with salmon and trout, spring and fall. Great smallmouth and panfish. Super place for families and children."

STAN MOAK, TROUT UNLIMITED

"Best bet on the Cape for Atlantic salmon."

STEVE HURLEY, MDFW

"Overall, the best Atlantic salmon pond on Cape Cod. Best method? Troll a 3" Rapala in blue and silver."

PETER MIRICK, EDITOR,
MASSACHUSETTS WILDLIFE

"The best salmon and trout lake on Cape Cod. Try shiners or troll from a canoe using spinners or spoons."

GENE BOURQUE, EDITOR, ON THE WATER

"Awesome for trout and smallmouth bass."

ROBERT JESSUP, THE SPORTING LIFE

"Some of the state's largest salmon are stocked here. Fish shiners, jigs, dry and wet flies from a boat."

CRAIG POOSIKIAN, CUSTOM ROD BUILDER

"Has most fish stocked on Cape. Great access points. Can use outboard up to 9.9 HP. Try crawlers, troll streamers – smelt imitations."

MARK PALMER, GOOSE HUMMOCK

"One of 3 best ponds on the Cape. Try a Wooly Bugger in early spring, on the bottom and slow."

STEVE HALLEY, ORVIS- BOSTON

"Cape's number 1 trout pond. Use worms, powerbait, corn."

DAVID GILMORE, RENOWNED CAPE COD ANGLER

LITTLE CLIFF POND

BREWSTER

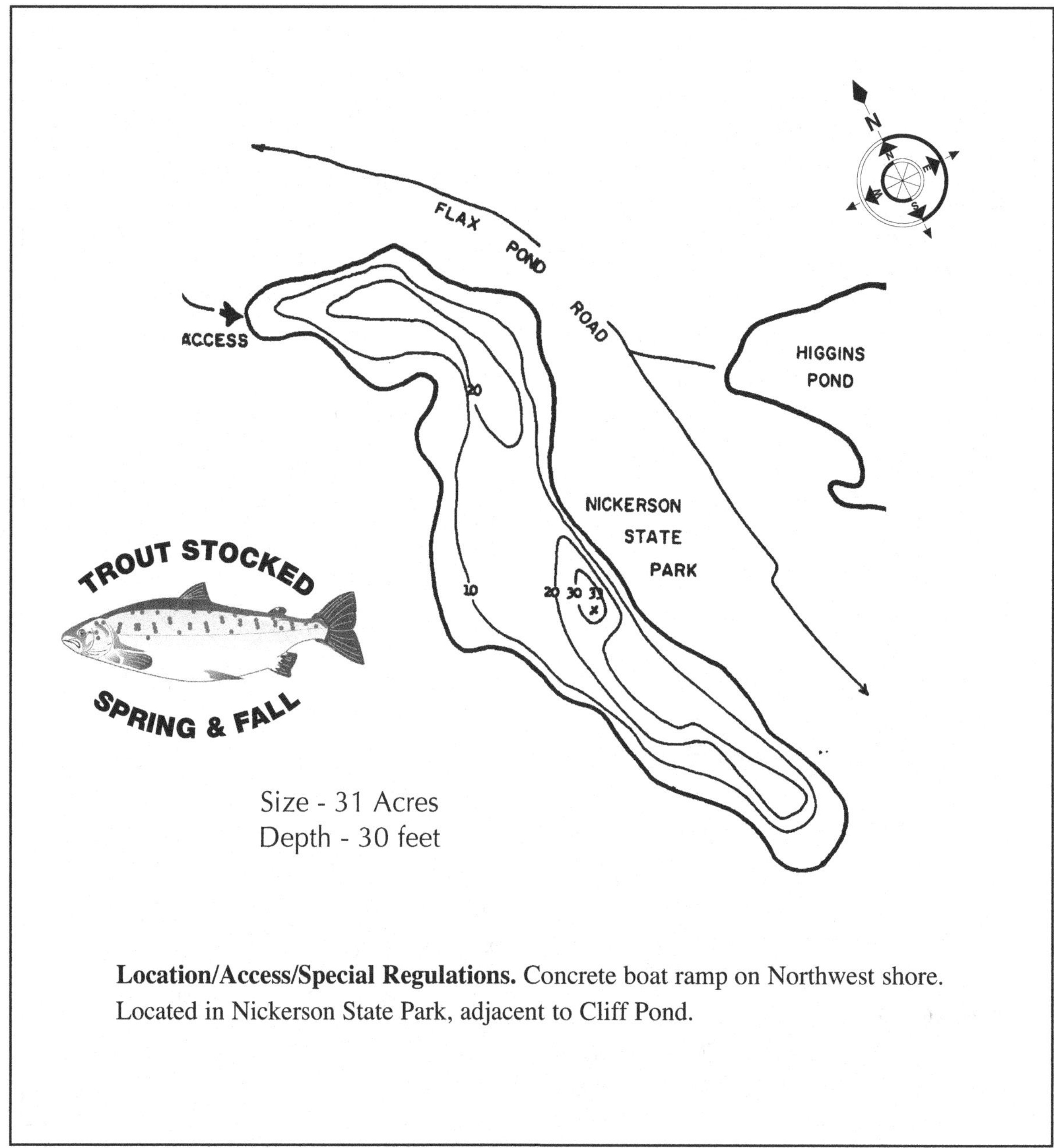

Location/Access/Special Regulations. Concrete boat ramp on Northwest shore. Located in Nickerson State Park, adjacent to Cliff Pond.

LITTLE CLIFF POND - TIPS FROM EXPERTS

" Cape's second best smallmouth pond.Try shiners, Mepps Spinners."

MARK PALMER, GOOSE HUMMOCK

"Another excellent trout pond."

ROD SCHOU, BUTTERWORTH MAPS

"Lots of trout and, unfortunately, overrun with largemouths."

CRAIG POOSIKIAN, CUSTOM ROD BUILDER

"Fly fish here for trout-good hatches, less pressure than Big Cliff."

GENE BOURQUE, EDITOR, ON THE WATER

"A top Cape trout pond. When Big Cliff is crowded, this is a great choice, especially in late May. Use same baits as Big Cliff."

PETER MIRICK, EDITOR, MASSACHUSETTS

"Great smallmouth and panfish. Good pond for bank fishing."

STAN MOAK, TROUT UNLIMITED

"Good trout pond. Try any gold and red lure, Thomas Cyclone, silver Phoebe, Colorado Spinner, gold Kastmaster, copper Canduit. I always cast into the wind when I am fishing with lures."

ELLA SCHULTZ, EXPERIENCED CAPE COD ANGLER

ELBOW POND

Brewster

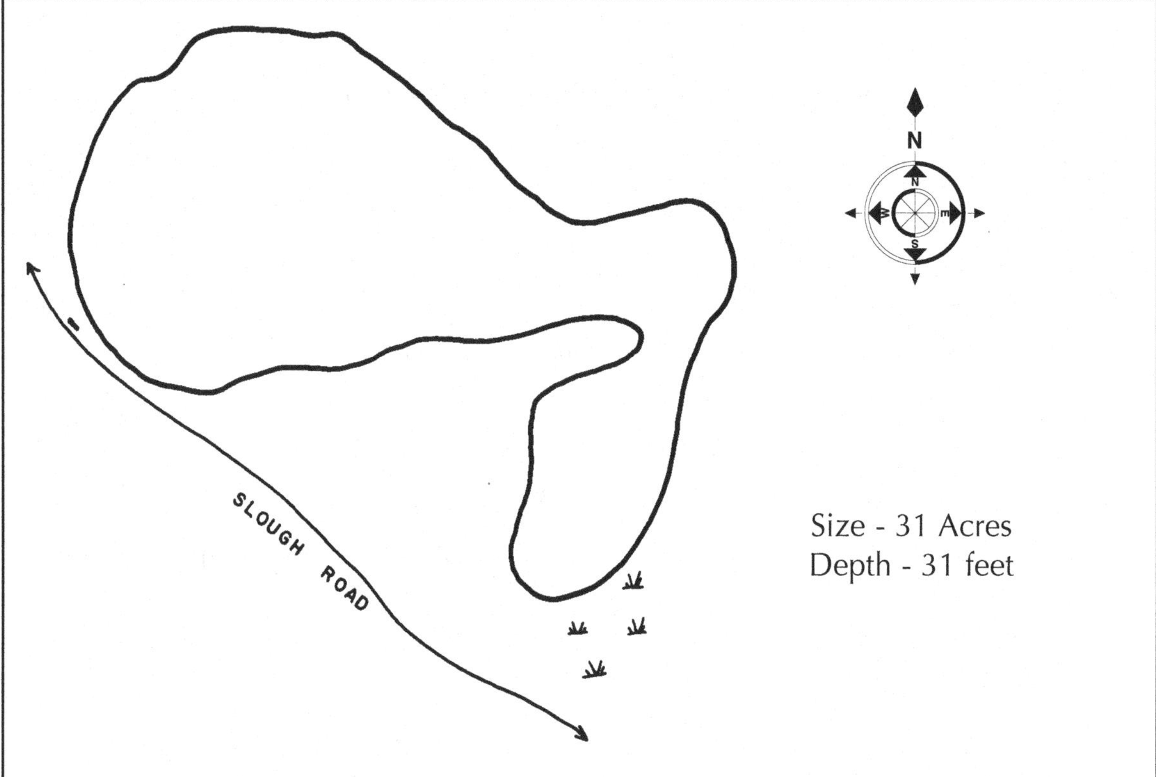

Location/Access/Special Regulations. Located in southwest corner of Brewster, north of Route 6 and east of Airline Road. Public access via Slough Pond Road. Essentially undeveloped shoreline. Several sizeable cranberry bogs and town owned pieces of property adjacent to pond. Pond actually is elbow shaped.

"Try worms, spinners for good panfish, pic kerel, and bass fishing."

Mark Palmer, Goose Hummock

"Good largemouth bass fishing in years past. Return all fish."

Robert Jessup, The Sporting Life

FLAX POND

Brewster

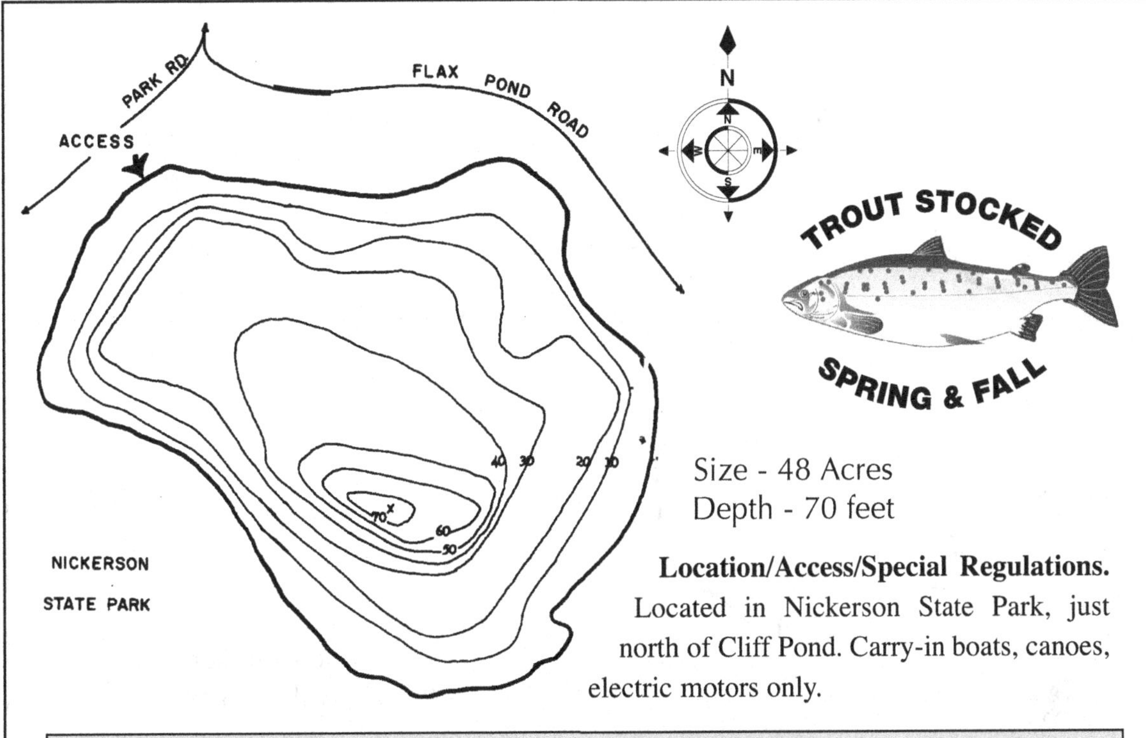

Size - 48 Acres
Depth - 70 feet

Location/Access/Special Regulations. Located in Nickerson State Park, just north of Cliff Pond. Carry-in boats, canoes, electric motors only.

"Very good bass and trout pond. Another great family pond."

Stan Moak, TROUT UNLIMITED

"Mostly trout. Fish the same as Cliff Pond. A more wadable pond."

Craig Poosikian, Custom Rod Builder

"Good waters for trout on flies. I often fish my way all around the pond."

Ella Schultz, Experienced angler

"Good trout pond and fair smallmouth bass fishing. Also holds yellow perch and pumpkinseed."

Steve Hurley, MDFW

"Good trout fishery. Drops off nicely near shore so you can bait fish in summer and get down to deeper water rather easily."

Mark Palmer, Goose Hummock

GRIFFITHS POND

BREWSTER

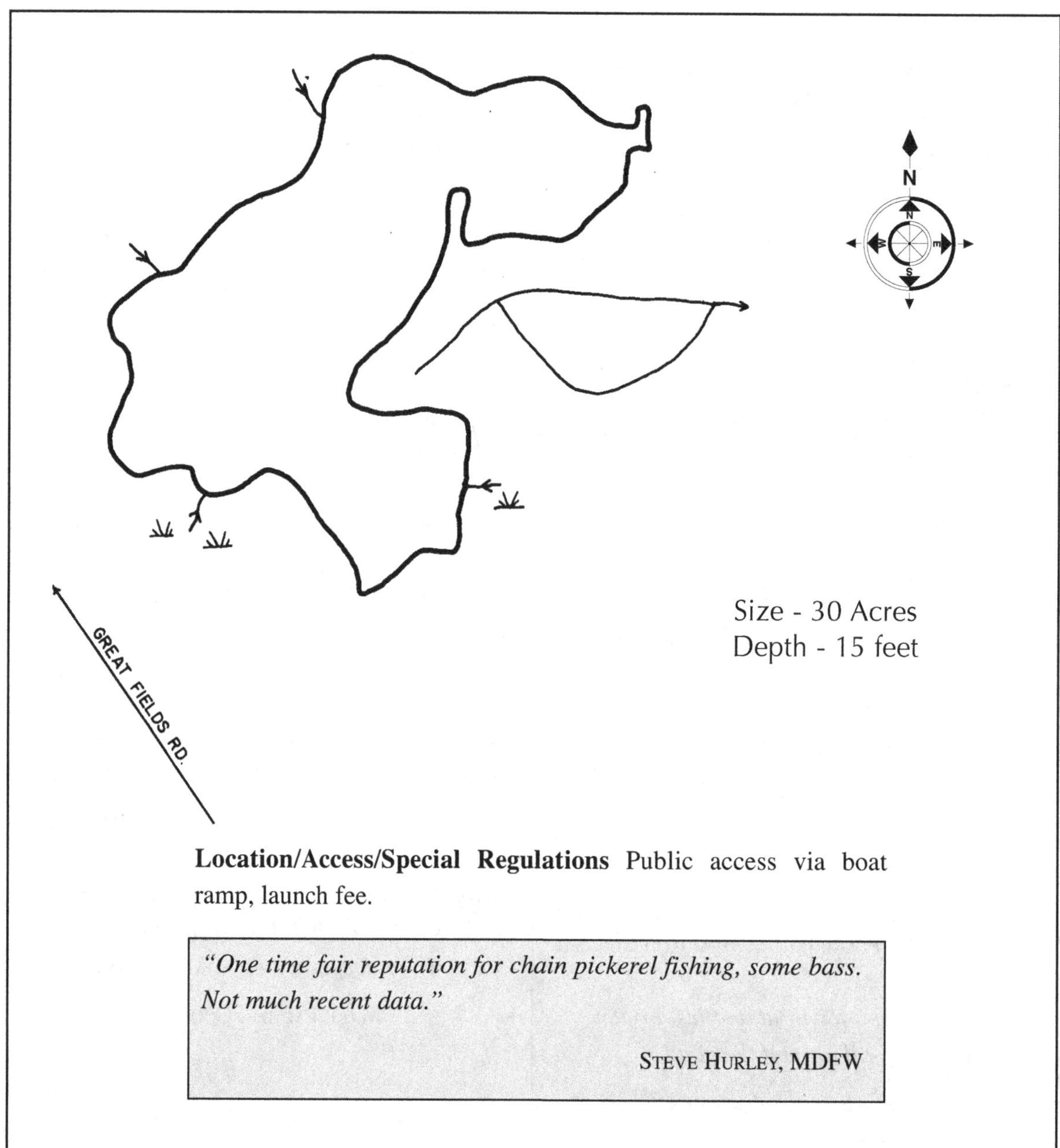

Location/Access/Special Regulations Public access via boat ramp, launch fee.

> *"One time fair reputation for chain pickerel fishing, some bass. Not much recent data."*
>
> STEVE HURLEY, MDFW

HIGGINS POND

BREWSTER

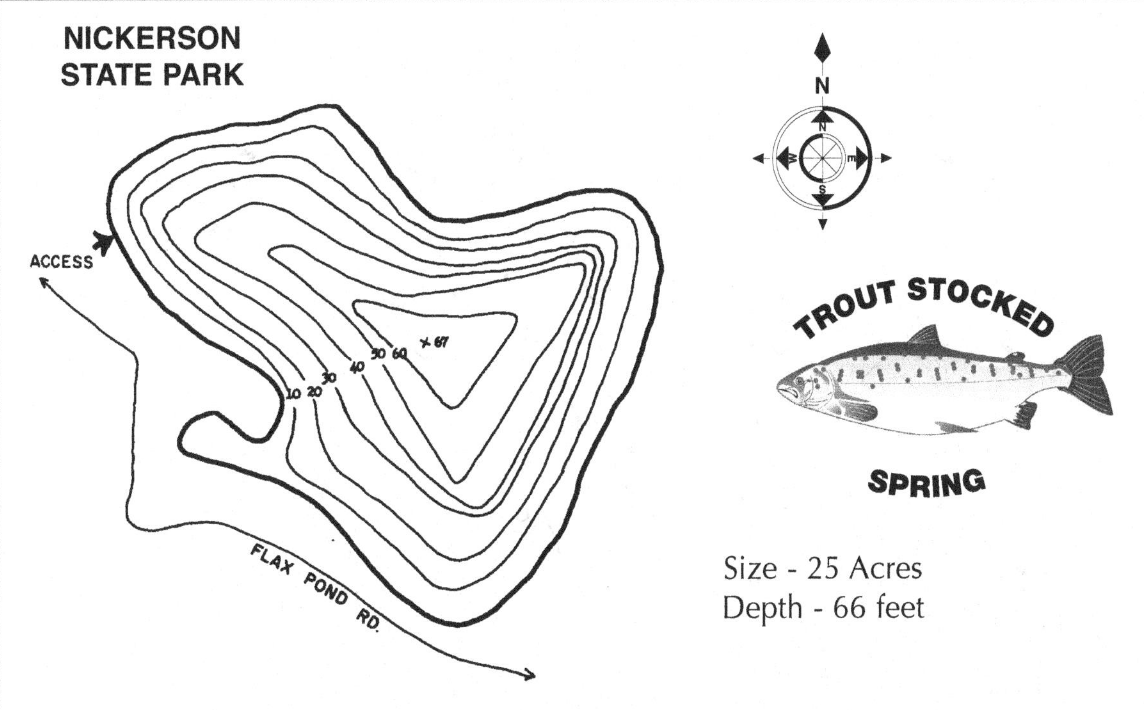

Location/Access/Special Regulations Located in Nickerson State Park, east of Little Cliff Pond. No launch, carry in. Electric motors only. Reclaimed trout pond. Stocked at one time with Temiscamee brook trout which grow to 8 pounds. Also tiger trout.

> *"Hard to reach.- limited shore fishing."*
>
> STAN MOAK, TROUT UNLIMITED
>
> *"Best fishing is for trout. Cast a Thomas Cyclone. One October I fished this pond all the time and had great trout fishing. I don't think they stock it anymore as the road to the pond is all washed away."*
>
> ELLA SCHULTZ, EXPERIENCED ANGLER

LONG POND

Brewster & Harwich (see also Harwich)

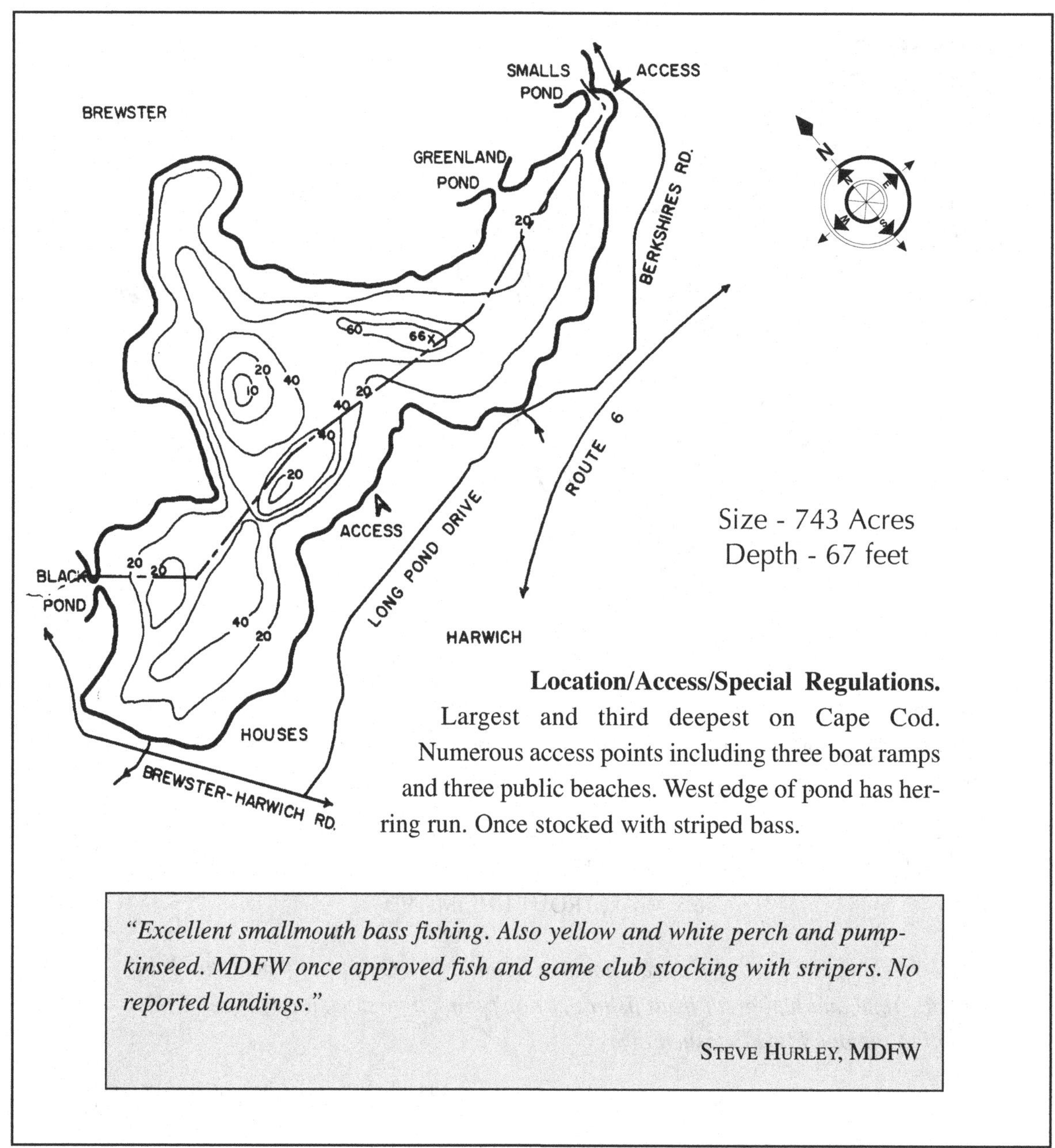

Size - 743 Acres
Depth - 67 feet

Location/Access/Special Regulations. Largest and third deepest on Cape Cod. Numerous access points including three boat ramps and three public beaches. West edge of pond has herring run. Once stocked with striped bass.

> *"Excellent smallmouth bass fishing. Also yellow and white perch and pumpkinseed. MDFW once approved fish and game club stocking with stripers. No reported landings."*
>
> Steve Hurley, MDFW

LONG POND: TIPS FROM PANEL OF EXPERTS

"Best species-large and smallmouth bass."

DAVID GILMORE, RENOWNED BASS ANGLER

"For smallies, largemouths fish live herring. BIG bait-BIG fish!"

CRAIG POOSIKIAN, CUSTOM ROD BUILDER

"Lots of smallmouth bass can be fished from gas powered outboards, along structure and where rocky banks prevail. Try Gitzits, shiners. Fish move out to deeper water when weather warms."

MARK PALMER, GOOSE HUMMOCK

"Fair smallmouth, white and yellow perch. I've had best luck with light color, short (<31/2") twister tail jigs. Fishing is generally slow, but most trips will produce a couple of good 'smallies' and, sometimes, a stringer of perch. Grass shrimp should work well here."

PETER MIRICK, EDITOR, MASSACHUSETTS WILDLIFE

"Excellent bass fishing, year 'round, easy access."

ROD SCHOU, BUTTERWORTH MAPS

"Caught my biggest Cape Cod smallmouth bass here- 3 1/2 pounds- on a green Roostertail. Fought so hard I thought I hooked a new world record!"

PETER BUDRYK, A FISHERMAN

BE EXTRA KIND TO THIS POND. The CCC water quality assessment estimated only 2 undeveloped parcels existed along the entire shoreline in 2000, and that approximately 92 cesspools or leechfields exist within 200 feet of the shoreline, resulting in regular water quality problems that threaten the environmental health and enjoyment of the pond.

Long Pond, looking west, from the Harwich-Brewster border. Route 6 through Harwich is on the left. The pond is the Cape's largest freshwater lake. (Steve Heaslip photo 8/8/97)

(LOWER) MILL POND

Brewster

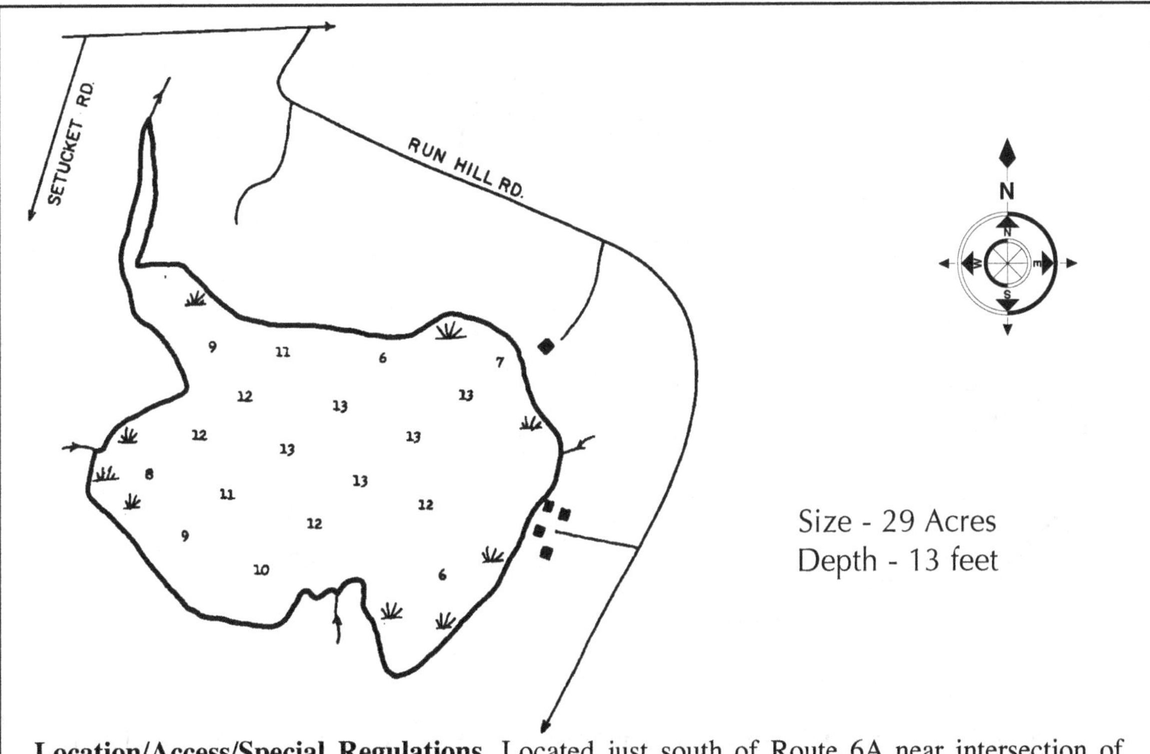

Location/Access/Special Regulations. Located just south of Route 6A near intersection of Satucket and Stoney Brook Roads. Pond water is recharged by a surface outlet from Upper Mill Pond. It is dammed at northern tip where it discharges water into the Stoney brook herring run. An historic grist mill is operated at this dam site. Informal access across town owned land.

"A good place to catch chain pickerel."

Steve Hurley, MDFW

"Fish here with live herring for largemouth bass and pickerel. Again: BIG bait=BIG fish."

Craig Poosikian, Custom Rod Builder

"Best species are bass and panfish. Use shiners, spinners. Doesn't get a lot of pressure. Lots of 2-3 pound largemouths."

Mark Palmer, Goose Hummock

(UPPER) MILL POND

Brewster

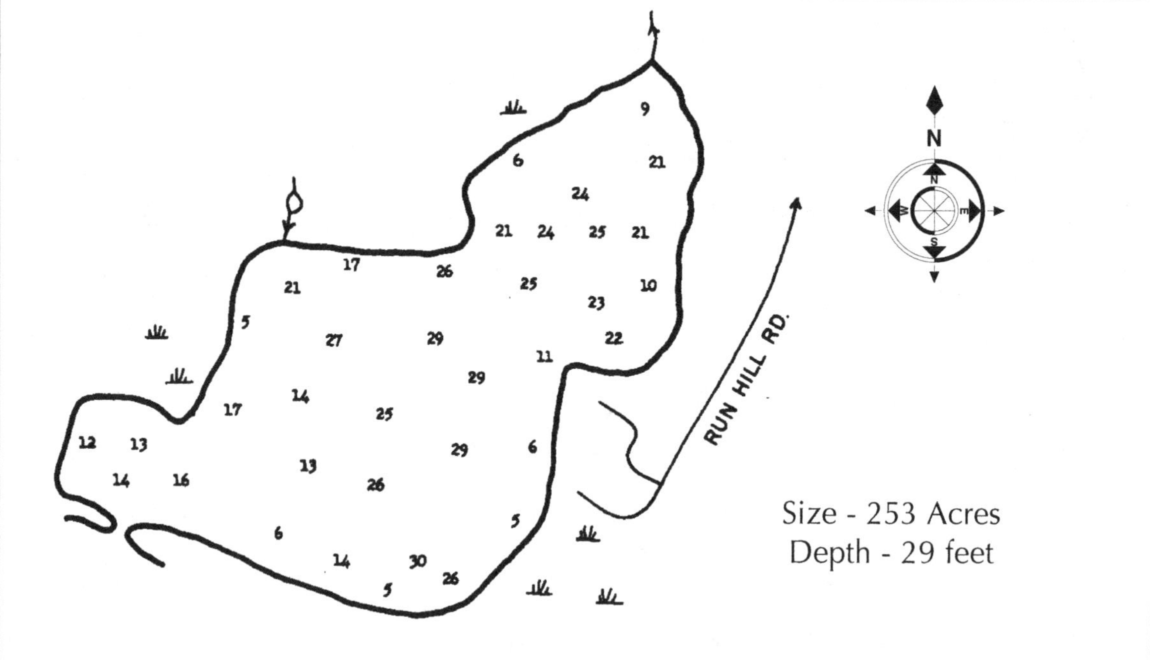

Location/Access/Special Regulations. Joins Walkers pond, easy access via town dump to Run Hill road . Unimproved launch area. 3 HP limit. Has an inlet and an outlet.

"Best species- yellow perch. Also holds largemouth bass, white perch, pickerel, pumpkinseed."

Steve Hurley, MDFW

"Best species-bass. Good top water action. Shiners. Good pond-fun with canoe or kayak."

Mark Palmer, Goose Hummock

"Best species-yellow perch. Use worms, shiners. Can produce a nice bucket of yellows on the right day."

Peter Mirick, Editor, MASSACHUSETTS WILDLIFE

SHEEP POND

BREWSTER

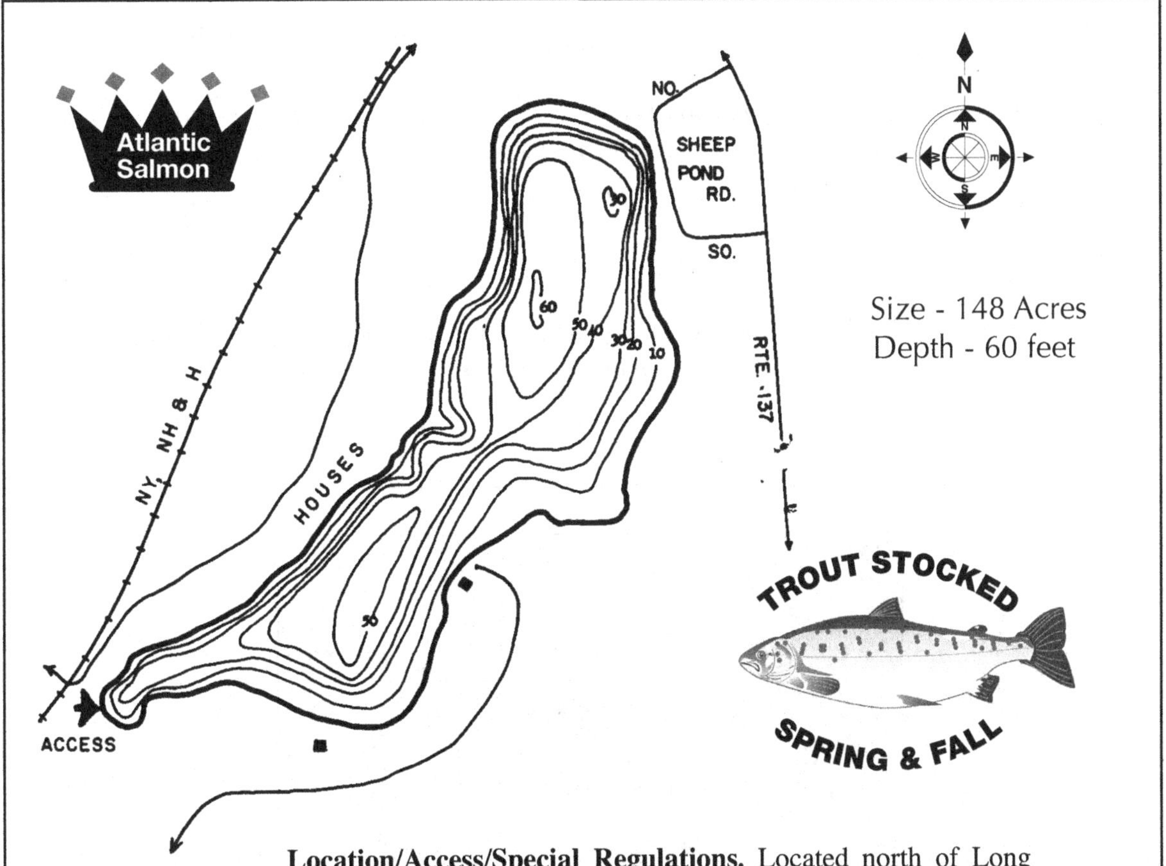

Location/Access/Special Regulations. Located north of Long pond, midway between Routes 124 and 137. Easy access via Fisherman's Landing. Concrete public boat ramp. 3 HP limit.

> *"In addition to excellent trout fishing, this is one of only three Cape waters with stocked Atlantic salmon. Also provides good smallmouth bass fishing."*
>
> STEVE HURLEY, MDFW

SHEEP POND: TIPS FROM EXPERTS

"Patience and perseverance fishing Mooselook Wobblers, shiners, or Rapalas can land you salmon up to 15 pounds here, but it gets a lot of pressure."

MARK PALMER, GOOSE HUMMOCK

"A best salmon pond that also produces bass and trout. Best fished from a boat, canoe, or float tube. I like a streamer fly tied with either flourescent root beer or purple Ersatz, size 6 or 8, with a 4X tippet."

STAN MOAK, TROUT UNLIMITED

"This pond is loaded with fish, some very large, stocked brutes. Best fishing during off season; no pressure, very pleasant during the winter months. Quiet!"

ROBERT JESSUP, THE SPORTING LIFE

Gene Bourque, angler, instructor, guide, author, editor of On The Water Magazine, and one of this book's expert panelists.

SLOUGH POND

BREWSTER

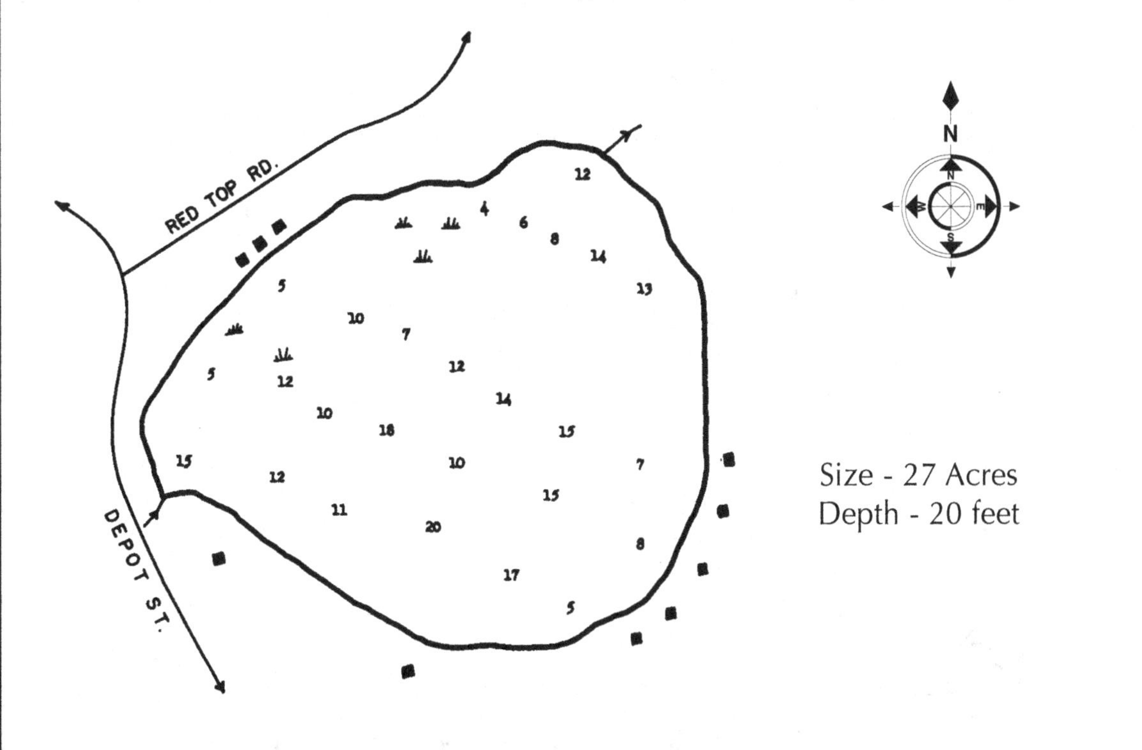

Location/Access/Special Regulations. Public boat ramp, cartop

"A good yellow perch pond."

STEVE HURLEY, MDFW

"A good bass, perch and sunfish pond."

DAVID GILMORE, RENOWNED BASS ANGLER

"Fish here for bass, pickerel with poppers,spinners. Lots of fish with occasional surprises."

MARK PALMER, GOOSE HUMMOCK

"Good pickerel fishing with live bait."

JEFF CAPUTE, AWARD WINNING ANGLER

WALKER POND

BREWSTER

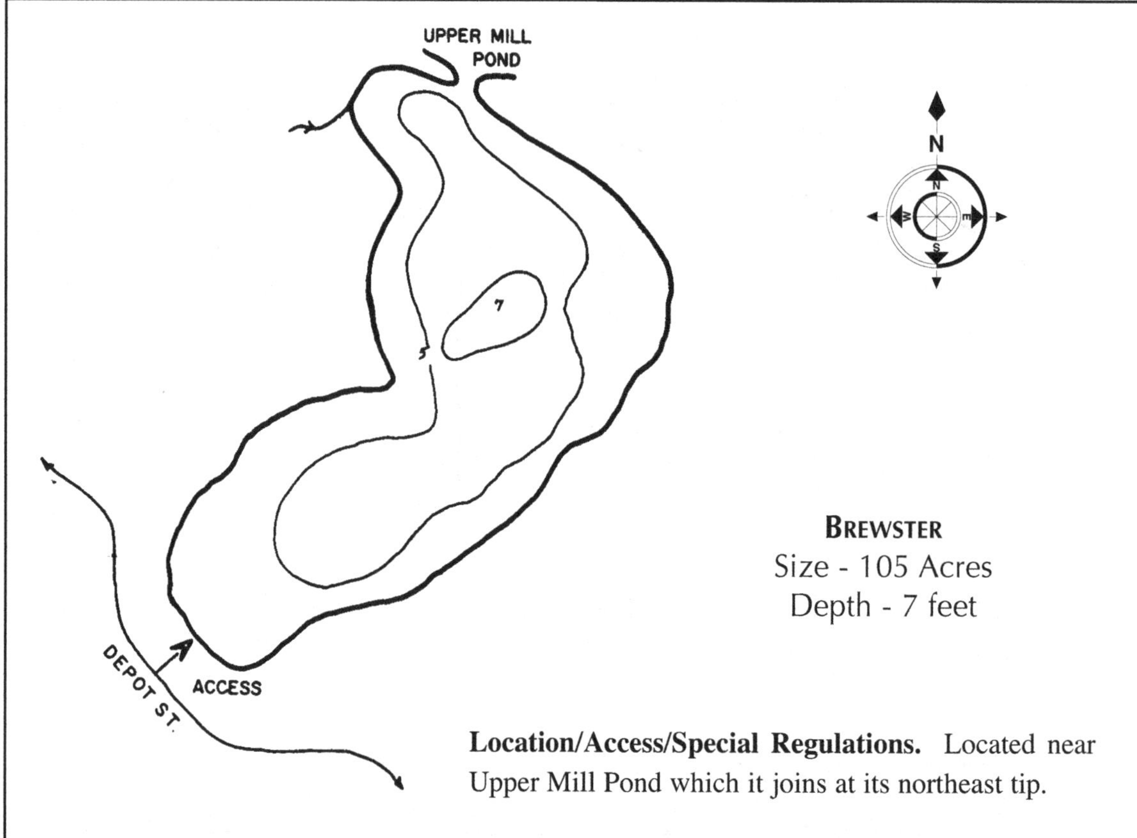

BREWSTER
Size - 105 Acres
Depth - 7 feet

Location/Access/Special Regulations. Located near Upper Mill Pond which it joins at its northeast tip.

"Good largemouth bass and pickerel fishing. Also holds white and yellow perch and pumpkinseed."

STEVE HURLEY, MDFW

"A good yellow perch pond. Live bait."

JEFF CAPUTE, AWARD WINNING ANGLER

"Best species-yellow perch.. Worms, shiners. Rarely get many, but does produce a corker yellow or white perch now and then. Bass fishing I rate only 'OK'".

PETER MIRICK, EDITOR,
MASSACHUSETTS WILDLIFE

Tony Stetzko, expert Cape Cod guide, angler, world record-holder, and proprietor of Cape Cod Shoppe, Orleans.

> *"Everyday I see the head of the largest trout I ever hooked, but did not land."*
>
> THEODORE GORDON (1914)

Cast 15:

CHATHAM

Ponds & Lakes

Total Land Area (sq. miles) 15.88

Total Area of Ponds (acres) 298

Total numbers of Ponds 44

Number of Ponds by size:

Size	Number
<1 acres:	9
1-5 acres:	24
5-10 acres:	4
10-20 acres:	2
20-50 acres:	5
50-100 acres:	0
>100 acres:	0

Pond groups:

- **Town of Chatham Water Quality Lab**
- **Chatham High School**

Devices for bottom bait fishing for trout in Cape Cod ponds. Note bobbers clipped on slack between reel and first guide. When fish takes bait, bobber rises, alerting angler to put down drink and set hook.

CHATHAM

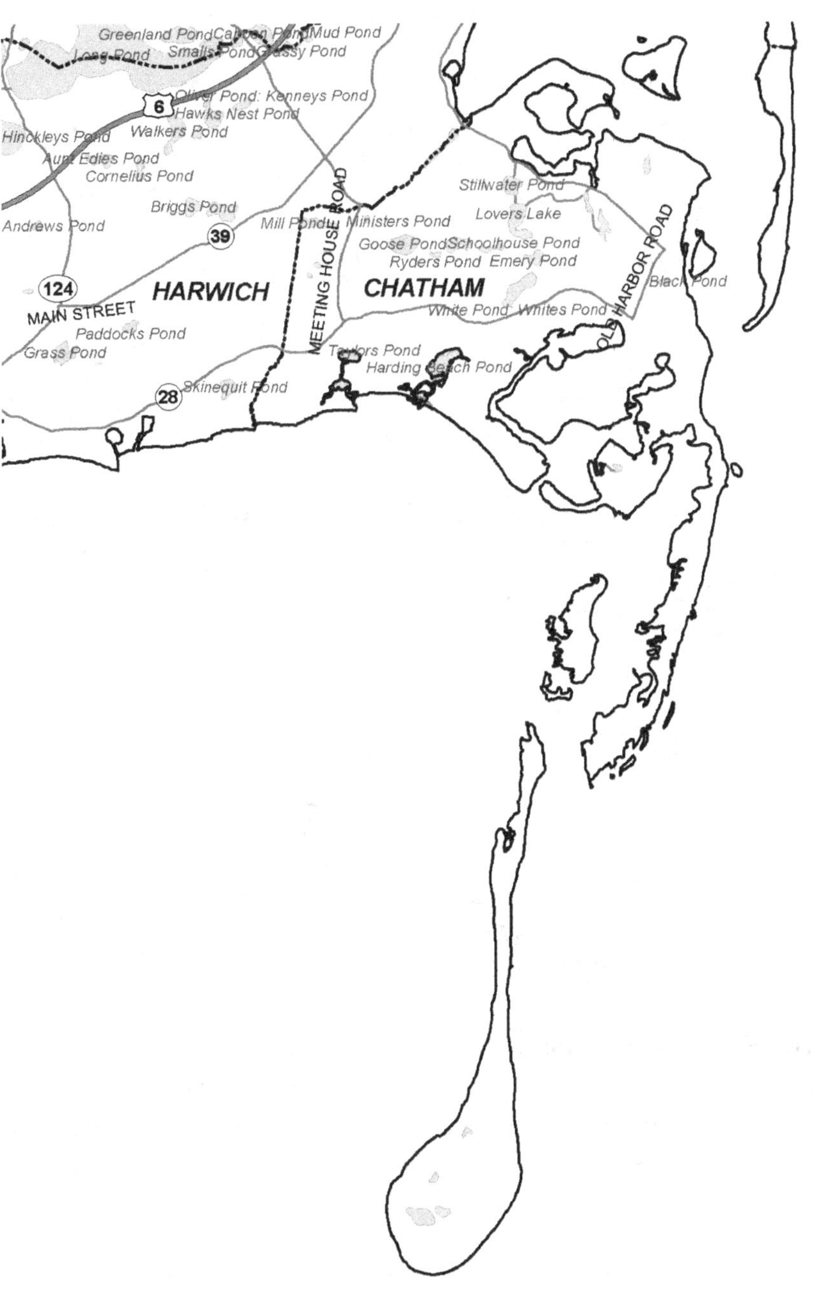
Greenland Pond
Mud Pond
Long Pond
Smalls Pond
Kenneys Pond
6
Hawks Nest Pond
Walkers Pond
Hinckleys Pond
Aunt Edies Pond
Cornelius Pond
Briggs Pond
Andrews Pond
39
124
MAIN STREET
HARWICH
Paddocks Pond
Grass Pond
28
Skinequit Pond
Mill Pond
MEETING HOUSE ROAD
Ministers Pond
Stillwater Pond
Lovers Lake
Goose Pond
Schoolhouse Pond
Ryders Pond
Emery Pond
CHATHAM
White Pond
Whites Pond
OLD HARBOR ROAD
Black Pond
Taylors Pond
Harding Beach Pond

GOOSE POND

CHATHAM

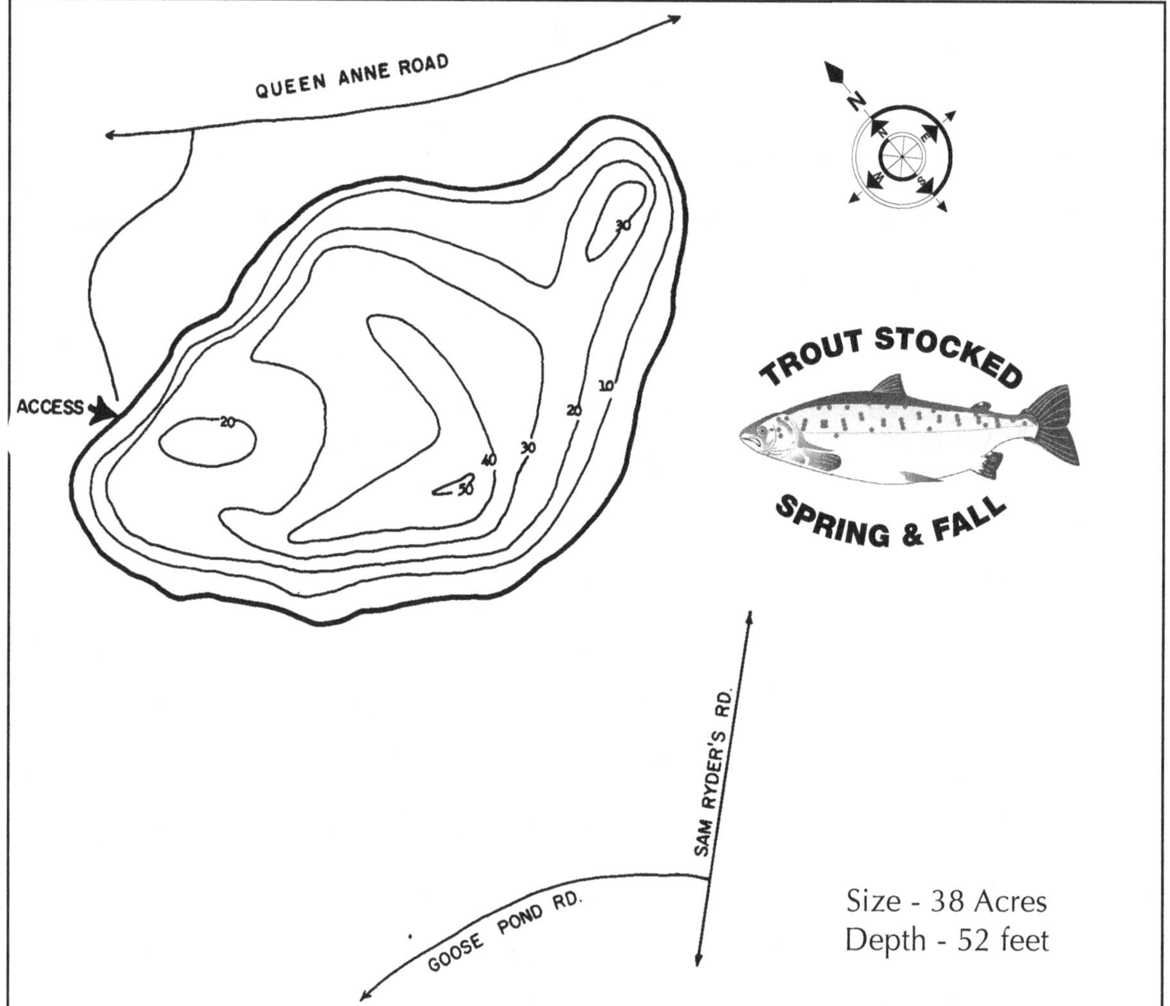

Size - 38 Acres
Depth - 52 feet

Location/Access/Special Regulations. Largest pond in Chatham. Clear to depth of 26 feet. Located south of Queen Anne Road and east of Route 137. Unimproved launch site. Electric motors only. Two town tracts of land protect northwest shore where a Fisherman's Landing is located. Wooded and undeveloped shoreline. Watch for Lady Slippers in spring.

GOOSE POND: TIPS FROM EXPERTS

"Good trout and largemouth bass pond."

DAVID GILMORE, RENOWNED BASS ANGLER

"Best trout pond in Chatham."

STEVE HURLEY, MDFW

"A good pond. Best species- striped bass! Best bait-live trout (legal?) from a boat. Check it out. Stripers are in Goose."

CRAIG POOSIKIAN, CUSTOM ROD BUILDER

"Well stocked with trout. Try shiners, spinners. Match the hatch in late spring/summer-midges, gnats"

MARK PALMER, GOOSE HUMMOCK

"Best town pond for trout. Spin fish small silver Krokodile, red & gold Thomas Buoyant, green Buoyant, Cyclone, all colors. Fly fish black Wooly Bugger."

ELLA SCHULTZ, EXPERIENCED ANGLER

Goose Pond, another lovely innermost water.

LOVERS LAKE

CHATHAM

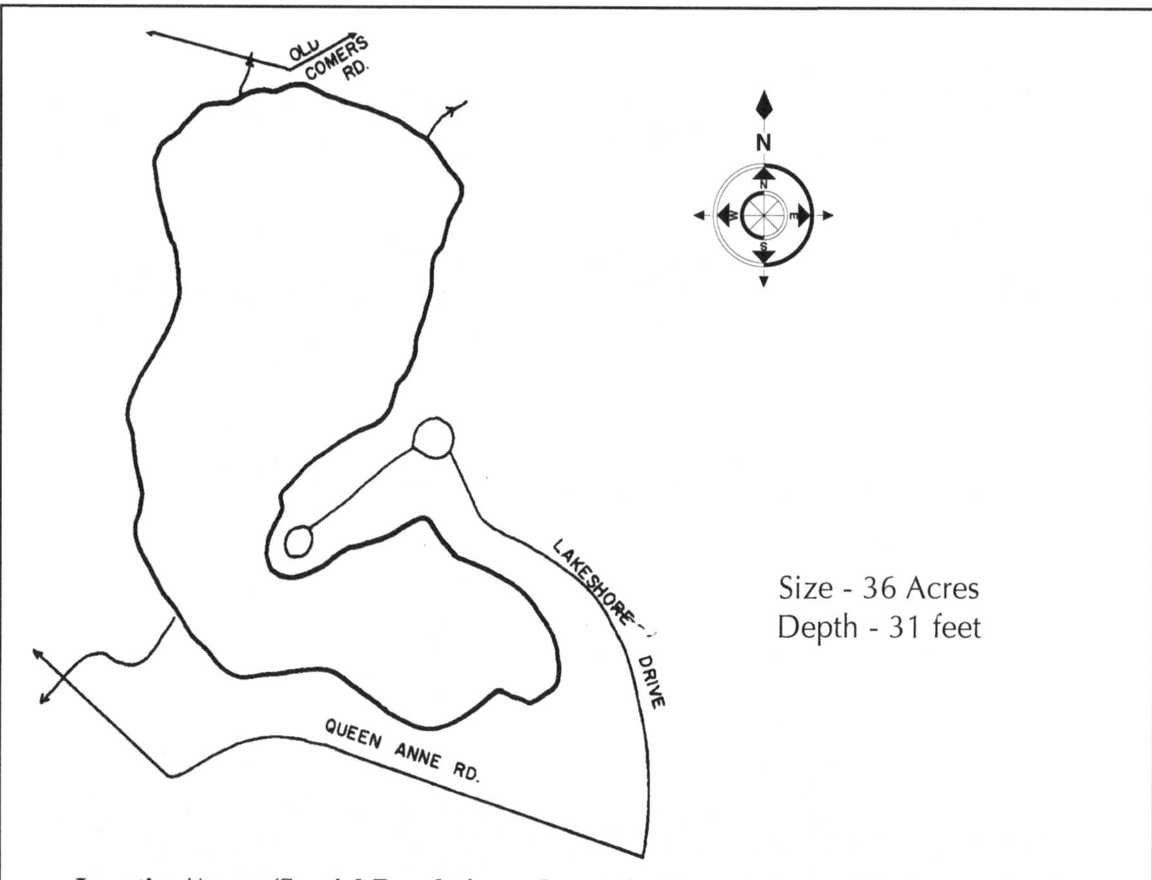

Location/Access/Special Regulations. Located midway between Old Comers Road and Queen Anne Road , just south of Ryders Cove. Poor access. West and north shores undeveloped. South and west shore developed with single family homes. Some conservation property and a municipal water supply.

> *"Chain pickerel, some bass."*
>
> STEVE HURLEY, MDFW

NOTE: "LOVERS LAKE PRESENTS AS A HIGHLY IMPACTED POND WITH SIGNIFICANT WATER QUALITY PROBLEMS." CAPE COD COMMISSION

MILL POND

CHATHAM

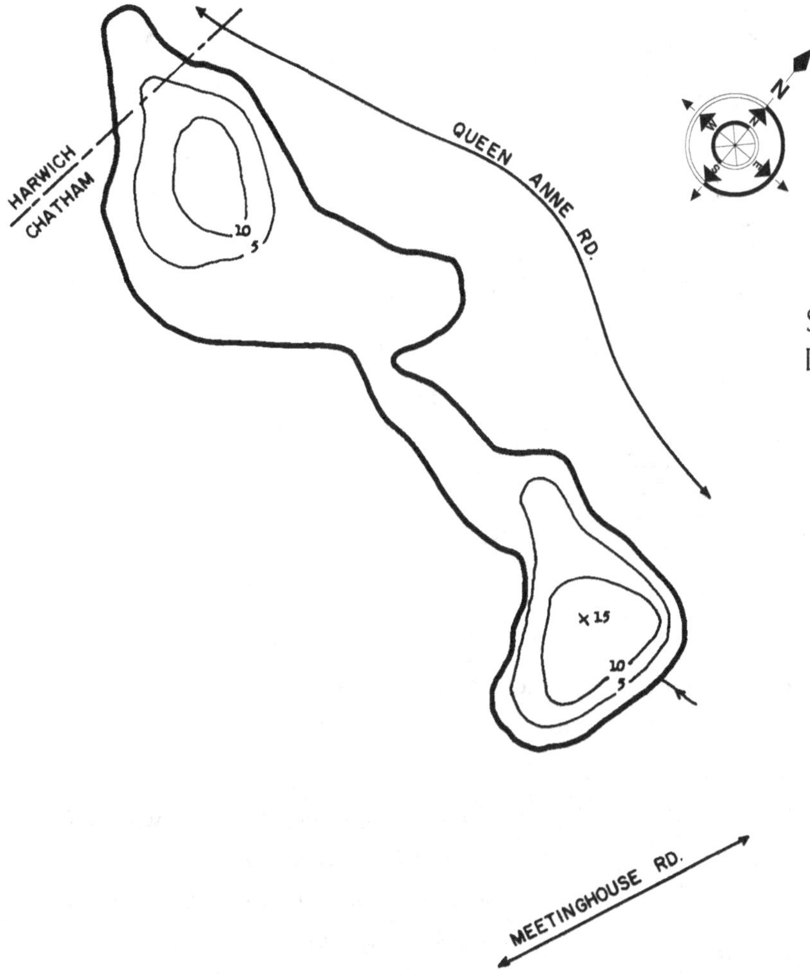
HARWICH
CHATHAM
QUEEN ANNE RD.
10
5
x15
10
5
MEETINGHOUSE RD.
N

Size - 22 Acres
Depth - 16 feet

Location/Access/Special Regulations. Located in northwest corner of Chatham near intersection of Queen Anne Road and Route 137. Poor public access.

SCHOOLHOUSE POND

CHATHAM

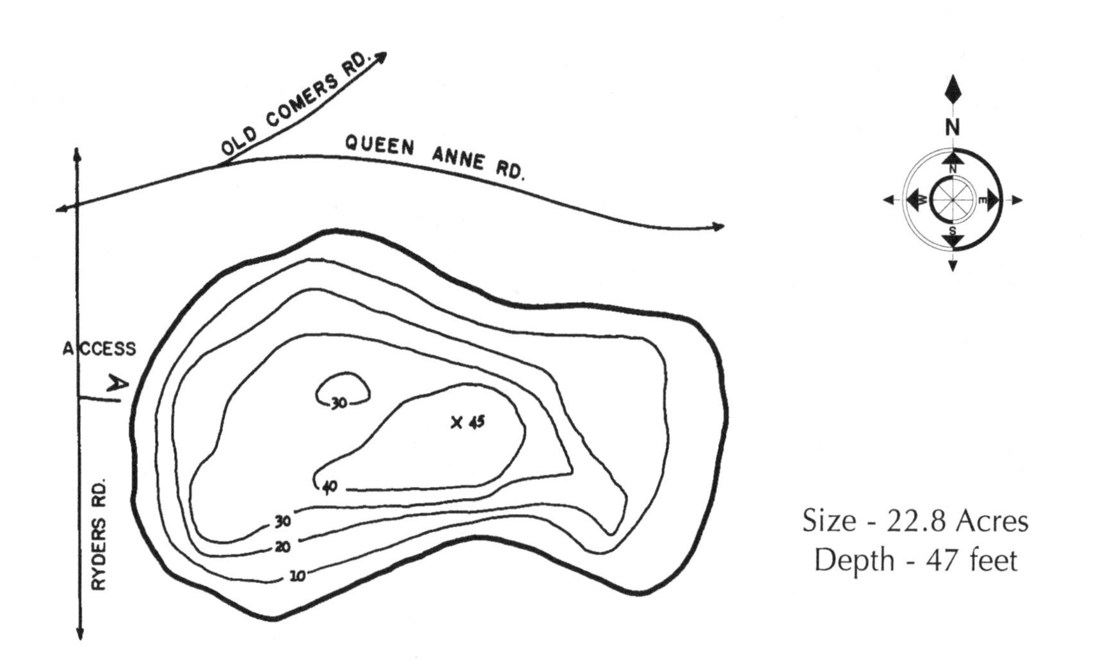

Location/Access/Special Regulations. Located south of Quenn Anne Road and east of Sam Ryder Road. Town beach on west shore connects pond with Ryder Pond.

"A good trout pond."

Steve Hurley, MDFW

"A good largemouth bass pond."

David Gilmore, Acclaimed Bass Angler

"A good trout pond.. Spin fish with red and gold Thomas Buoyant,green Buoyant, red and gold Canduit. Fly fish a black Wooly Bugger, Montana Nymph, and Black Gnat. I have had good fishing using Black Gnats on the surface."

Ella Schultz, Accomplished Angler

WHITE POND

CHATHAM

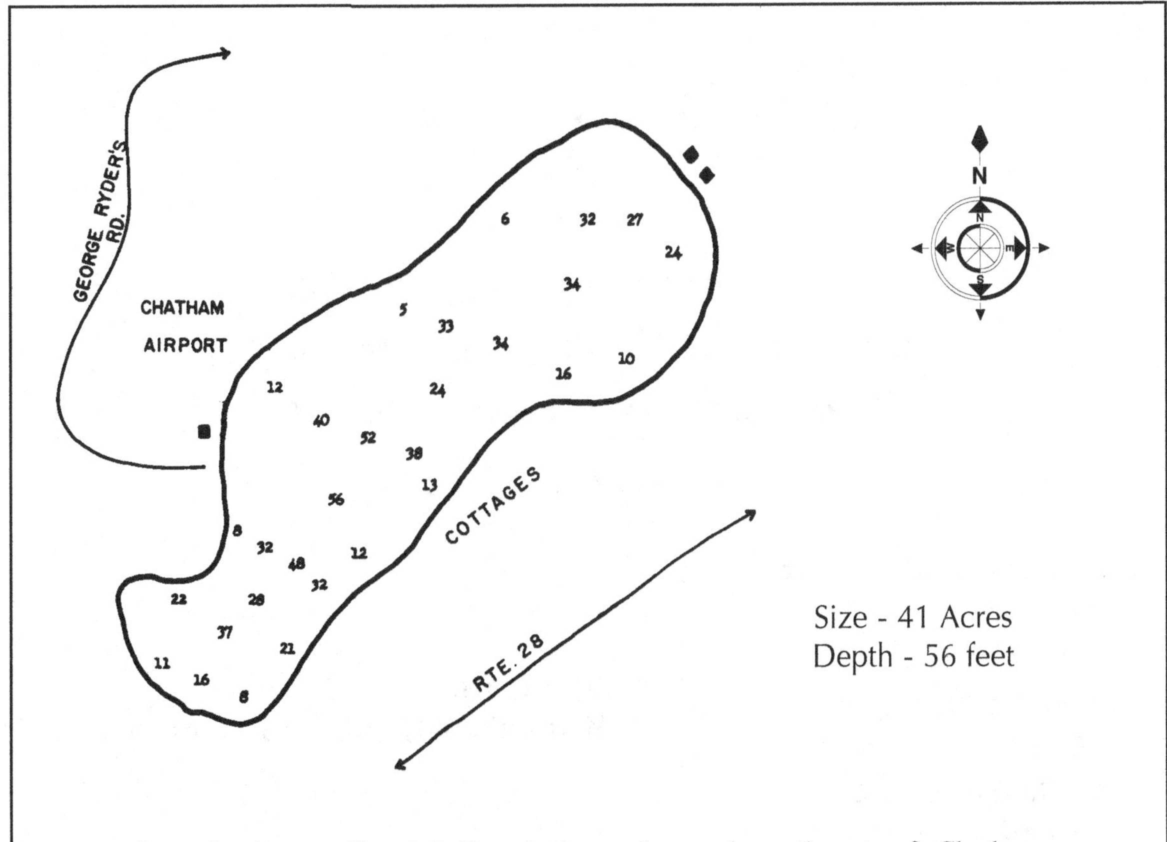

Location/Access/Special Regulations. Located southwest of Chatham Municipal Airport. Public access via small town beach and boat ramp on north shore. Public boat ramp. Surface channel connects White Pond with Blue Pond at southwest corner during high water conditions.

> *"Holds bass and pickerel."*
>
> ROD SCHOU, BUTTERWORTH MAPS

Cast 16:

DENNIS

Ponds & Lakes

Total Land Area (sq. miles) **20.66**

Total Area of Ponds (acres) **275**

Total numbers of Ponds **57**

Number of Ponds by size:

<1 acres:	27
1-5 acres:	14
5-10 acres:	10
10-20 acres:	3
20-50 acres:	2
50-100 acres:	1
>100 acres:	0

Pond groups:

Water Quality Advisory Committee

DENNIS

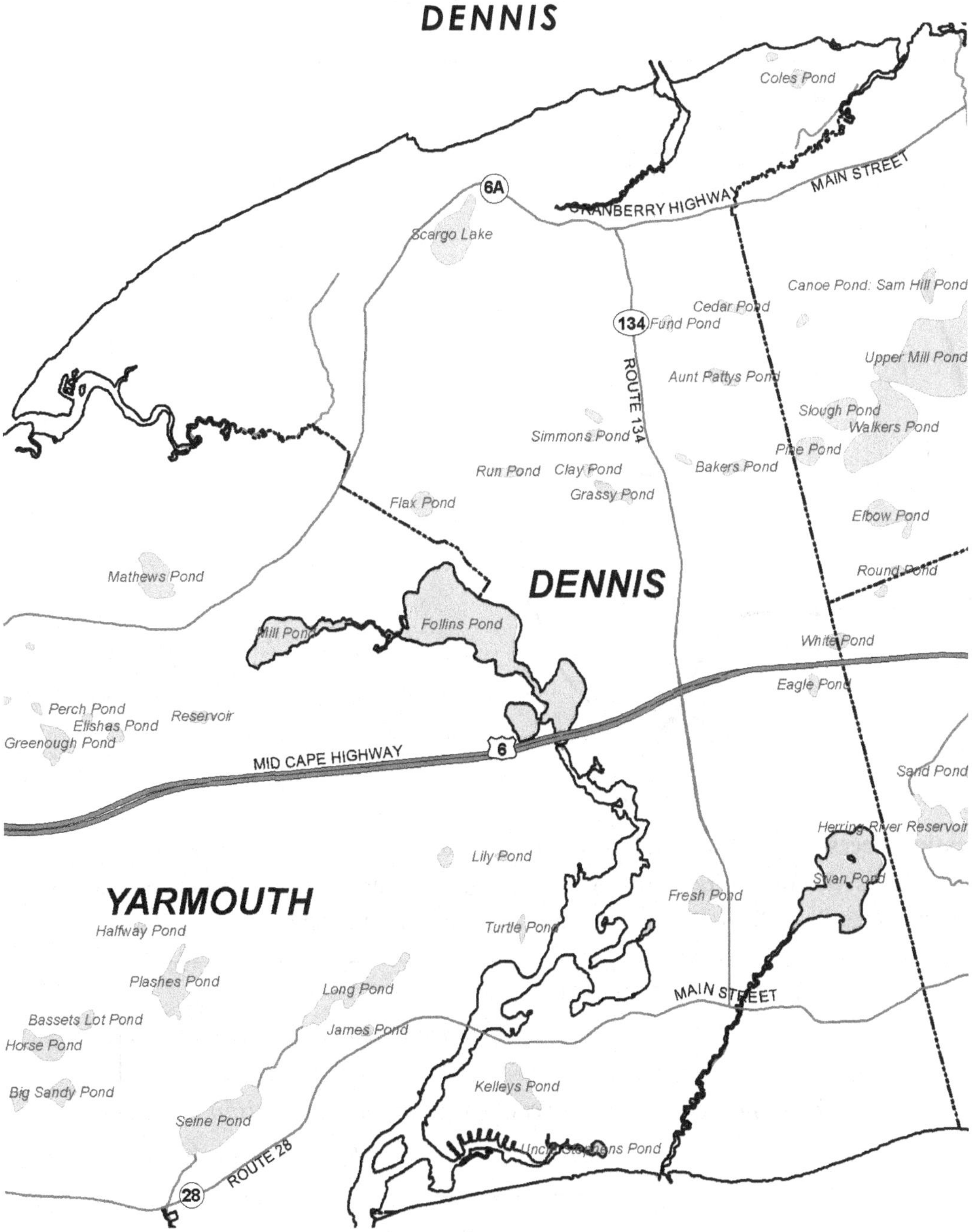

Coles Pond
6A
CRANBERRY HIGHWAY
MAIN STREET
Scargo Lake
Canoe Pond: Sam Hill Pond
Cedar Pond
134
Fund Pond
ROUTE 134
Upper Mill Pond
Aunt Pattys Pond
Slough Pond
Walkers Pond
Simmons Pond
Pine Pond
Run Pond
Clay Pond
Bakers Pond
Grassy Pond
Flax Pond
Elbow Pond
Mathews Pond
DENNIS
Round Pond
Follins Pond
Mill Pond
White Pond
Eagle Pond
Perch Pond
Elishas Pond
Reservoir
Greenough Pond
MID CAPE HIGHWAY
6
Sand Pond
Herring River Reservoir
Lily Pond
Swan Pond
YARMOUTH
Fresh Pond
Halfway Pond
Turtle Pond
Plashes Pond
Long Pond
MAIN STREET
Bassets Lot Pond
James Pond
Horse Pond
Kelleys Pond
Big Sandy Pond
Seine Pond
ROUTE 28
28

FRESH POND

DENNIS

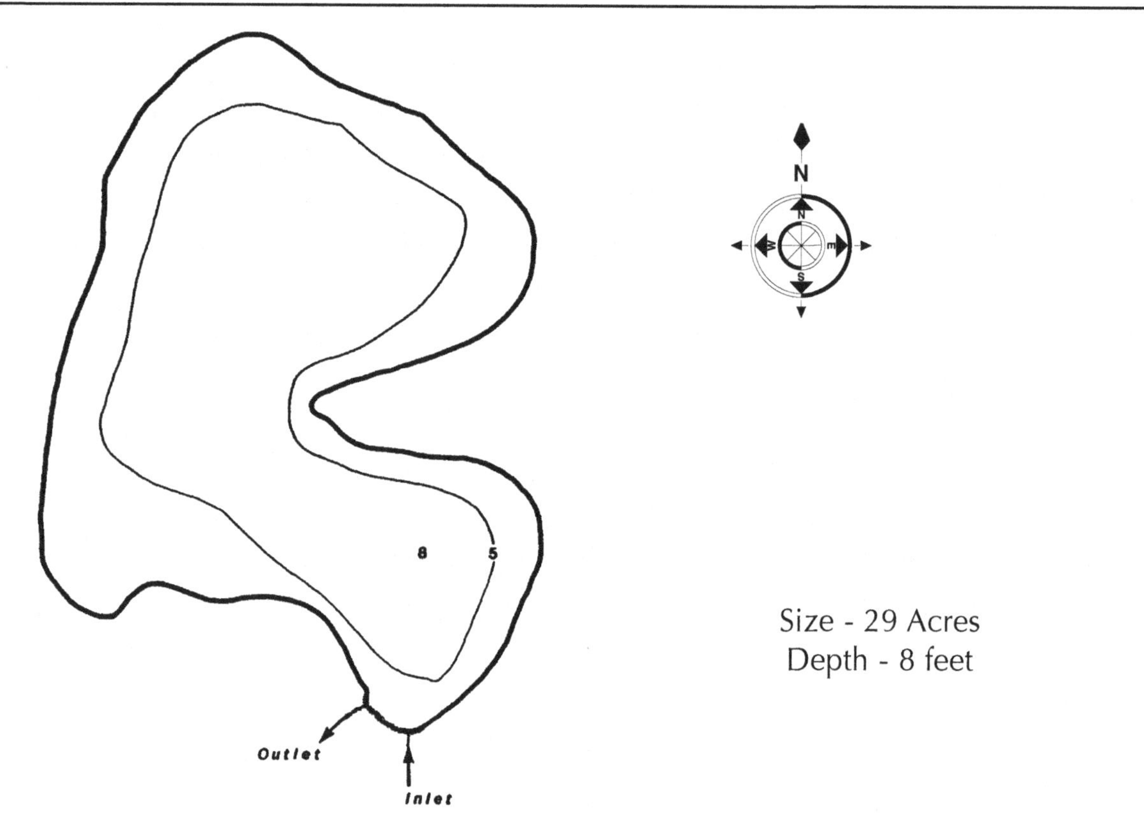

Location/Access/Special Regulations. Located just north and west of Routes 134 and 28. Public access via conservation area off Route 134. Discharges surface water through an outlet that runs to the Bass River. Shoreline surrounded by conservation area and wetlands.

> *"This pond is partially tidal."*
>
> Rod Schou, Butterworth Maps
>
> *"Yellow perch, but water is very acidic, probably poor fishing."*
>
> Steve Hurley, MDFW

SCARGO LAKE

DENNIS

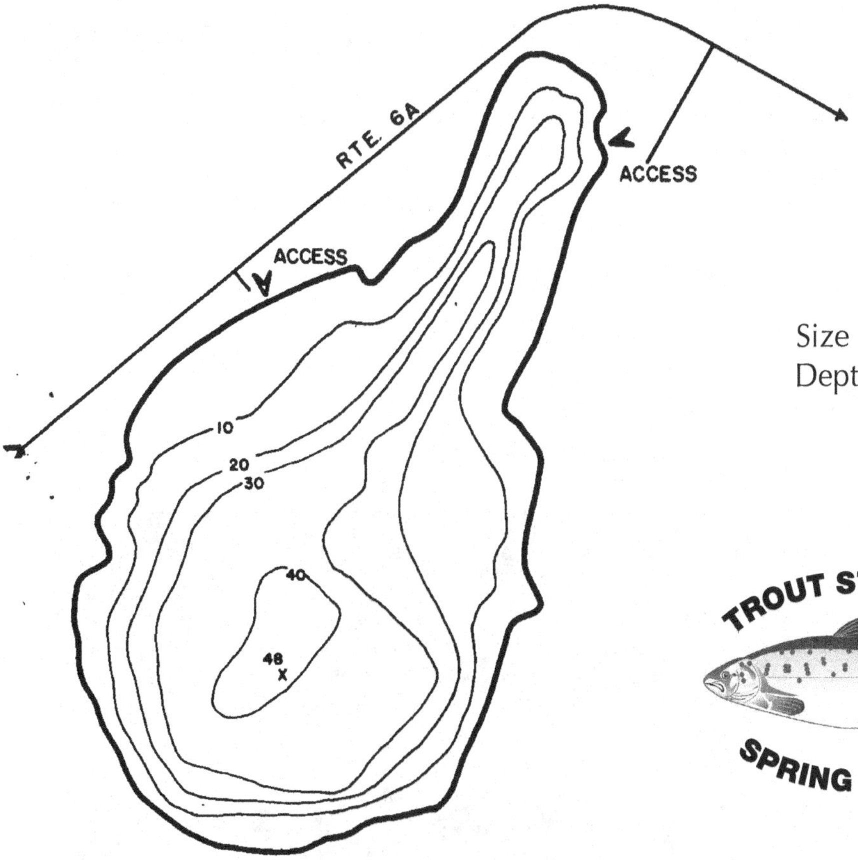
RTE. 6A
ACCESS
ACCESS
10
20
30
40
48
X

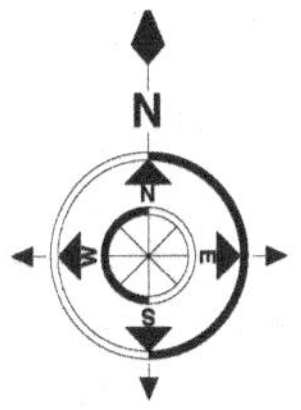
N

Size - 53 Acres
Depth - 44 feet

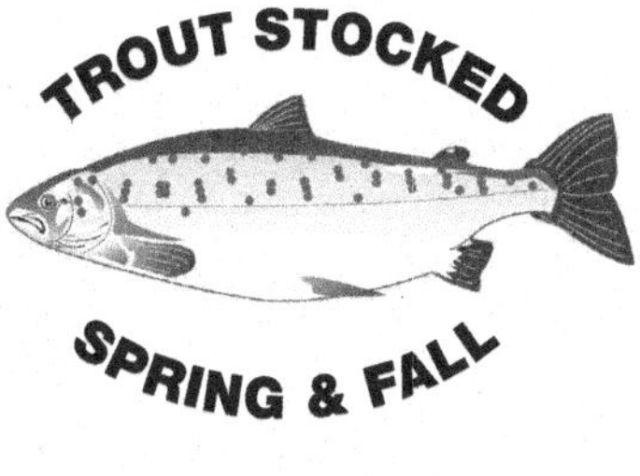
TROUT STOCKED
SPRING & FALL

Location/Access/Special Regulations. Clarity to 13 feet. Located south side of Dennis just south of Rote 6 A. Unimproved public boat ramp. 7.5 HP limit. Fisherman's Landing on Route 6A. Herring run at north end of lake leading to Sesuit Creek.

SCARGO LAKE: TIPS FROM EXPERTS

"Best town water for trout-all varieties- and smallies. Use live shiners, Wooly Buggers. Check out nearby Scargo Tower for an awesome view and, nearby Buckies Biscotti for an awesome brew (coffee that is)."

CRAIG POOSIKIAN, CRAIG'S CUSTOM RODS

"Nice mixture of trout and smallmouth bass. Never know what you will get. Try Colorado Spinner, Mepps Spinner, Sluggos on bass."

MARK PALMER, GOOSE HUMMOCK

"Excellent trout pond. Use all the standard flies."

STAN MOAK, TROUT UNLMITED

"Good trout water. Powerbait early. Fly fishing ."

GENE BOURQUE, EDITOR, ON THE WATER

"Cape Cod pond shoreline—loaded with baitfish, bass and pickerel. Fish the edges with top-water lures or bait under a bobber, cast into the vegetation with weedless plastic baits."

State record holder and Cape Cod fishing expert: Michael Shelton, Mashpee.

I started fishing on the cape in 1986. I was quite surprised with the quality of fresh water fishing on the cape. I soon discovered that there were quite a few ponds that supported excellent trout and bass. Over the 18 years fishing on the cape I have certainly had my share of fun and success fishing for trout, salmon, and bass. There are plenty of trout in the 3 to 4 pound range to be taken as well as salmon in the 4 to 8 pound range. It is not uncommon for much bigger fish within these species.

I personally like to catch and release my fish. I respect the environment in and around these beautiful ponds and would hope that visitors and native fish enthusiasts will do the same.

For fly rod enthusiasts, do not over look the opportunity of casting poppers from shore for bass from mid July through August. If you are seeking a trophy trout or salmon grab a handful of Joe's Flies, have fun and be diligent.

Cast 17:

EASTHAM

Ponds & Lakes

Total Land Area (sq. miles) → **14.25**

Total Area of Ponds (acres) → **258**

Total numbers of Ponds → **23**

Number of Ponds by size:

<1 acres:	7
1-5 acres:	7
5-10 acres:	4
10-20 acres:	2
20-50 acres:	2
50-100 acres:	0
>100 acres:	1

Pond groups:

- **National Park Service**
- **Eastham Pond Monitoring Group**

> *"A man can be a fish hog with a fly rod as easily as he can with a cane pole. Easier perhaps."*
>
> H.G. Tapply, The Sportsman's Notebook (1964)

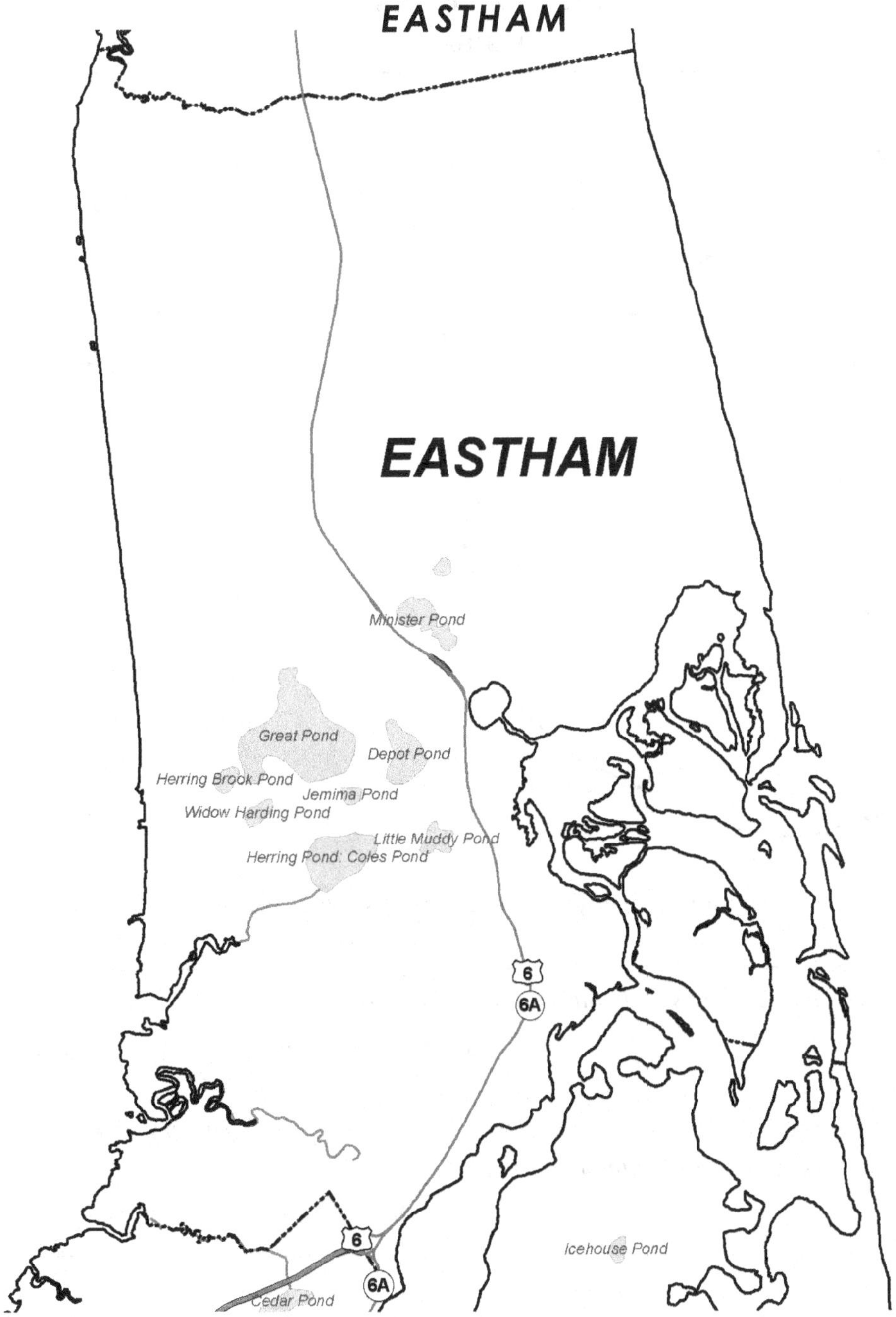

EASTHAM

EASTHAM

Minister Pond

Great Pond

Depot Pond

Herring Brook Pond

Jemima Pond

Widow Harding Pond

Little Muddy Pond

Herring Pond; Coles Pond

6

6A

Icehouse Pond

6

6A

Cedar Pond

DEPOT POND

EASTHAM

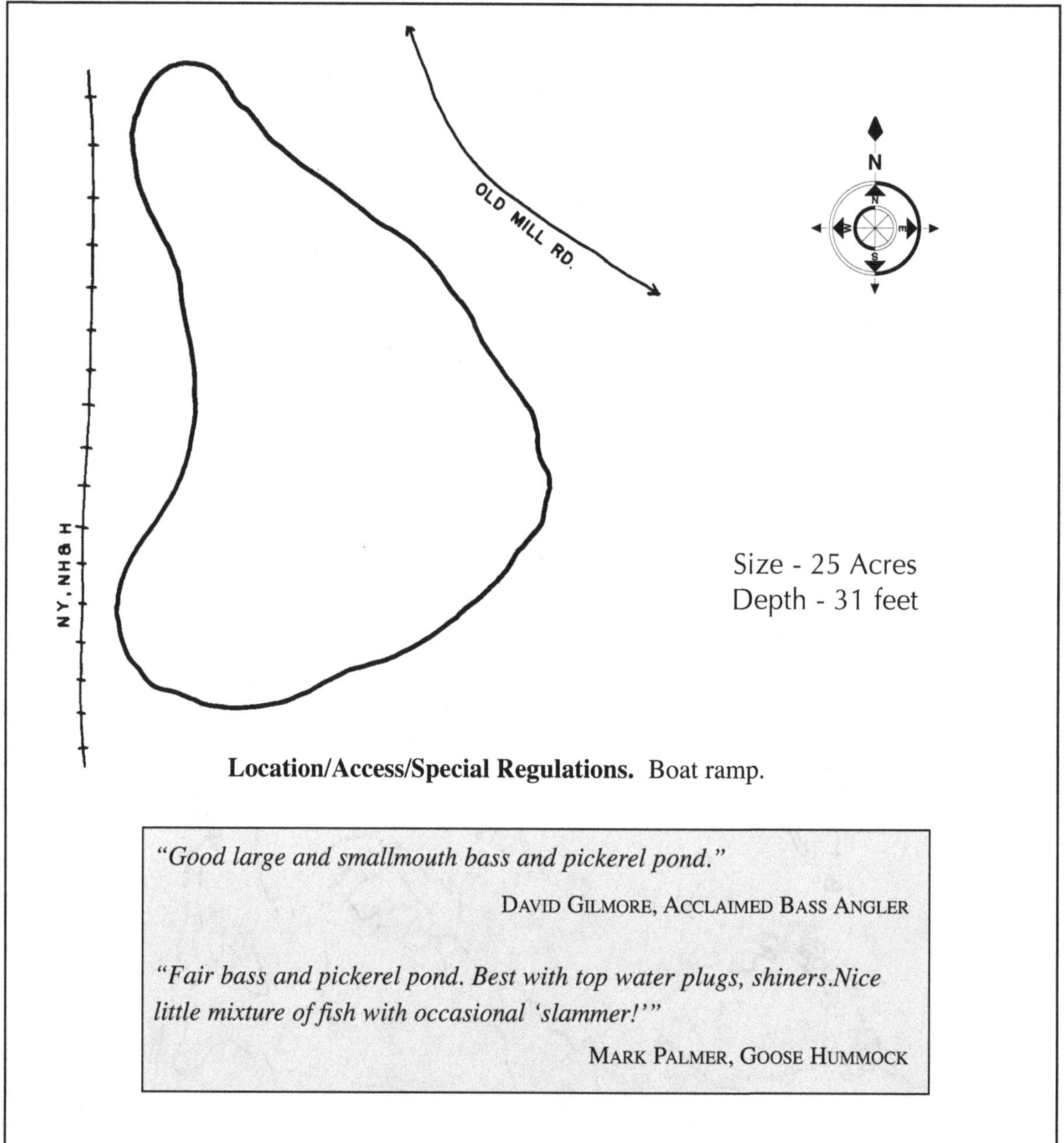

Location/Access/Special Regulations. Boat ramp.

> *"Good large and smallmouth bass and pickerel pond."*
>
> DAVID GILMORE, ACCLAIMED BASS ANGLER
>
> *"Fair bass and pickerel pond. Best with top water plugs, shiners.Nice little mixture of fish with occasional 'slammer!'"*
>
> MARK PALMER, GOOSE HUMMOCK

GREAT POND

EASTHAM

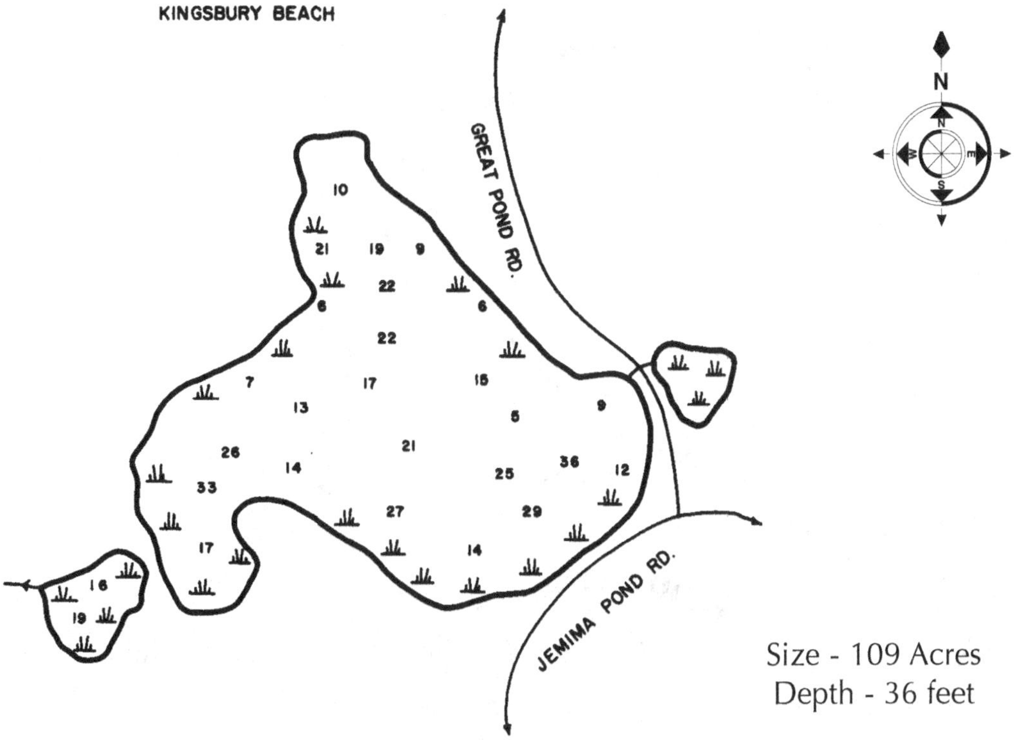

KINGSBURY BEACH

GREAT POND RD.

JEMIMA POND RD.

Size - 109 Acres
Depth - 36 feet

Location/Access/Special Regulations. Located midway between Cape Cod Bay and Salt Pond, west of Route 6 and east of Herring Brook Road. Public access via beach at Wiley Park, off Herring Brook Road, and at a boat ramp off Great Pond Road.

HERRING POND

EASTHAM

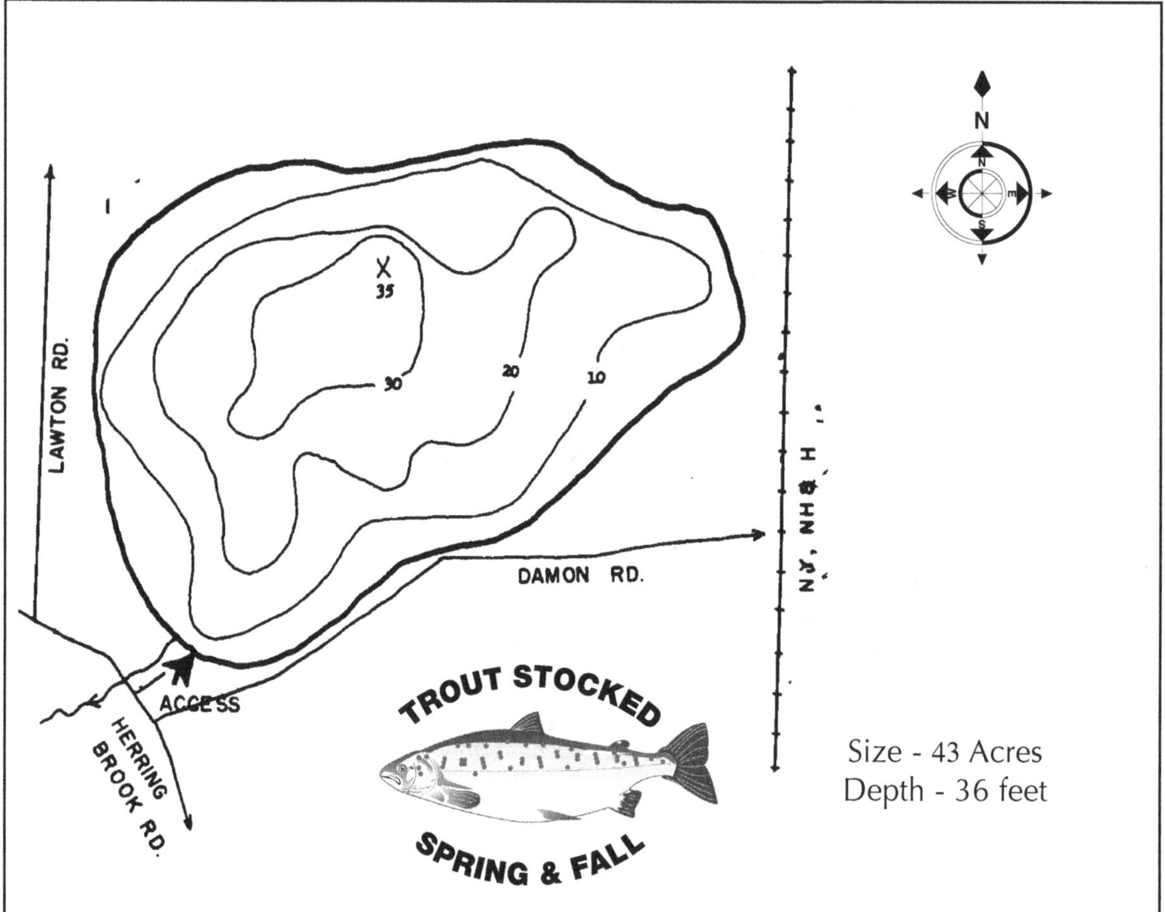

Location/Access/Special Regulations. Boat carry in. 3 HP limit. Located midway between Herring River and Salt Pond, west of Route 6 and east of Herring Brook Road. Public access via boat ramp On Herring Brook Road near the herring run. Herring run connected to pond at southwest corner of pond, discharging water to the Herring River.

Herring churn up the shallow waters of the run as they make their way towards Herring Pond in Eastham. (Photo: Steve Heaslip, Cape Cod Times)

"Eastham's best trout pond. Fair pickerel fishing. Also holds yellow and white perch and pumpkinseed."

STEVE HURLEY, MDFW

"In addition to other species, pond also holds largemouth bass."

DAVID GILMORE, ACCLAIMED BASS ANGLER

"Pond is hard to wade so a boat really helps when you fish as you use live herring to catch giant pickerel and stripers."

CRAIG POOSIKIAN, CRAIG'S CUSTOM RODS

"Trout are best bet in this pond. Use herring imitations. Well stocked. Tough access. Good for canoe or wading. Occasional BIG pickerel."

MARK PALMER, GOOSE HUMMOCK

MINISTERS POND / SCHOOLHOUSE POND

EASTHAM

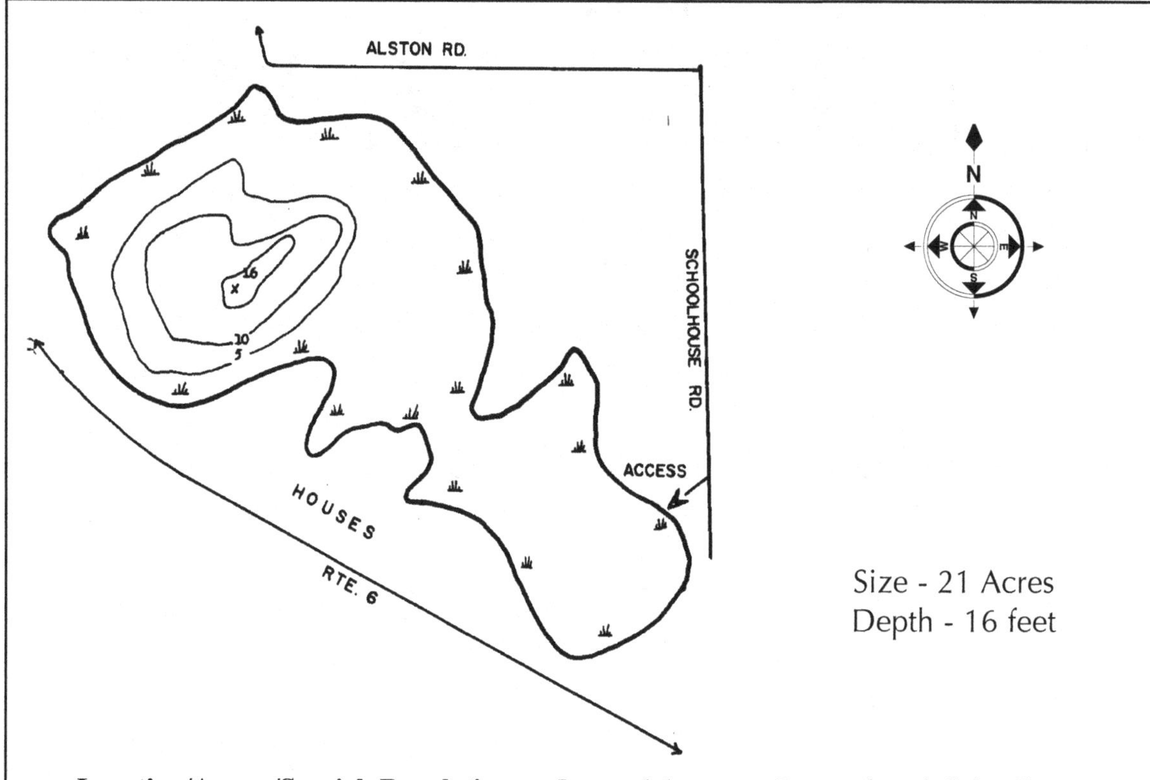

Size - 21 Acres
Depth - 16 feet

Location/Access/Special Regulations. Located between Route 6 and Schoolhouse Road. Access via Schoolhouse Road. Boat ramp on southeast shore. Both ponds are joined at narrow neck.

"Fair chain pickerel fishing."

Steve Hurley, MDFW

"A good pond for bass, pickerel, perch and sunfish."

David Gilmore. Acclaimed Bass Angler

"Good fishing here for bass and pickerel. Best bets are shiners, poppers, other top water artificials."

Mark Palmer, Goose Hummock

Another tip: attach a chartreuse crappie jig 18" - 24" below a conventional bobber or even a Sponge Bob Square Pants on days when pond surface has slight waves. The bouncing jig entices largemouth bass.

"But ah, to fish with a worm, and then not catch your fish! To fail with a fly is no disgrace: your art may have been impeccable, your patience faultless to the end. But the philosophy of worm fishing is that of results, of having something tangible in your basket when the day's work is done."

BLISS PERRY, FISHING WITH A WORM

"I know of no sport so ridden with taboos, so gangrenous with snobbery, so reeking with cant, as fly fishing."

HOWARD WALDEN (1972)

Cast 18:

FALMOUTH

Ponds & Lakes

Total Land Area (sq. miles) **44.25**

Total Area of Ponds (acres) **1,016**

Total numbers of Ponds **141**

Number of Ponds by size:

<1 acres:	**68**
1-5 acres:	**40**
5-10 acres:	**10**
10-20 acres:	**12**
20-50 acres:	**7**
50-100 acres:	**2**
>100 acres:	**2**

Pond groups:

Coonamesset Pond Association

> *"Quite possibly this is the key to fishing: the ability to see glamour in whatever species one may fish for."*
>
> Harold Blaisdell, The Philosophic Fisherman (1969)

FALMOUTH

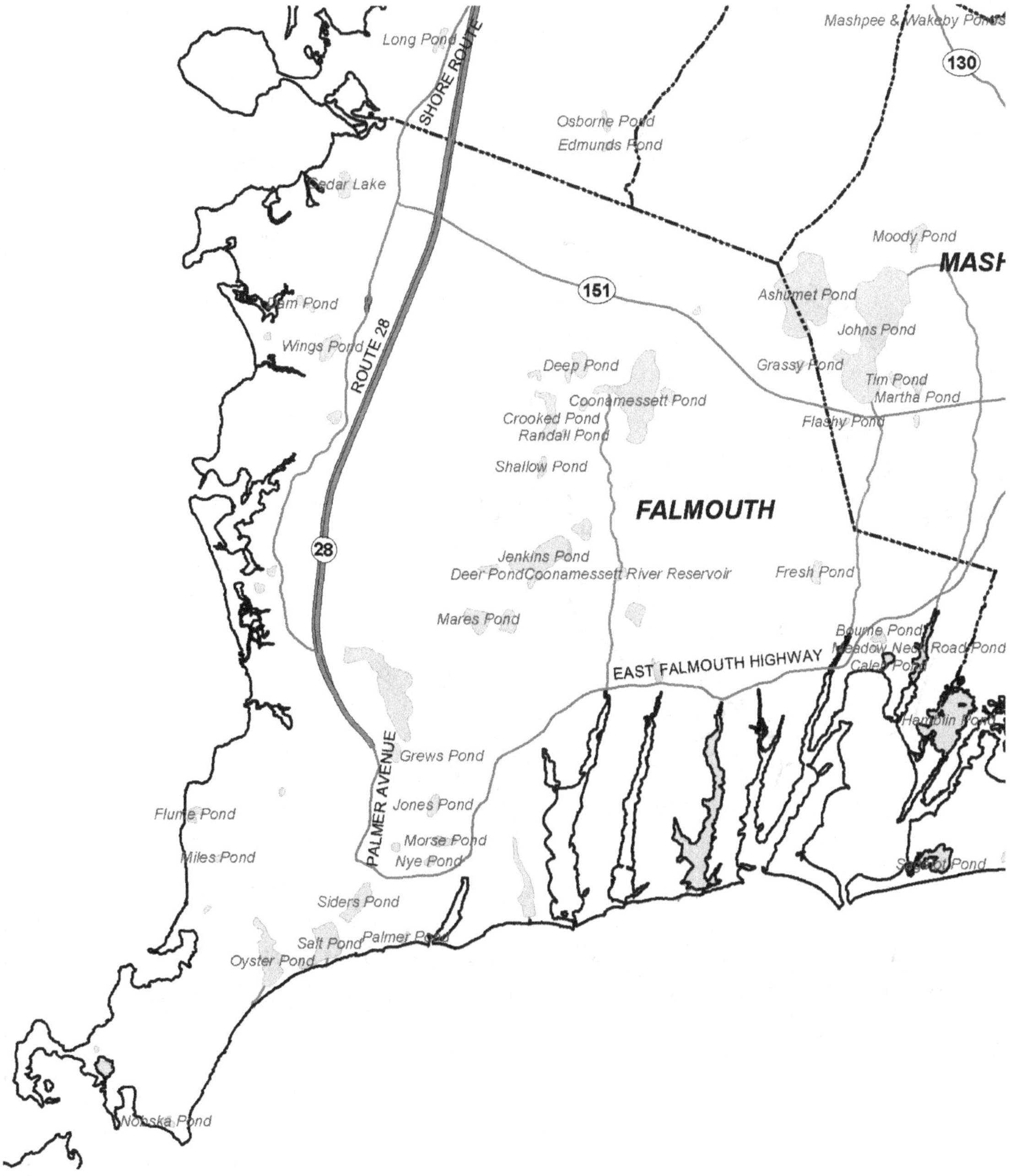

Long Pond
SHORE ROUTE
Mashpee & Wakeby Ponds
130
Osborne Pond
Edmunds Pond
Cedar Lake
Moody Pond
MASH
151
Ashumet Pond
Johns Pond
Wings Pond
ROUTE 28
Deep Pond
Grassy Pond
Tim Pond
Martha Pond
Coonamessett Pond
Crooked Pond
Randall Pond
Flashy Pond
Shallow Pond
FALMOUTH
28
Jenkins Pond
Deer Pond
Coonamessett River Reservoir
Fresh Pond
Mares Pond
Bourne Pond
Meadow Neck Road Pond
EAST FALMOUTH HIGHWAY
Caleb Pond
Hamblin Pond
PALMER AVENUE
Grews Pond
Jones Pond
Flume Pond
Morse Pond
Nye Pond
Miles Pond
Siders Pond
Salt Pond
Palmer Pond
Oyster Pond
Nobska Pond

COONAMESSETT POND

FALMOUTH

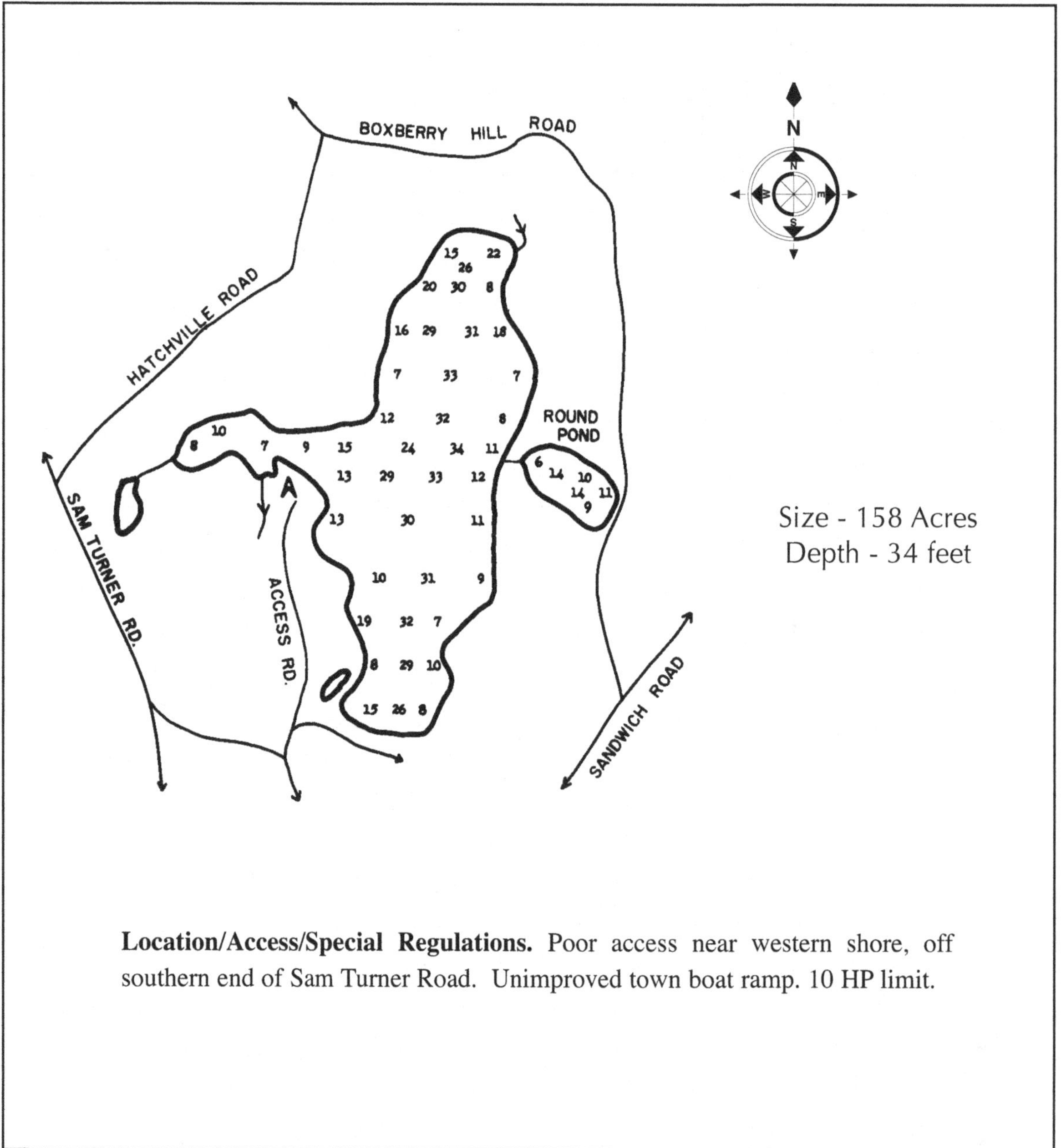

Size - 158 Acres
Depth - 34 feet

Location/Access/Special Regulations. Poor access near western shore, off southern end of Sam Turner Road. Unimproved town boat ramp. 10 HP limit.

COONAMESSETT POND: TIPS FROM EXPERTS

"Best pond in Falmouth for largemouth bass. Also good fishing for smallmouth bass. Also holds yellow and white perch, bluegills and pumpkinseed."

STEVE HURLEY, MDFW

"Once known as a very productive largemouth bass pond, it has changed over the years because of development. It is still Falmouth's best largemouth pond. Spinnerbaits,, small, white and chartreuse are great !"

CURT JESSUP, THE SPORTING LIFE

"A good largemouth and smallmouth bass pond.that also has perch and crappies. Fish edges-need a canoe or kayak to fish effectively. Best lures here are plastic baits-Sluggo, Fin-S, etc."

GENE BOURQUE, EDITOR, ON THE WATER

Hefty bluegill caught on Silver Wabler from Coonamessett Pond.

DEEP POND
FALMOUTH

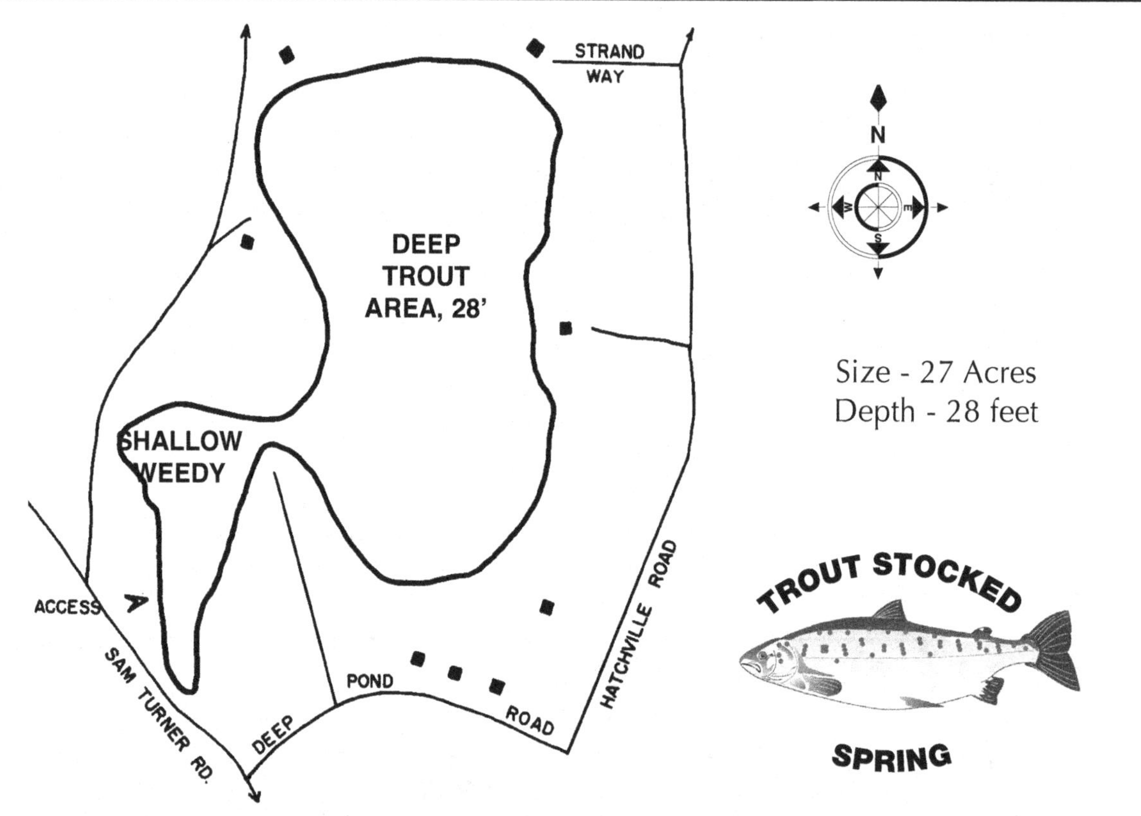

Location/Access/Special Regulations. Located south of Route 151 and east of Sam Turner Road. Two public access points: southern access is off Sam Turner Road via a swamp and impassable in low water conditions; northern access is off Pondview Road and includes a small beach and steep boat ramp. Electric motors only.

"A good pond for trout. Stocked in spring only. Fishes best April-June. Best bets are worms, powerbait."

GENE BOURQUE, EDITOR, ON THE WATER

"A good trout and largemouth bass pond. Also holds yellow perch and pumpkinseed."

STEVE HURLEY, MDFW

GREWS POND

FALMOUTH

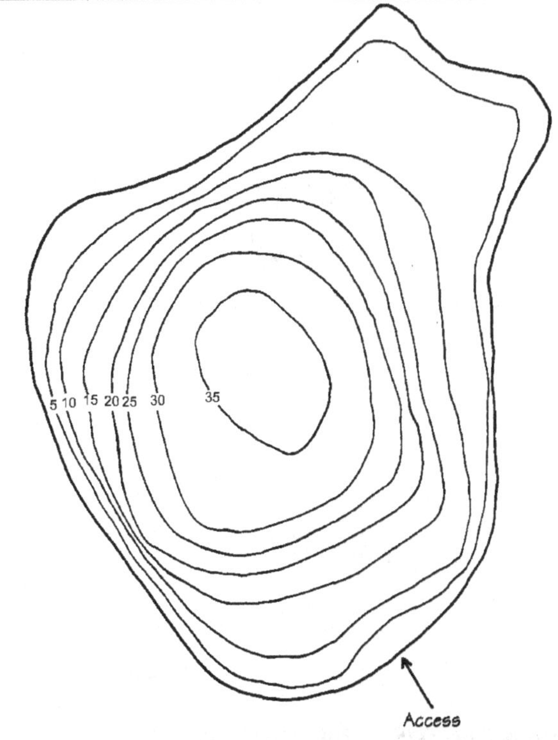

Size - 13 Acres
Depth - 42 feet

SPRING

Location/Access/Special Regulations. Located east of Route 28. Unimproved town boat ramp-carry in- off southeast shore. Electric motors only.

"Good trout and smallmouth bass pond. Also has yellow perch and pumpkinseed."

STEVE HURLEY, MDFW

"In the spring time or after a light snow there is no more beautifulsetting. The pond is set in a deep impression and the water is deep. Best bet is a Mepps Aglia, countdown method, slow retrieve, hang on!"

CURT JESSUP, THE SPORTING LIFE

"A good trout pond. Good winter caddis hatch. All methods work. Pond is heavily stocked, heavily fished, and has good access."

GENE BOURQUE, EDITOR, ON THE WATER

"A good trout pond. Use powerbaits or lures."

JEFF CAPUTE, AWARD WINNING ANGLER

JENKINS POND

FALMOUTH

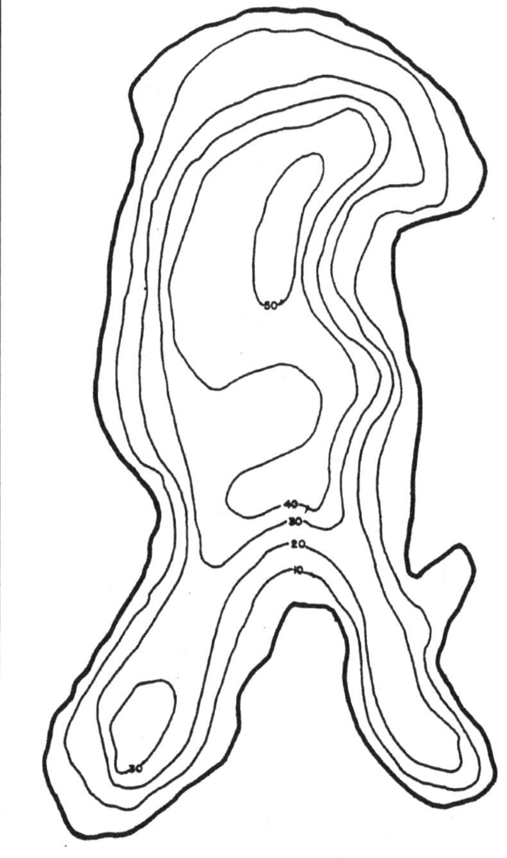

Size - 87 Acres
Depth - 51 feet

Location/Access/Special Regulations. Located west of Sandwich Road. Carry in. Electric motors only.

"A good fishing pond that holds trout, bass, pickerel, and white perch."

ROD SCHOU, BUTTERWORTH MAPS

"A good smallmouth bass pond. Also white and yellow perch."

STEVE HURLEY, MDFW

"A good pond for smallmouth bass, pickerel, and yellow perch. Use stick-baits, shiners."

GENE BOURQUE, EDITOR, ON THE WATER

MARES POND

FALMOUTH

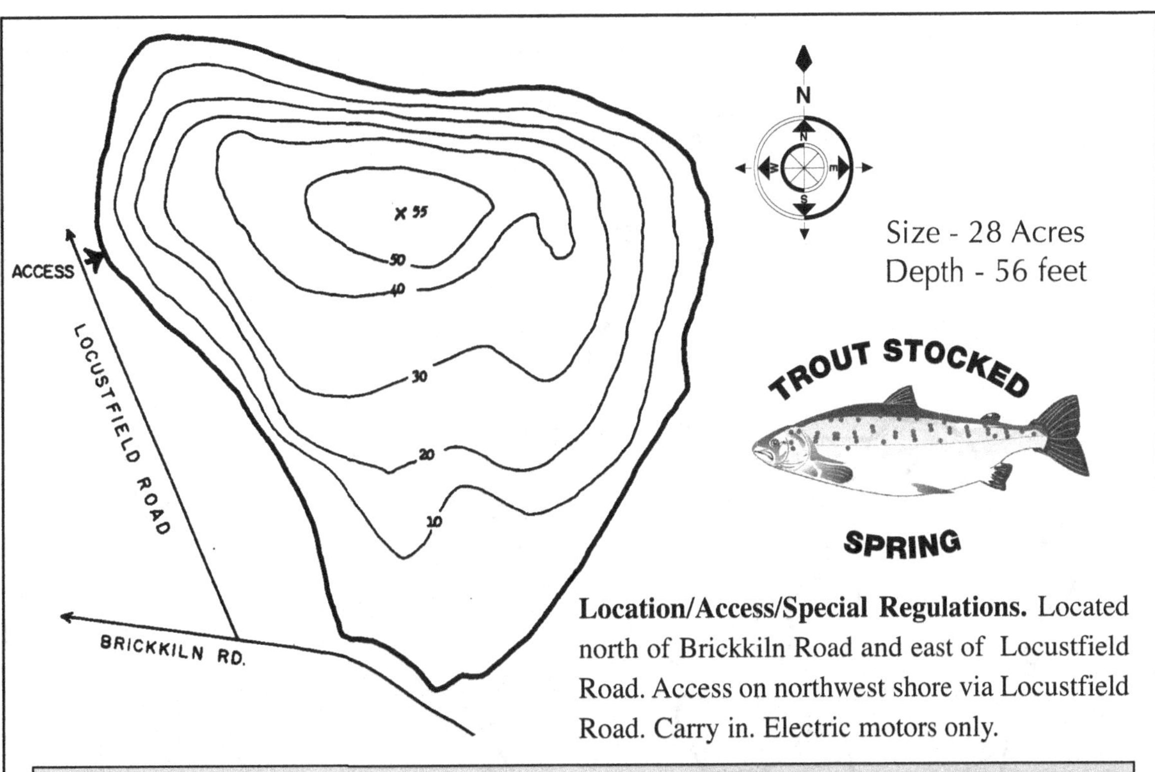

Location/Access/Special Regulations. Located north of Brickkiln Road and east of Locustfield Road. Access on northwest shore via Locustfield Road. Carry in. Electric motors only.

"One of the best little trout ponds in the state. Any small, flashy lure will work, but it's hard to beat pink powerbait or brown 'hatchery formula" powerbait. 2-2 1/2 inch streamers with silver and red are also good bets."

PETER MIRICK, EDITOR, MASSACHUSETTS WILDLIFE

"A good trout pond. Powerbait is best bait."

JEFF CAPUTE, AWARD WINNING ANGLER

"A good pond for trout, largemouth and smallmouth bass."

STEVE HURLEY, MDFW

"Small but nice. Although private, good kayak access. Use grubs and worms. Great for kids."

CURT JESSUP, THE SPORTING LIFE

"Fish same way as Deep Pond."

GENE BOURQUE, EDITOR, ON THE WATER

POND #14

FALMOUTH (Coonamessett River Reservoir)

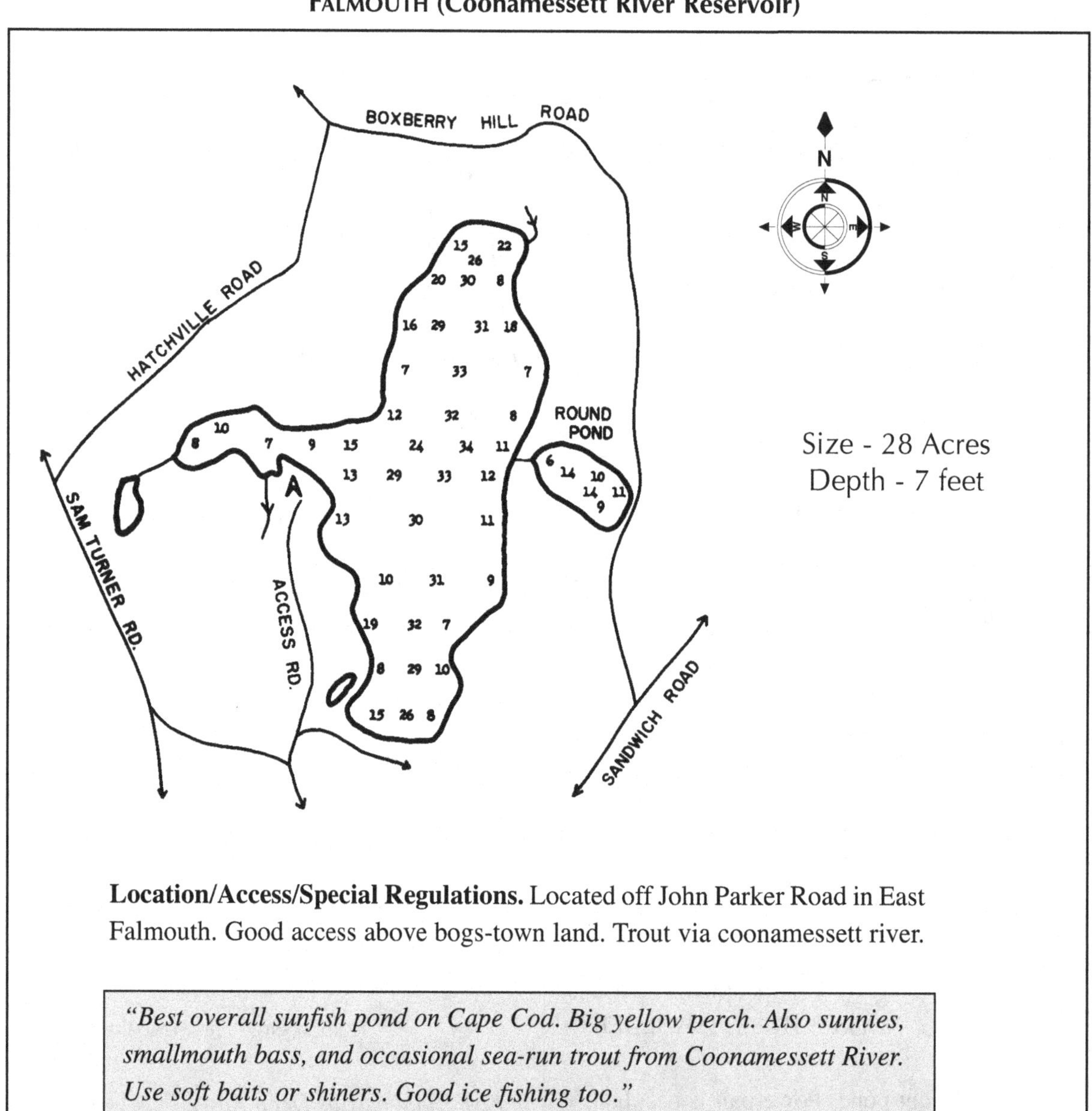

Size - 28 Acres
Depth - 7 feet

Location/Access/Special Regulations. Located off John Parker Road in East Falmouth. Good access above bogs-town land. Trout via coonamessett river.

> *"Best overall sunfish pond on Cape Cod. Big yellow perch. Also sunnies, smallmouth bass, and occasional sea-run trout from Coonamessett River. Use soft baits or shiners. Good ice fishing too."*
>
> GENE BOURQUE, EDITOR, ON THE WATER

SIDERS POND

FALMOUTH

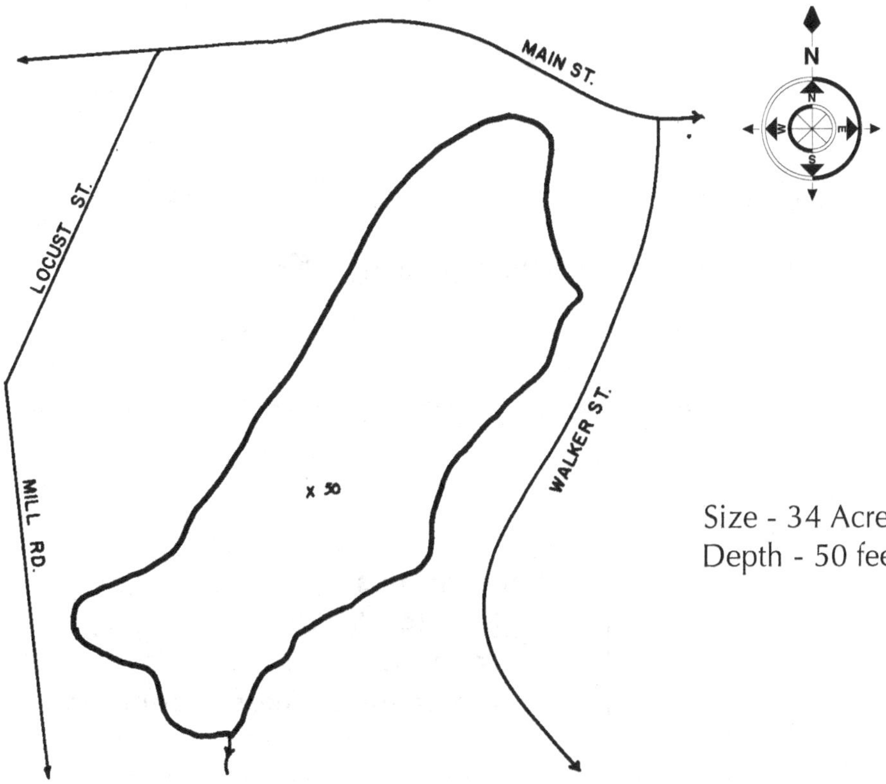

MAIN ST.
LOCUST ST.
MILL RD.
WALKER ST.
N
x 50

Size - 34 Acres
Depth - 50 feet

Location/Access/Special Regulations. Located south of Main Street, east of Locust Street and Mill Road, west of Walker Street. Town boat ramp at southern tip of pond, near an outlet.

Cast 19:

HARWICH

Ponds & Lakes

Total Land Area (sq. miles) → **20.93**

Total Area of Ponds (acres) → **850**

Total numbers of Ponds → **63**

Number of Ponds by size:

Size	Number
<1 acres:	29
1-5 acres:	9
5-10 acres:	5
10-20 acres:	10
20-50 acres:	8
50-100 acres:	1
>100 acres:	1

Pond groups:

- Harwich SMWQC
- Long Pond Watershed Association
- Great Sand Lakes Association

> *"Only those become weary of angling who bring nothing to it but the idea of catching fish."*
>
> Rafael Sabatine

HARWICH

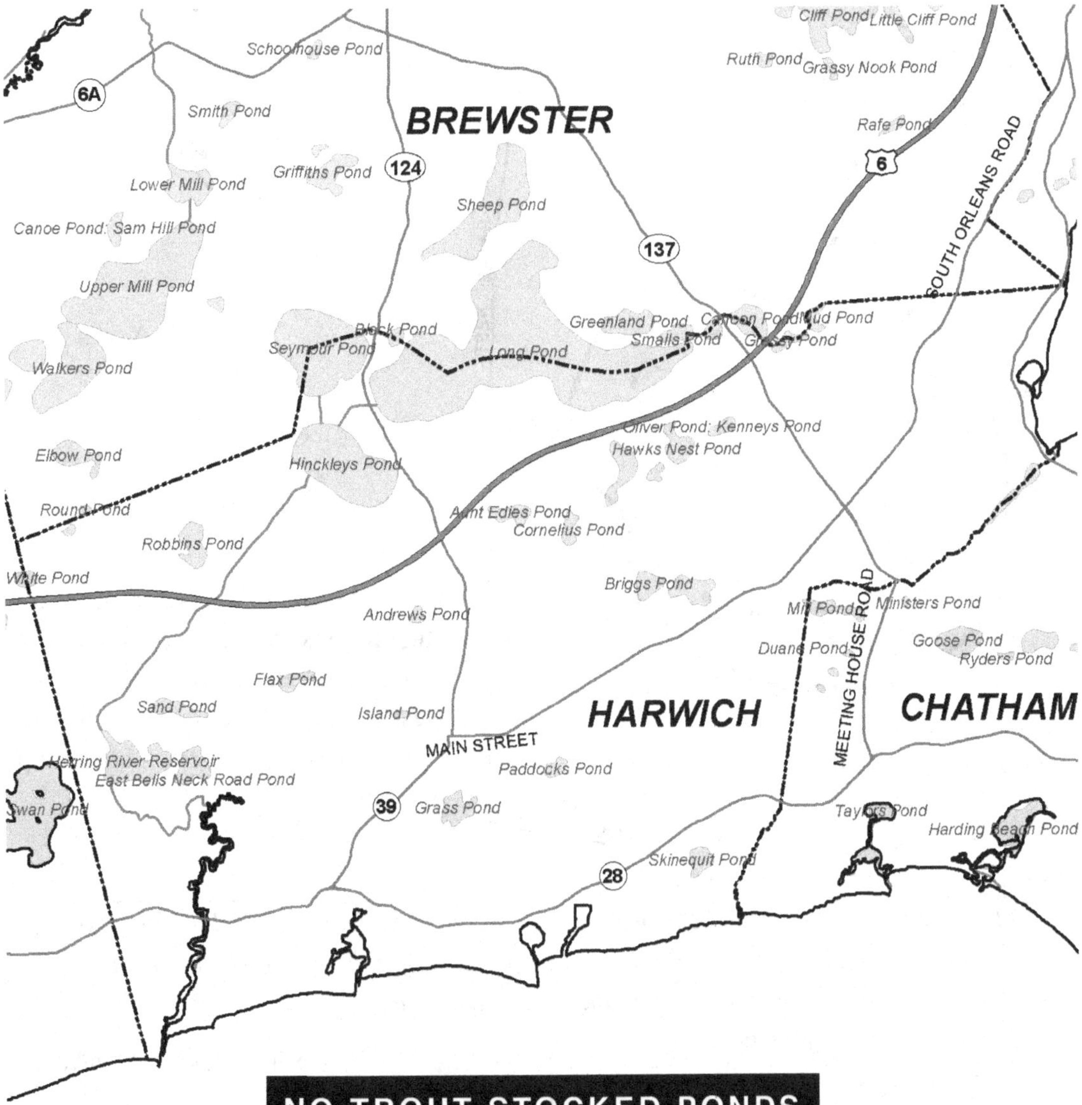

NO TROUT STOCKED PONDS

BUCKS/HAWKS NEST POND

HARWICH

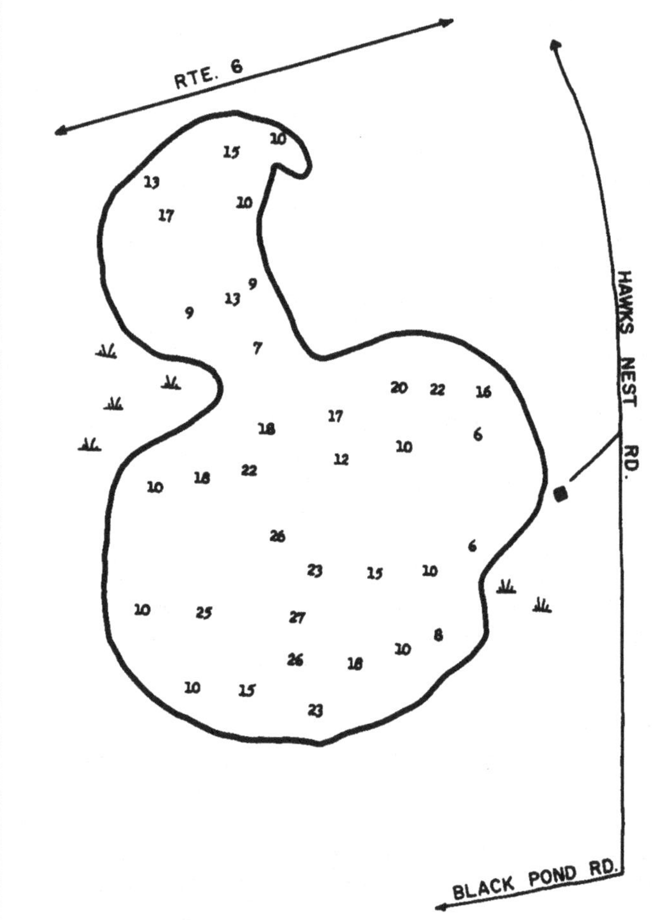

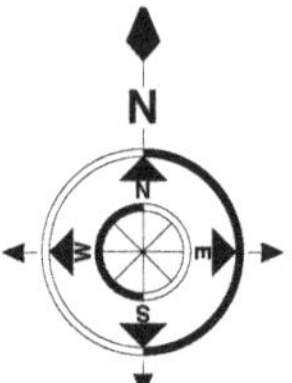

Size - 29 Acres
Depth - 36 feet

Location/Access/Special Regulations. Located south of Route 6, north of Black Pond Road, and west of Hawks Nest Road. Access off Hawks Nest Road to town boat ramp on eastern shore.

"This is a good largemouth bass pond that does not get a lot of pressure but has nice fish. Best lures are spinners or, dawn and dusk, surface lures for top water action."

MARK PALMER, GOOSE HUMMOCK

"Reputed to be a fair smallmouth bass pond. Also holds pickerel Not much recent data."

STEVE HURLEY, MDFW

ELDREDGE POND/WALKERS POND

Harwich

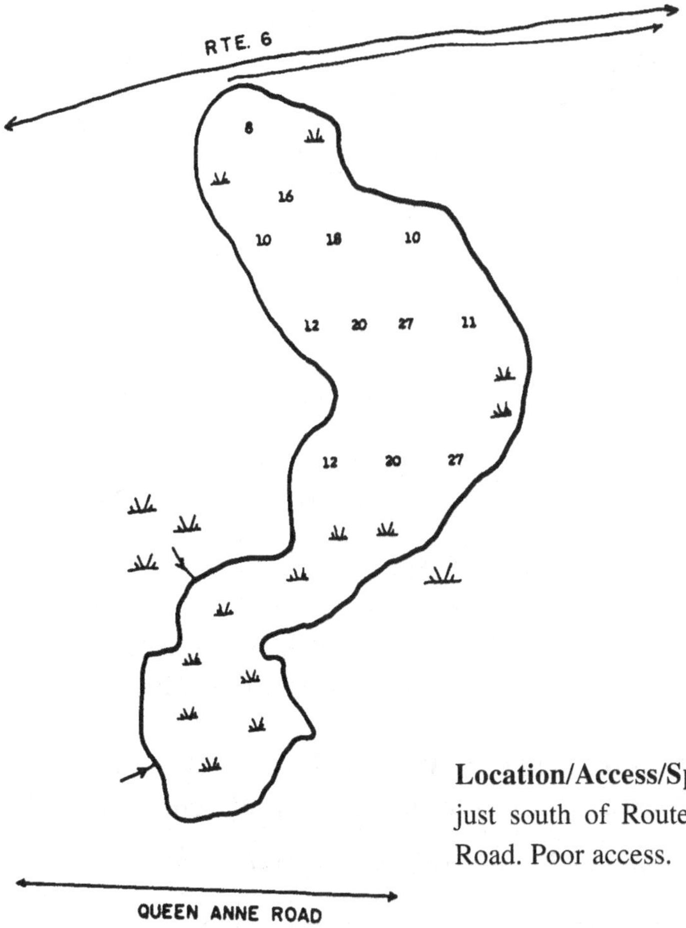

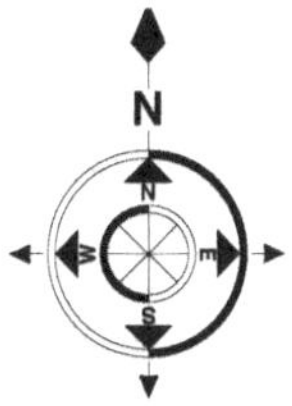

RTE. 6

QUEEN ANNE ROAD

Size - 25 Acres
Depth - 27 feet

Location/Access/Special Regulations. Located just south of Route 6 and north of Queen Anne Road. Poor access.

> *"Eldredge holds pickerel, but has poor access."*
>
> Rod Schou, Butterworth Maps

WEST & EAST RESERVOIRS (Herring River Reservoirs)

HARWICH

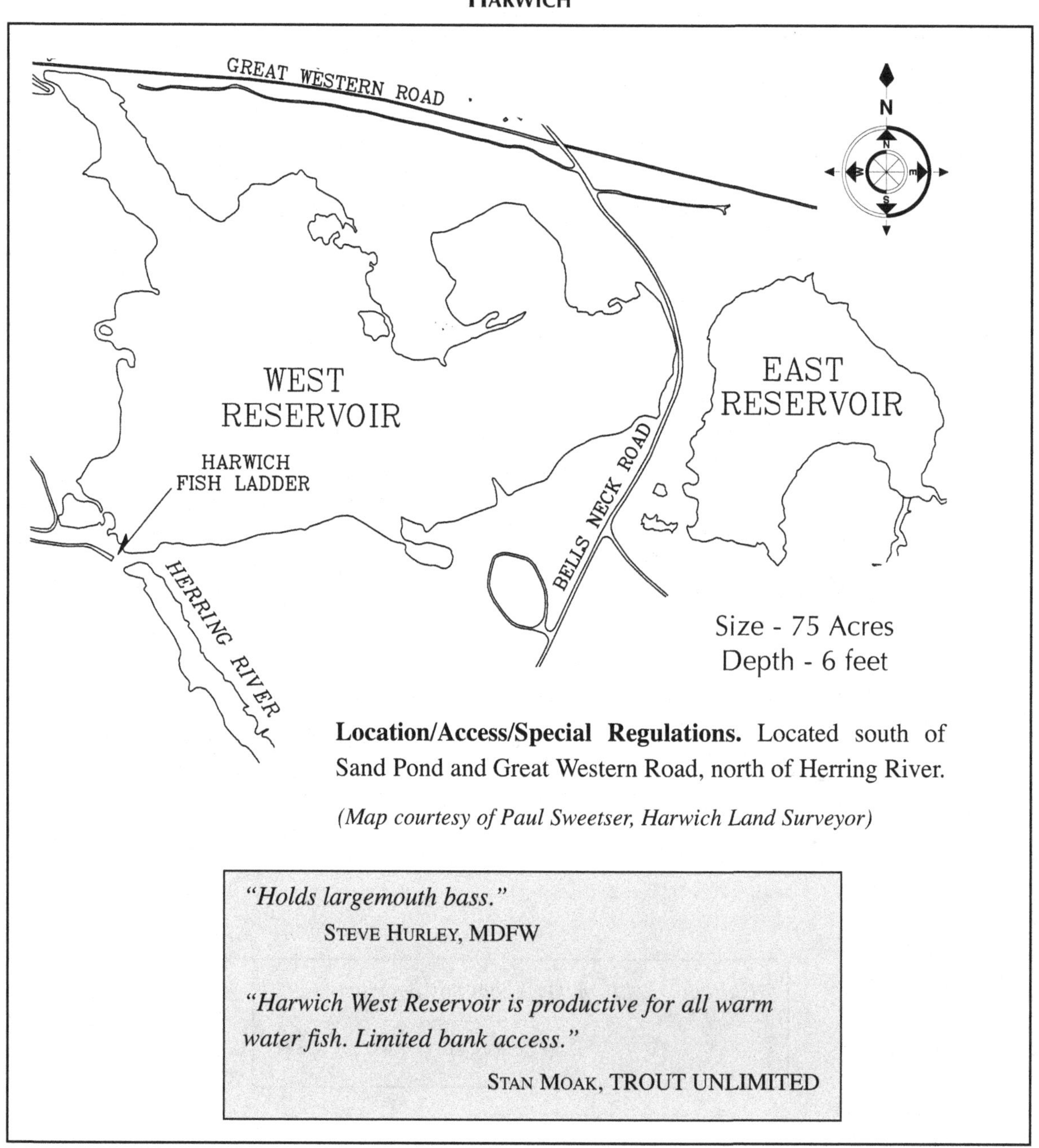

Size - 75 Acres
Depth - 6 feet

Location/Access/Special Regulations. Located south of Sand Pond and Great Western Road, north of Herring River.

(Map courtesy of Paul Sweetser, Harwich Land Surveyor)

"Holds largemouth bass."
STEVE HURLEY, MDFW

"Harwich West Reservoir is productive for all warm water fish. Limited bank access."
STAN MOAK, TROUT UNLIMITED

HINCKLEYS POND aka PLEASANT LAKE

Harwich

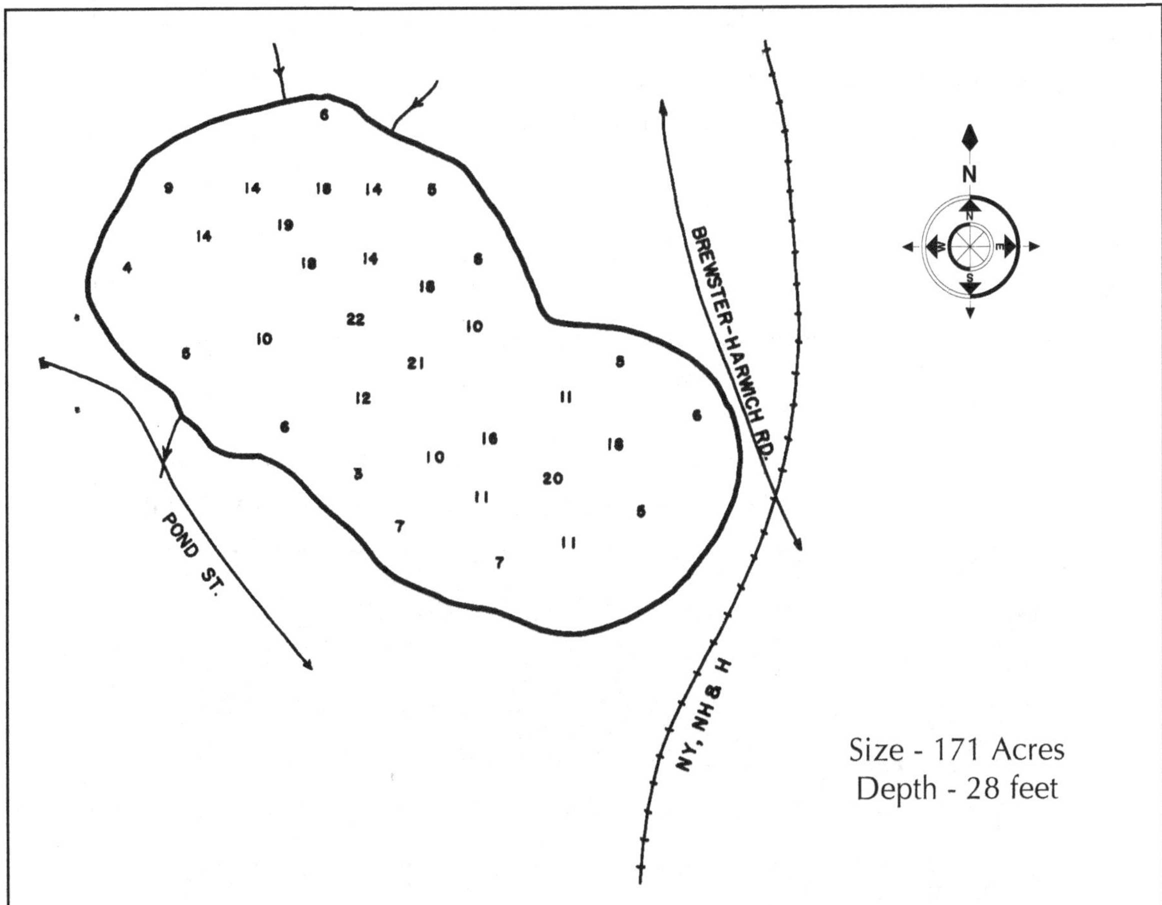

Location/Access/Special Regulations. Located 1/2 mile northwest of intersection of Route 6 and Route 124. Harwich town beach is just west of Route 124. Access is from a dirt road off pond street on west side of pond, south of a cranberry bog. Informal town boat launch area. 6 HP limit. Pond receives water from Long Pond via Herring River in north and discharges water into Herring River in west near Pond Road.

> *"Holds bass, pickerel, and white perch."*
>
> Rod Schou, Butterworth Maps

HINCKLEY'S POND: TIPS FROM EXPERTS

"Good largemouth bass fishing."

STEVE HURLEY, MDFW

"Holds pickerel and white perch. Poor access."

ROD SCHOU, BUTTERWORTH MAPS

"Largemouth bass. Big fish. Best bait-shiners. Lures-Jitterbug, crankbaits."

MARK PALMER, GOOSE HUMMOCK

"A good pond for smallmouth bass and yellow perch. Best methods: drift shiners, worms; cast dark plastic jigs into early June. The northeastern 'flat' in the middle of the pond holds lots of smallmouth in spring.
One of our best perch ponds in terms of quantity, though average is about 9 inches."

PETER MIRICK, EDITOR, MASSACHUSETTS WILDLIFE

Bass bait, alive for the moment.

"As the old fisherman remarked after explaining the various ways to attach a frog to a hook, it's all the same to the frog."

PAUL SCHULLERY, MOUNTAIN TIME

LONG POND

Brewster & Harwich

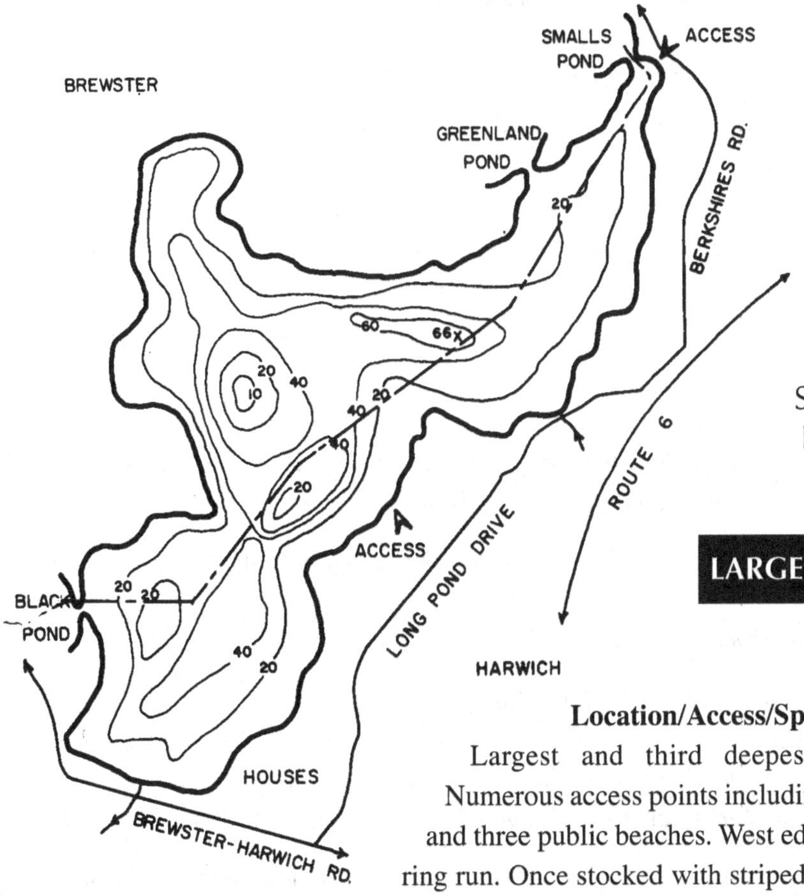

SMALLS POND
ACCESS
BREWSTER
GREENLAND POND
BERKSHIRES RD.
ROUTE 6
ACCESS
LONG POND DRIVE
BLACK POND
HARWICH
HOUSES
BREWSTER-HARWICH RD.

Size - 743 Acres
Depth - 67 feet

LARGEST ON CAPE COD

Location/Access/Special Regulations. Largest and third deepest on Cape Cod. Numerous access points including three boat ramps and three public beaches. West edge of pond has herring run. Once stocked with striped bass.

> *"Excellent smallmouth bass fishing. Also yellow and white perch and pumpkinseed. MDFW once approved fish and game club stocking with stripers. No reported landings."*
>
> Steve Hurley, MDFW

LONG POND: TIPS FROM EXPERTS

"Best species-large and smallmouth bass."

DAVID GILMORE, RENOWNED BASS ANGLER

"For smallies, largemouths fish live herring. BIG bait-BIG fish!"

CRAIG POOSIKIAN, CUSTOM ROD BUILDER

"Lots of smallmouth bass can be fished from gas powered outboards, along structure and where rocky banks prevail. Try Gitzits, shiners. Fish move out to deeper water when weather warms."

MARK PALMER, GOOSE HUMMOCK

"Fair smallmouth, white and yellow perch. I've had best luck with light color, short (<31/2") twister tail jigs. Fishing is generally slow, but most trips will produce a couple of good 'smallies' and, sometimes, a stringer of perch. Grass shrimp should work well here."

PETER MIRICK, EDITOR, MASSACHUSETTS WILDLIFE

"Excellent bass fishing, year 'round, easy access."

ROD SCHOU, BUTTERWORTH MAPS

"Caught my biggest Cape Cod smallmouth bass here- 3 1/2 pounds- on a green Roostertail. Fought so hard I thought I hooked a new world record!"

PETER BUDRYK, A FISHERMAN

BE EXTRA KIND TO THIS POND. The CCC water quality assessment estimated only 2 undeveloped parcels existed along the entire shoreline in 2000, and that approximately 92 cesspools or leechfields exist within 200 feet of the shoreline, resulting in regular water quality problems that threaten the environmental health and enjoyment of the pond.

SAND POND

Harwich

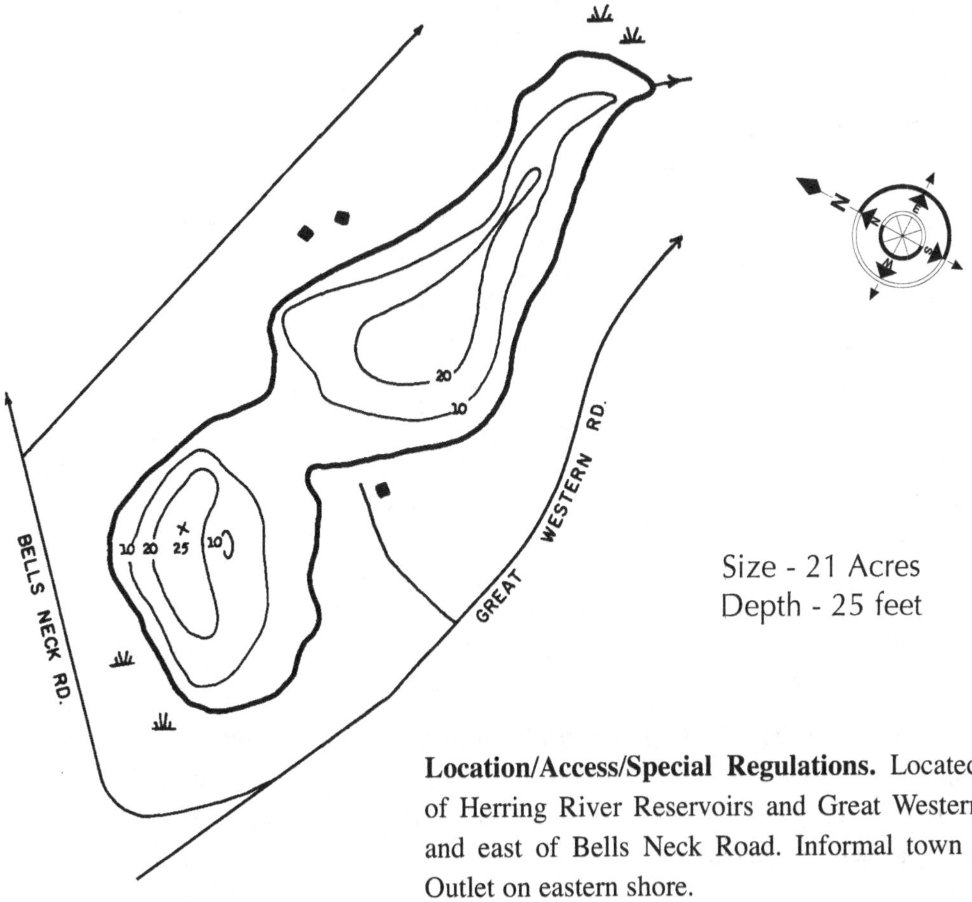

Size - 21 Acres
Depth - 25 feet

Location/Access/Special Regulations. Located north of Herring River Reservoirs and Great Western Road and east of Bells Neck Road. Informal town access. Outlet on eastern shore.

> *"Holds chain pickerel. No recent data."*
>
> Steve Hurley, MDFW
>
> *"A pond that holds bass and pickerel. Boat launch."*
>
> Rod Schou, Butterworth maps

SEYMOUR POND

Brewster & Harwich

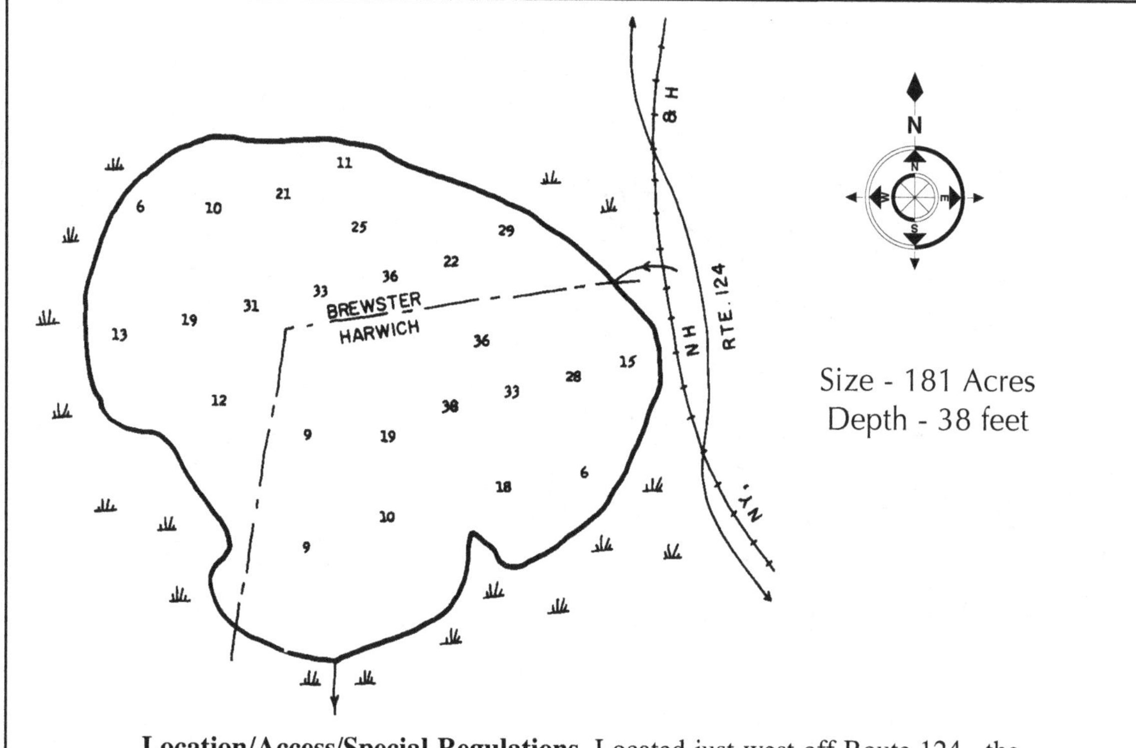

Location/Access/Special Regulations. Located just west off Route 124, the Cape Cod Bicycle Trail, and across Route 124 from Long Pond. Access by town beach on western shore near bike trail. Carry in for boats. 3 HP limit. Pond has herring run outlet.

"Smallmouth bass are best species in pond. Good fishing for largemouth bass. Fair chain pickerel fishing. Also holds white and yellow perch and pumpkinseed."

Steve Hurley, MDFW

"Fish off point on southern shore with spinner/worm combination, small yellow plastic jig, or dark Roostertails for schools of 10-12 inch yellow perch."

Peter Budryk, A Fisherman

CAUGHT A TIGER–NOT BY THE TAIL

State record Tiger Trout 9 pounds, 7 ounces caught by Michael Shelton Peter's Pond, Sandwich, 2004 (Photo: Shelton)

I have no real secrets that I employ when I troll for trout. I will tell you how I fish for them and you are welcome to use it in your book. There are 3 methods commonly used to troll for trout. The first, which is what most people do, is a spinning rod with either a lure or worm/spinner combination. The second, is basically the same as the first except that a leaded line is used instead of monofilament line. The third, which I use, is a fly rod with sinking line, trolling a "Joe's Fly." I use this method over the others because it is much more exciting to catch a fish on a light weight fly rod than any of the other options. It also takes a little more skill and knowledge to successfully land the fish especially the bigger ones.

To be successful one must learn to observe what is going on around them when they are fishing. Are there bugs hatching out of the water? Are there fish jumping or feeding at the top of the surface? If either of these two conditions are happening then you do not have to fish your bait as deep to catch fish. I also take notice of the color and types of bugs hatching and try to match them with one of my files. The important thing is the color of the bugs.

The water temperature, time of day, cloud cover and wind speed are also important things to be considered. The warmer the water the deeper the trout go (to get deeper troll slower). If there is bright sunshine (middle of the day) the fish will be deeper also. If it is cloudy or windy enough to make surface choppy then the trout may not be as deep.

Once someone understands these techniques they will learn the proper depth to fish, the type and color of the fly, the speed at which to troll, and find that they will be catching more fish. It takes a lot of practice, experimentations, observations and determination but you will be successful.

Cast 20:

MASHPEE

Ponds & Lakes

Total Land Area (sq. miles) → **23.86**

Total Area of Ponds (acres) → **1,614**

Total numbers of Ponds → **56**

Number of Ponds by size:

Size	Number
<1 acres:	30
1-5 acres:	13
5-10 acres:	4
10-20 acres:	4
20-50 acres:	1
50-100 acres:	0
>100 acres:	4

Pond groups:

- **Mashpee Environmental Coalition**
- **Ashumet Valley Property Owners**

> *"Greedy little minds are ever busy turning landscapes into slag heaps, housing tracts, canals, freeways and shopping malls, a perversion they zealously, pursue under the ragged banner of progress."*
>
> Sheridan Anderson, The Curtis Creek Manifesto (1978)

MASHPEE

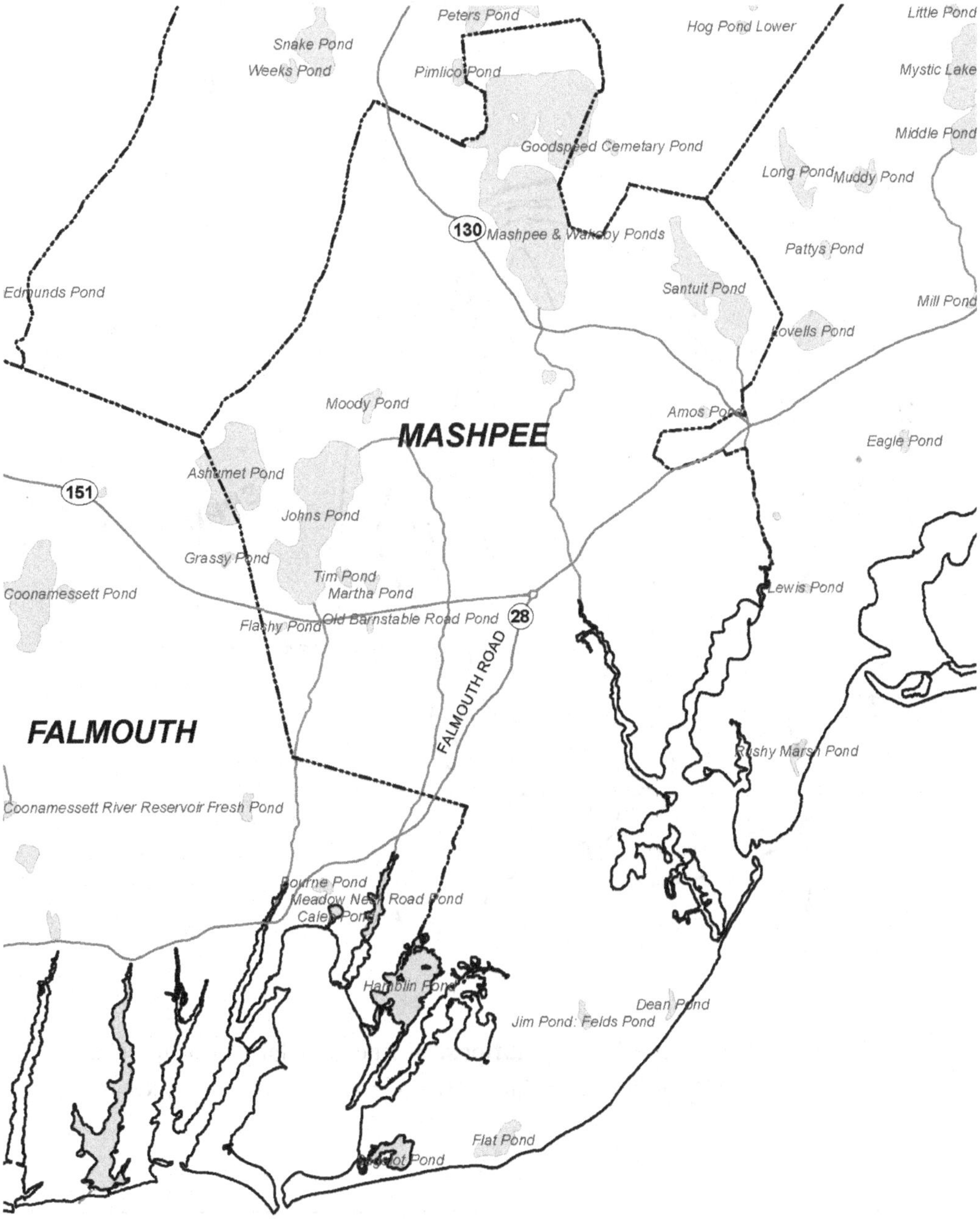

Peters Pond
Little Pond
Hog Pond Lower
Snake Pond
Weeks Pond
Pimlico Pond
Mystic Lake
Middle Pond
Goodspeed Cemetary Pond
Long Pond
Muddy Pond
130
Mashpee & Wakeby Ponds
Pattys Pond
Edmunds Pond
Santuit Pond
Mill Pond
Lovells Pond
Moody Pond
Amos Pond
MASHPEE
Eagle Pond
Ashumet Pond
151
Johns Pond
Grassy Pond
Tim Pond
Martha Pond
Lewis Pond
Coonamessett Pond
Flashy Pond
Old Barnstable Road Pond
28
FALMOUTH ROAD
FALMOUTH
Rushy Marsh Pond
Coonamessett River Reservoir Fresh Pond
Bourne Pond
Meadow Neck Road Pond
Caleb Pond
Hamblin Pond
Dean Pond
Jim Pond: Felds Pond
Flat Pond

ASHUMET POND

Mashpee / Falmouth

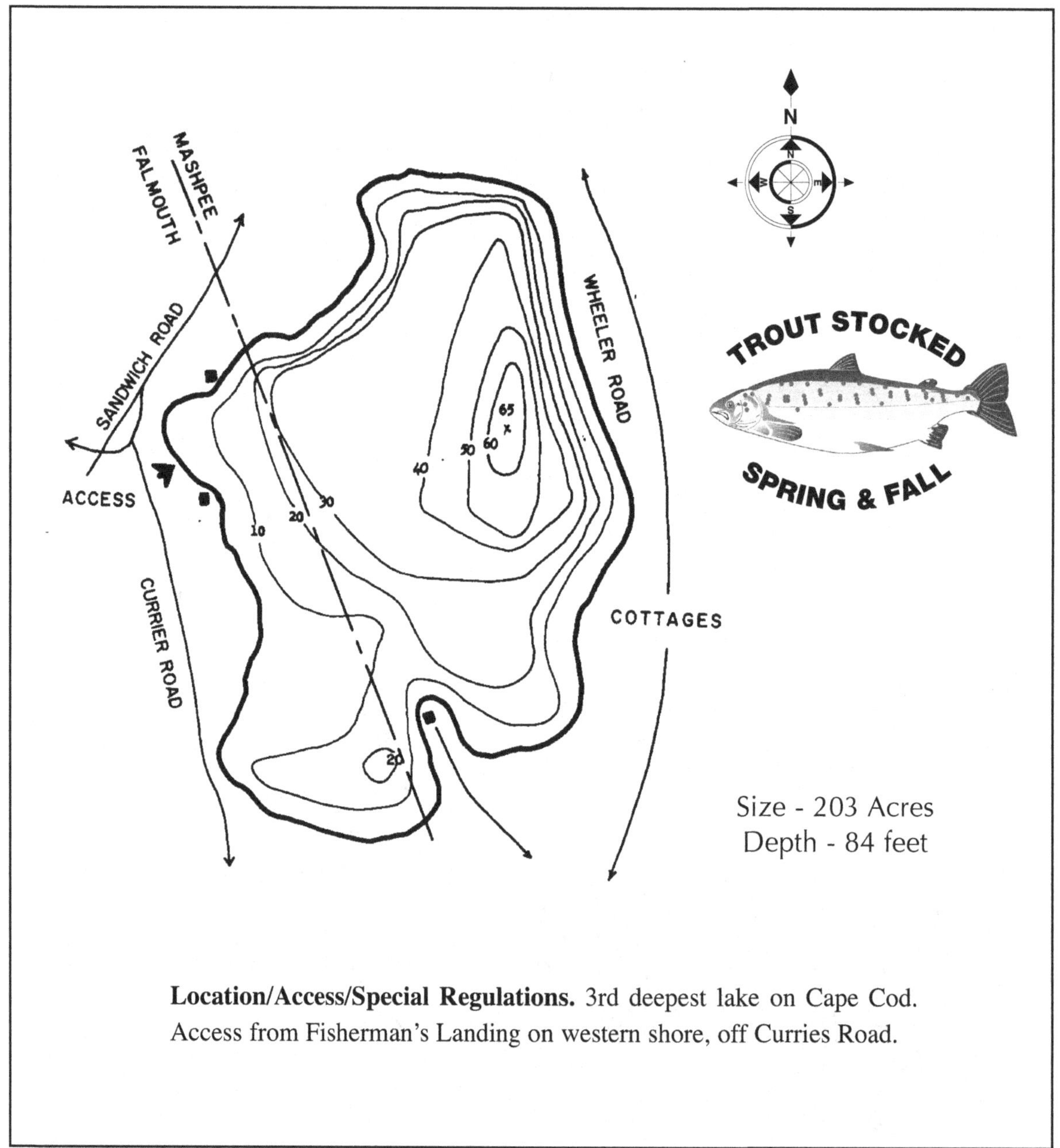

Location/Access/Special Regulations. 3rd deepest lake on Cape Cod. Access from Fisherman's Landing on western shore, off Curries Road.

Angler fishes Ashumet Pond among iron filings bags designed to reduce phosphates from the nearby Air Force base. Originally under five feet of water, the bags were placed there as a pilot iron barrier project (by Air Force center for environment excellence) which will be continued. The drop of the water level at the time of the photo exposed the bags. (Information supplied by Steve Hurley, MDFW)

"One of the top trout ponds in town. Also good smallmouth bass fishing. Use bait early in season, flies late spring, spoons anytime."

GENE BOURQUE, EDITOR, ON THE WATER

"Excellent smallmouth bass fishing. Good trout and largemouth bass fishing. Also holds yellow perch."

STEVE HURLEY, MDFW

"Excellent for trout. Use lures or powerbait."

JEFF CAPUTE, AWARD WINNING ANGLER

JOHNS POND

MASHPEE

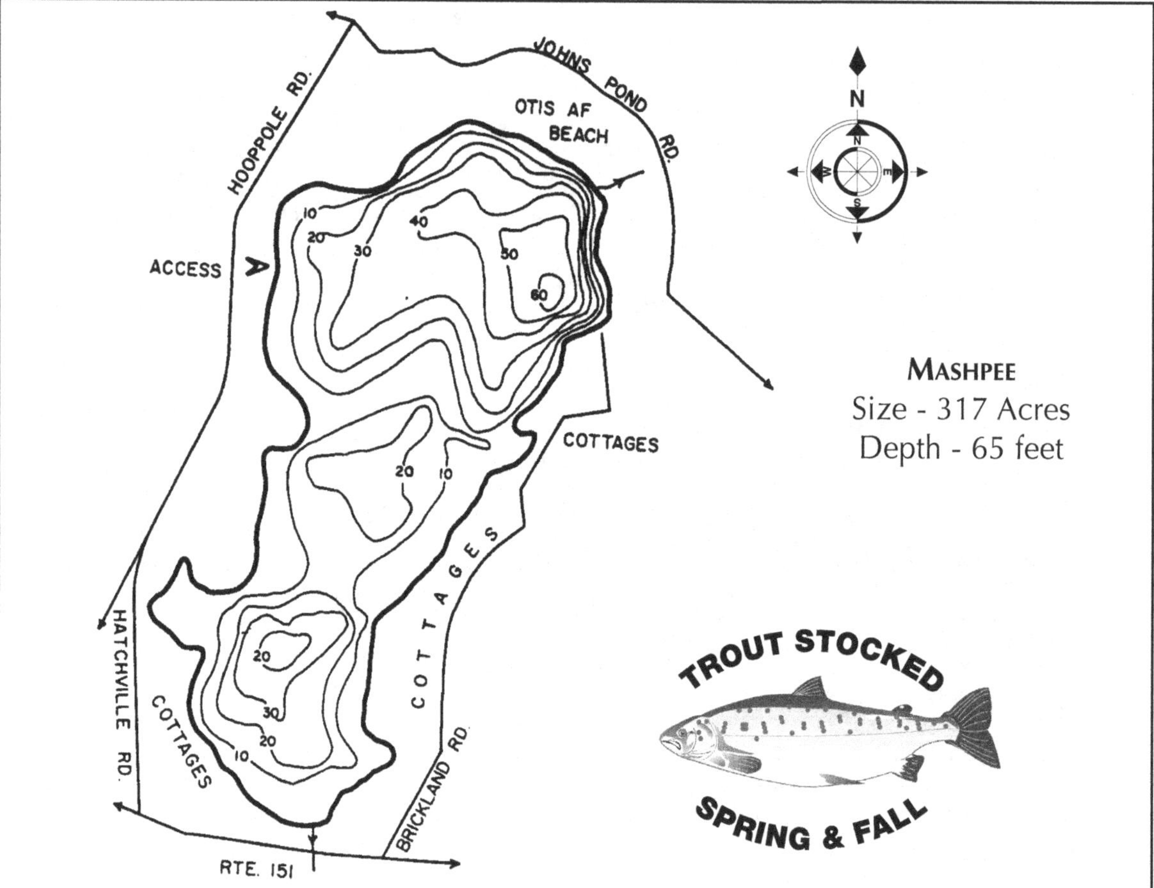

Location/Access/Special Regulations. Located in western Mashpee just southeast of Ashumet Pond and the MA Military reservation. Public paved boat ramp with small parking lot on northwest corner off Hooppole Road. Pond drains into Childs and Quashnet Rivers. Herring run.

HEALTH ALERT: Johns Pond is within a "pollution plume" from the nearby military base. Until corrected, consumption of any fish is <u>not</u> advised. Information? Write or call MDPH, 250 Washington St. 7th floor, Boston, MA 02108, (617) 624-5757

In short order they will be fly fishing and practicing catch and release.

"Excellent for smallmouth bass and good for trout and largemouth bass. Yellow and white perch and pumpkinseed."

STEVE HURLEY, MDFW

"A pond with excellent trout and bass fishing, as well as pickerel, and white perch."

ROD SCHOU, BUTTERWORTH MAPS

"A good pond for smallmouth and largemouth bass. Use spinnerbaits, grubs."

JEFF CAPUTE, AWARD WINNING ANGLER

"Good pond for trout and largemouth bass. Best fished from a boat or canoe, June-December."

GENE BOURQUE, EDITOR, ON THE WATER

MASHPEE-WAKEBY PONDS (Partially in Sandwich)

MASHPEE/SANDWICH

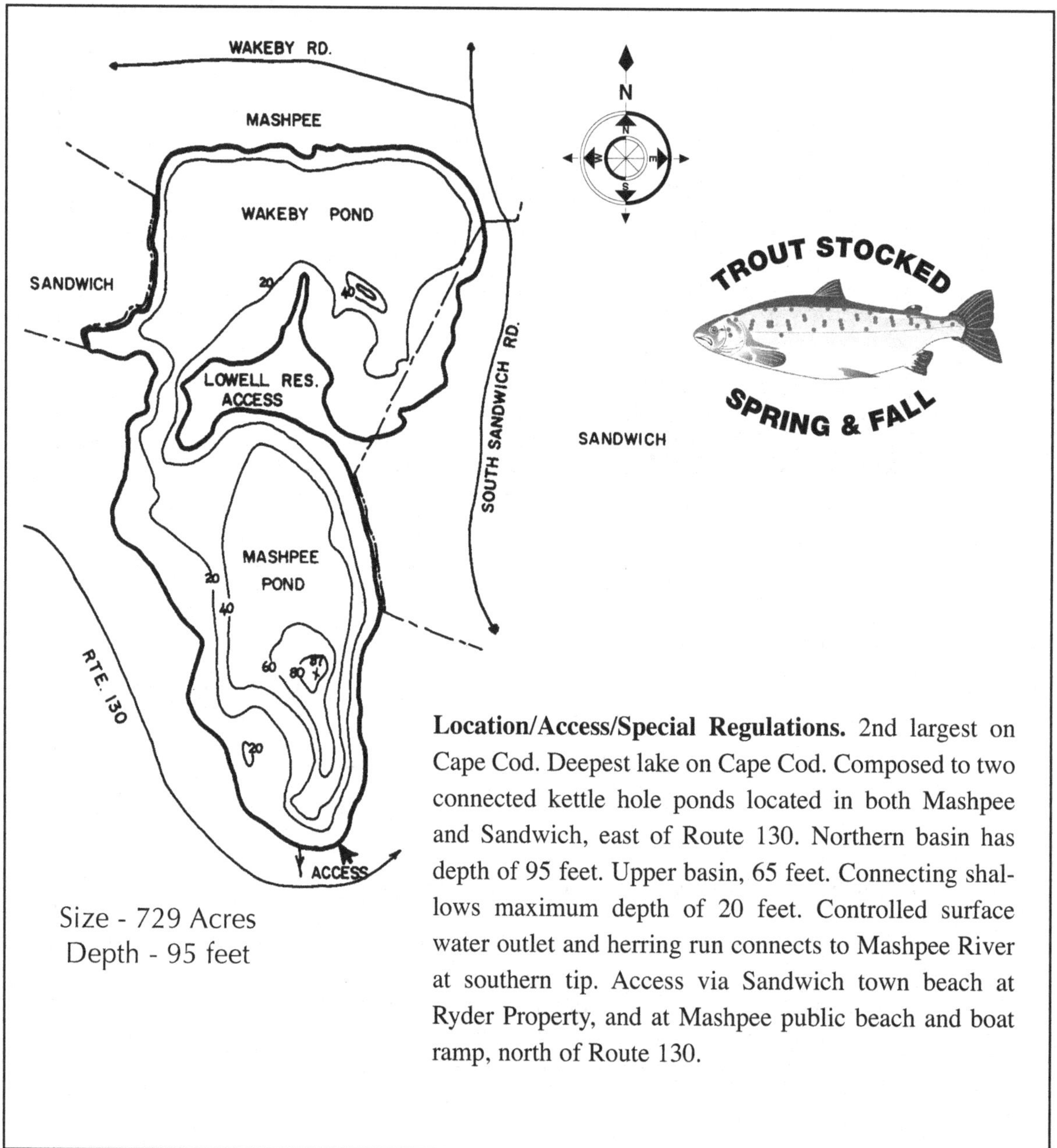

Size - 729 Acres
Depth - 95 feet

Location/Access/Special Regulations. 2nd largest on Cape Cod. Deepest lake on Cape Cod. Composed to two connected kettle hole ponds located in both Mashpee and Sandwich, east of Route 130. Northern basin has depth of 95 feet. Upper basin, 65 feet. Connecting shallows maximum depth of 20 feet. Controlled surface water outlet and herring run connects to Mashpee River at southern tip. Access via Sandwich town beach at Ryder Property, and at Mashpee public beach and boat ramp, north of Route 130.

MASHPEE-WAKEBY POND: TIPS FROM EXPERTS

" Probably best largemouth bass pond on the Cape. Best bets for me have been dark, 5 inch Senko worm rigged 'wacky' (hooked in the middle). Let sink (no weight) and jig back along bottom (like a jumping crayfish)"

PETER MIRICK, EDITOR, MASSACHUSETTS WILDLIFE .

"Good pond for smallies and largemouth bass. Sluggos. Sight fish shallows in spring."

CRAIG POOSIKIAN, CRAIG'S CUSTOM RODS

"Bass pros know the ins and out of this pond. Follow the rules for pre-spawn, et al. Near fallen timbers roll spinnerbaits, but jigging powerbaits is proven."

ROBERT JESSUP, THE SPORTING LIFE

"An excellent pond for trout and all warm water species.Heavily stocked with trout. All methods work-live baits, lures, flies, casting, trolling ,still fishing. Many boats and bass tournaments here on weekends."

GENE BOURQUE, EDITOR, ON THE WATER

Hamilton Reservoir (off Cape) 20 pounds northern pike caught by Mike Hansen. (Photo: MDFW)

SANTUIT POND

MASHPEE

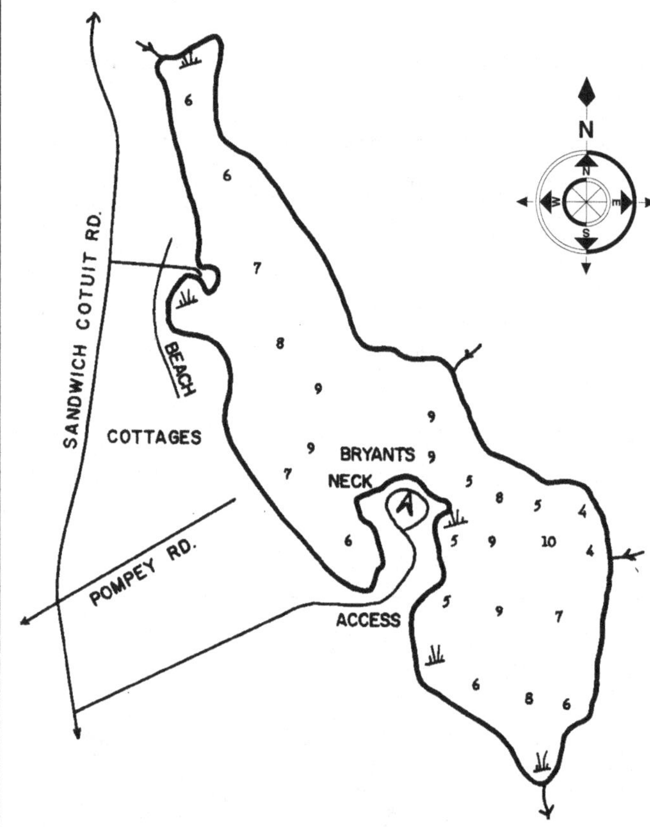

Size - 172 Acres
Depth - 10 feet

Location/Access/Special Regulations. Located approximately one mile north of Route 28 and east of Route 130 in northeastern Mashpee. Access off end of Hornbeam Street, which is off Sandwich/Cotuit Road, via town right of way to Bryants Neck. Dirt boat ramp.

"Not as good as it once was, but it still puts out its fair share of 3-5 pound largemouth bass and an occasional trophy. Have best luck with black or purple 9 inch rubber worm. Also happy with grey Sluggo. Need weedless lures by mid-May."

PETER MIRICK, EDITOR,
MASSACHUSETTS WILDLIFE

"A pond with good largemouth bass and chain pickerel fishing. Also can catch white and yellow perch and pumpkinseed."

STEVE HURLEY, MDFW

If it's a fight you're looking for, he'll oblige anytime, anywhere.

> *"But if the salmon and trout must be classified as elite in this mythical social structure then let the black bass be given permanent status as the working class of American game fish. He's tough and he knows it he's a bass sax, grumbling get down blue in the bayou. He's a factory worker, truck driver, wild catter, lumberjack, barroom bouncer, dock walloper, migrant farmhand, and bear wrestler. And if it's a fight you're looking for, he'll oblige anytime, anywhere. Whether it's a backwater at noon, a swamp at midnight, or dockside at dawn, he'll be there waiting. He's a pierce-eyed, foul-mouthed, tobacco-chewing redneck who has traveled to every corner of the nation, paying has way and giving no quarter."*
>
> PAT SMITH, OLD IRON JAW

Cast 21:

ORLEANS

Ponds & Lakes

Total Land Area (sq. miles) **13.94**

Total Area of Ponds (acres) **220**

Total numbers of Ponds **63**

Number of Ponds by size:

<1 acres:	**38**
1-5 acres:	**13**
5-10 acres:	**8**
10-20 acres:	**1**
20-50 acres:	**3**
50-100 acres:	**0**
>100 acres:	**0**

Pond groups:

- **Orleans Water Quality Task Force**
- **Friends of Crystal Lake**
- **Friends of Bakers Pond**
- **Friends of Pilgrim Lake**

> *"I object to fishing touraments less for what they do to fish than for what they do to fishermen."*
>
> Ted Williams (1984)

ORLEANS

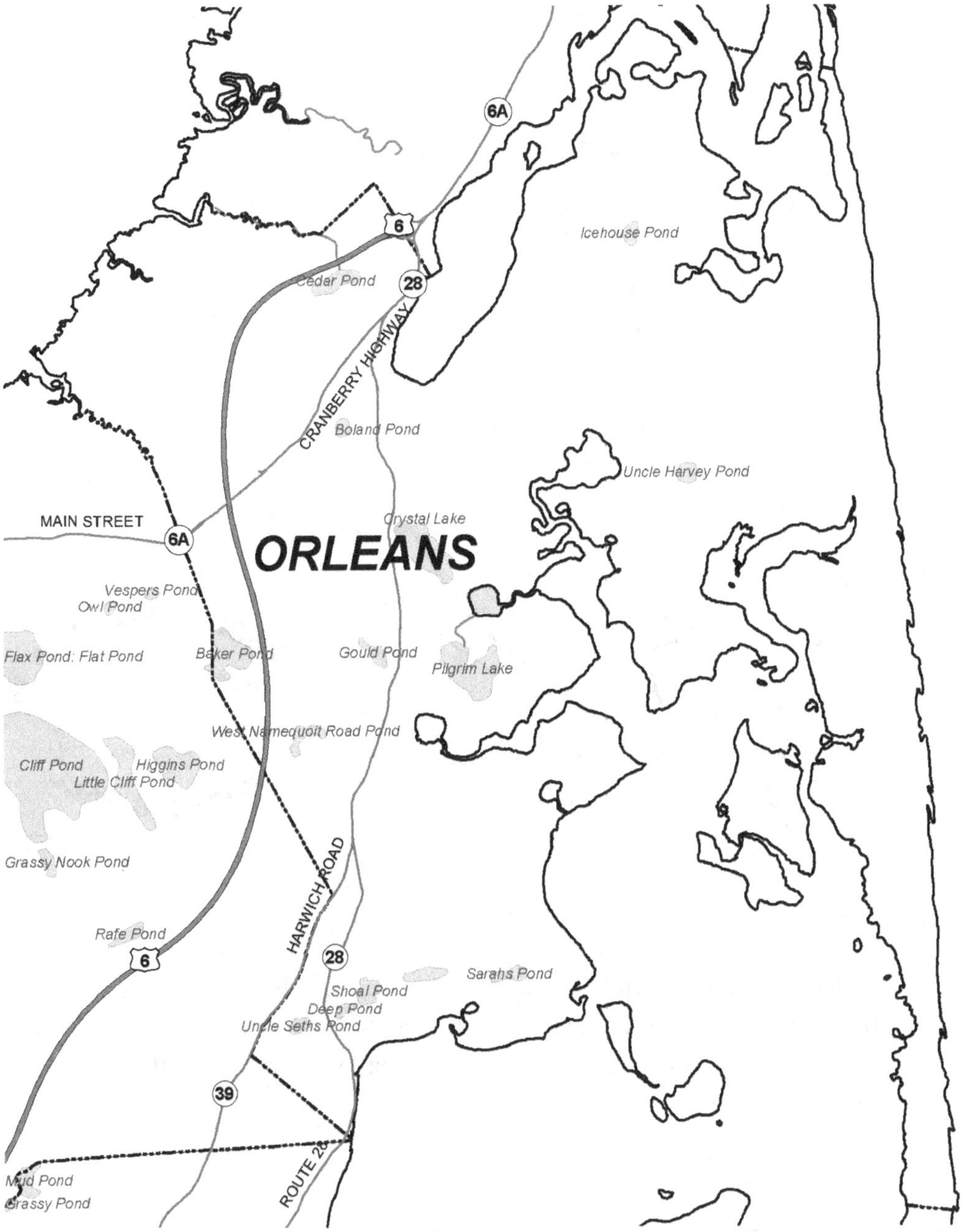

6A
6
Icehouse Pond
Cedar Pond
28
CRANBERRY HIGHWAY
Boland Pond
Uncle Harvey Pond
MAIN STREET
Crystal Lake
6A
ORLEANS
Vespers Pond
Owl Pond
Flax Pond: Flat Pond
Baker Pond
Gould Pond
Pilgrim Lake
West Namequoit Road Pond
Cliff Pond
Higgins Pond
Little Cliff Pond
Grassy Nook Pond
HARWICH ROAD
Rafe Pond
6
28
Sarahs Pond
Shoal Pond
Deep Pond
Uncle Seths Pond
39
ROUTE 28
Mud Pond
Grassy Pond

BAKERS POND

ORLEANS (Small portions of northern and western bays located in Brewster)

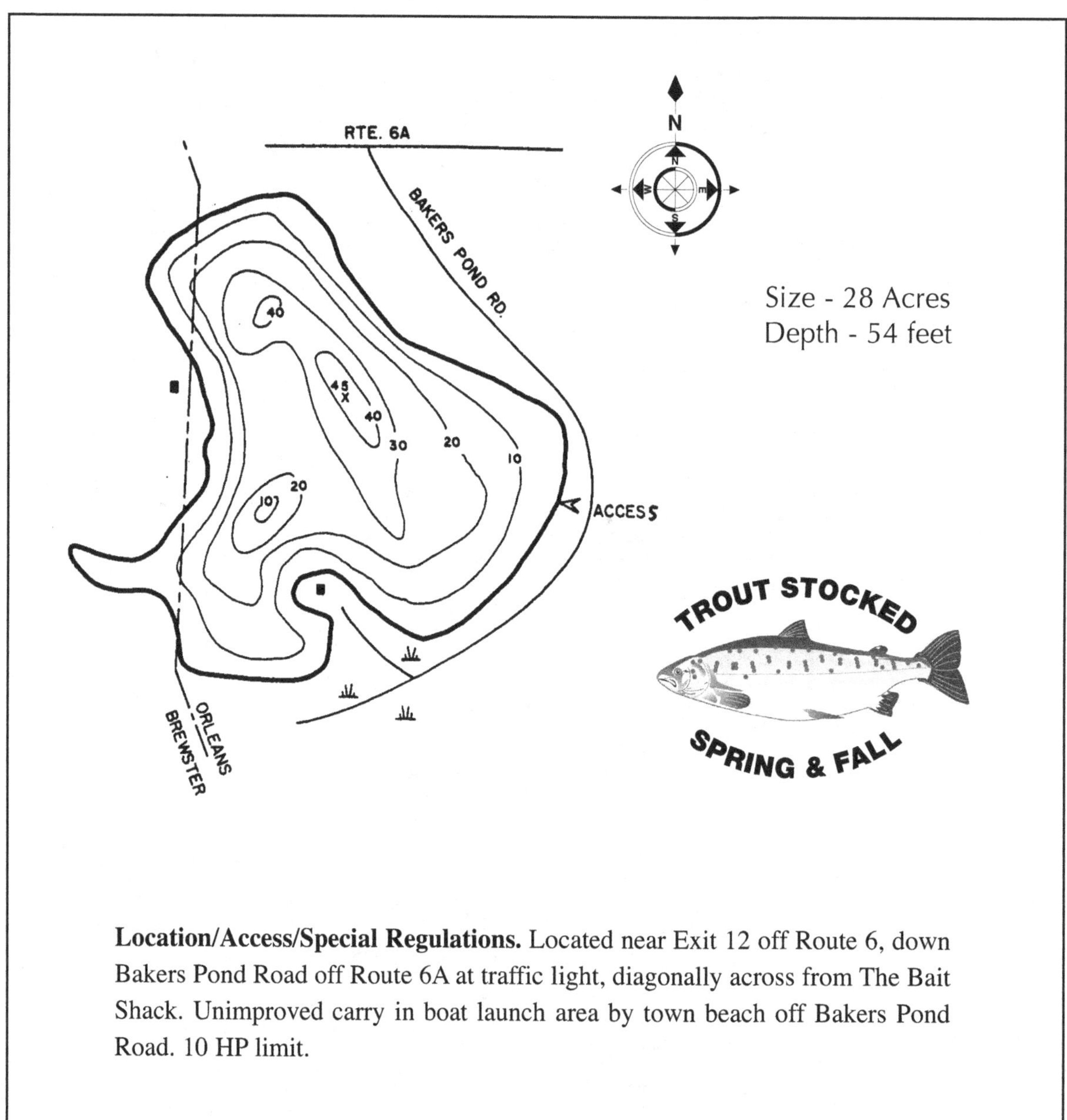

Location/Access/Special Regulations. Located near Exit 12 off Route 6, down Bakers Pond Road off Route 6A at traffic light, diagonally across from The Bait Shack. Unimproved carry in boat launch area by town beach off Bakers Pond Road. 10 HP limit.

BAKERS POND: TIPS FROM EXPERTS

"Best species in pond are the variety of trout and also smallmouth bass. Best-spoons, jigs, flies, wet or dry. Pond is easily wadable and holds a lot of fish."

CRAIG POOSIKIAN, CRAIG'S CUSTOM RODS

"A good trout and smallmouth bass pond. that also yields yellow perch and pumpkinseed."

STEVE HURLEY, MDFW

"This pond's best species is trout. Best method-casting a Thomas Cyclone, all colors."

ELLA SCHULTZ, EXPERIENCED ANGLER

"Best species-trout. Best bets- shiners at dark for big brown trout. Also Thomas Lures, Colorado Spinner.Occasional smallmouth. Good ice fishing pond."

MARK PALMER, GOOSE HUMMOCK

"Well stocked with trout in spring. Easy shore fishing. Good for families."

STAN MOAK, TROUT UNLIMITED

Bakers Pond, a trophy smallmouth bass caught with an inflated worm and released.

CRYSTAL LAKE

ORLEANS

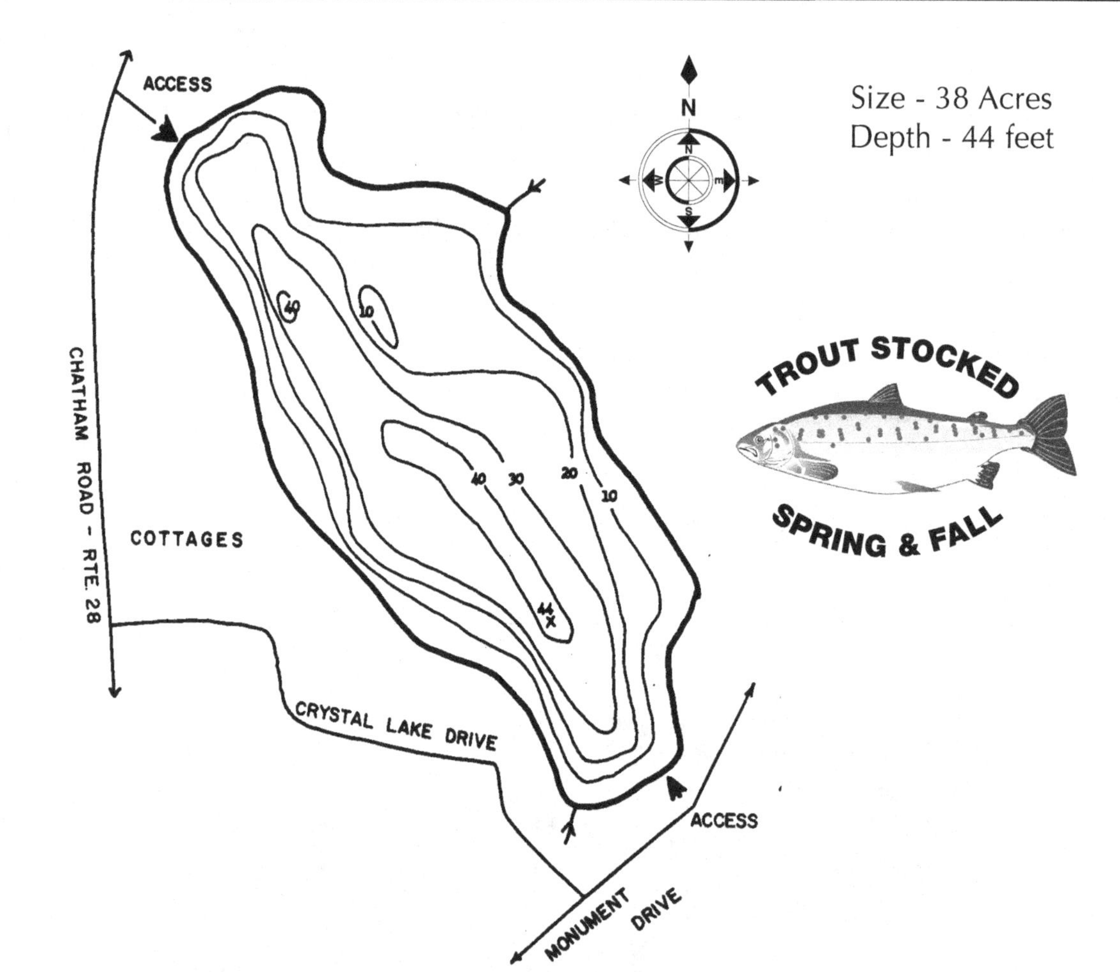

Location/Access/Special Regulations. Located off Route 28 near intersection of Pond Road. Padded boat launch area at this northwest access. Southeast access also off Monument Road by town beach and parking. 10 HP limit. On northeast shore an intermittent stream discharges into lake from a wetland area. In southwest corner a surface outlet drains into a cranberry bog ultimately leading into Keskayogansett Bay.

CRYSTAL LAKE: TIPS FROM EXPERTS

"Good pond for trout and monster eels.Fish live shiners or chubs. Probably next world record eel will come from Crystal Lake."

CRAIG POOSIKIAN, CRAIG'S CUSTOM RODS

"This is a good trout pond I fish with a gold Thomas Cyclone."

ELLA SCHULTZ, EXPERIENCED ANGLER

"Best species in here are trout. Powerbait, shiners, Mepps spinners all produce.Never used to be bass in here but lots of 1-2 pounders now."

MARK PALMER, GOOSE HUMMOCK

"Another good Orleans water for trout and bass. Stocked heavily in spring."

STAN MOAK, TROUT UNLIMITED

"Nice trout off beach and bass off other shores. Particularly good spot for kids early/late in day or cloudy/rainy days to avoid crowds, expecially during the summer."

PETER BUDRYK, A FISHERMAN

Crystal Lake, favored fishing water of late Governor Frank "Sarge" Sargent.

PILGRIM LAKE

ORLEANS

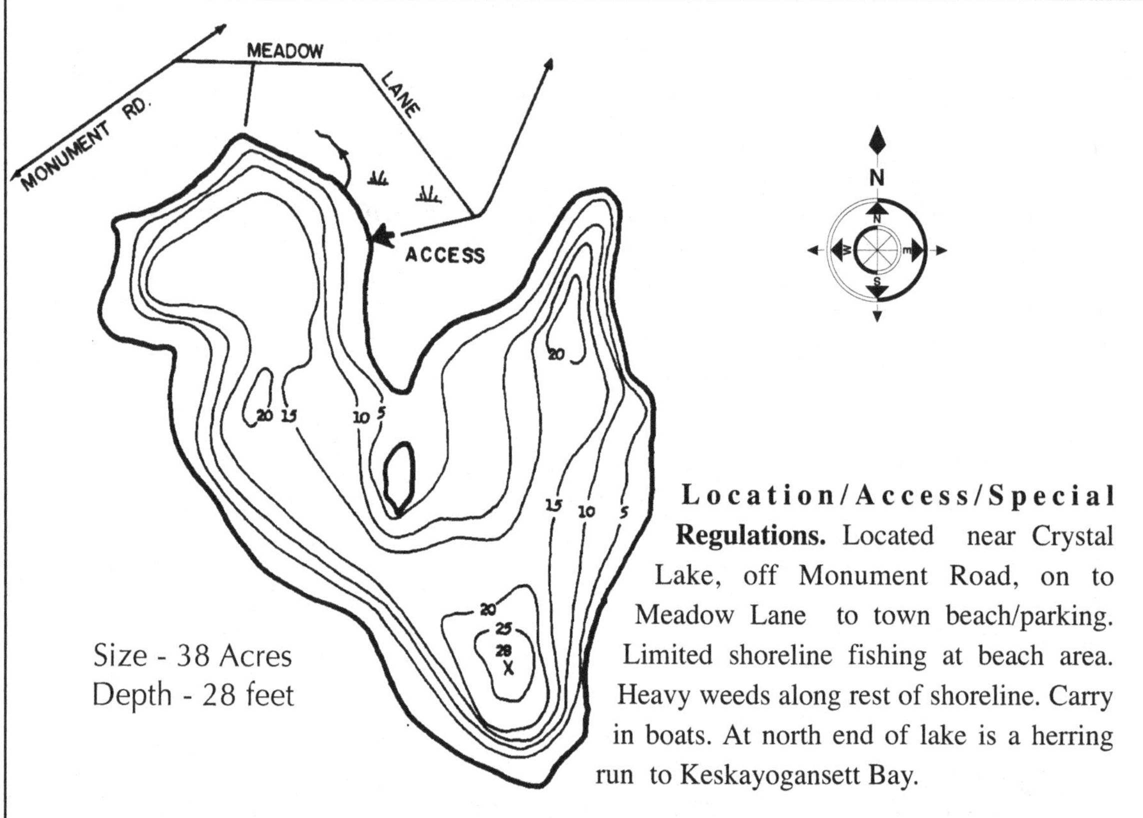

Size - 38 Acres
Depth - 28 feet

Location/Access/Special Regulations. Located near Crystal Lake, off Monument Road, on to Meadow Lane to town beach/parking. Limited shoreline fishing at beach area. Heavy weeds along rest of shoreline. Carry in boats. At north end of lake is a herring run to Keskayogansett Bay.

"A great warm water pond. Limited access from shore. Large and smallmouths are abundant with panfish and turtles."

STAN MOAK, TROUT UNLIMITED

"A good lake for largemouth bass, perch, and pickerel."

DAVID GILMORE, ACCLAIMED ANGLER

"Orleans" best waters for bass and pickerel. Best bets-worms, plugs, Sluggos, spinnerbaits. Bring your canoe or kayak."

CRAIG POOSIKIAN, CRAIG'S CUSTOM RODS

"Best bass pond in town. Use shiners, big herring imitations, Rapalas, flies."

MARK PALMER, GOOSE HUMMOCK

PANEL OF EXPERTS

Steve Hurley, MDFW, He and his staff put 'em in. (below)

Rob Jessup (above)
Rod Schou, Butterworth Maps (left)
Ella Schultz (below)

Jeff Capute (above)

Mark Palmer (above right), & Mike McCaskill (above left)

Cast 22:

PROVINCETOWN

Ponds & Lakes

Total Land Area (sq. miles) → **8.35**

Total Area of Ponds (acres) → **145**

Total numbers of Ponds → **31**

Number of Ponds by size:

<1 acres:	7
1-5 acres:	15
5-10 acres:	6
10-20 acres:	2
20-50 acres:	1
50-100 acres:	0
>100 acres:	0

NO TROUT STOCKED PONDS IN PROVINCETOWN. LIMITED WARM WATER FISHERY

PROVINCETOWN

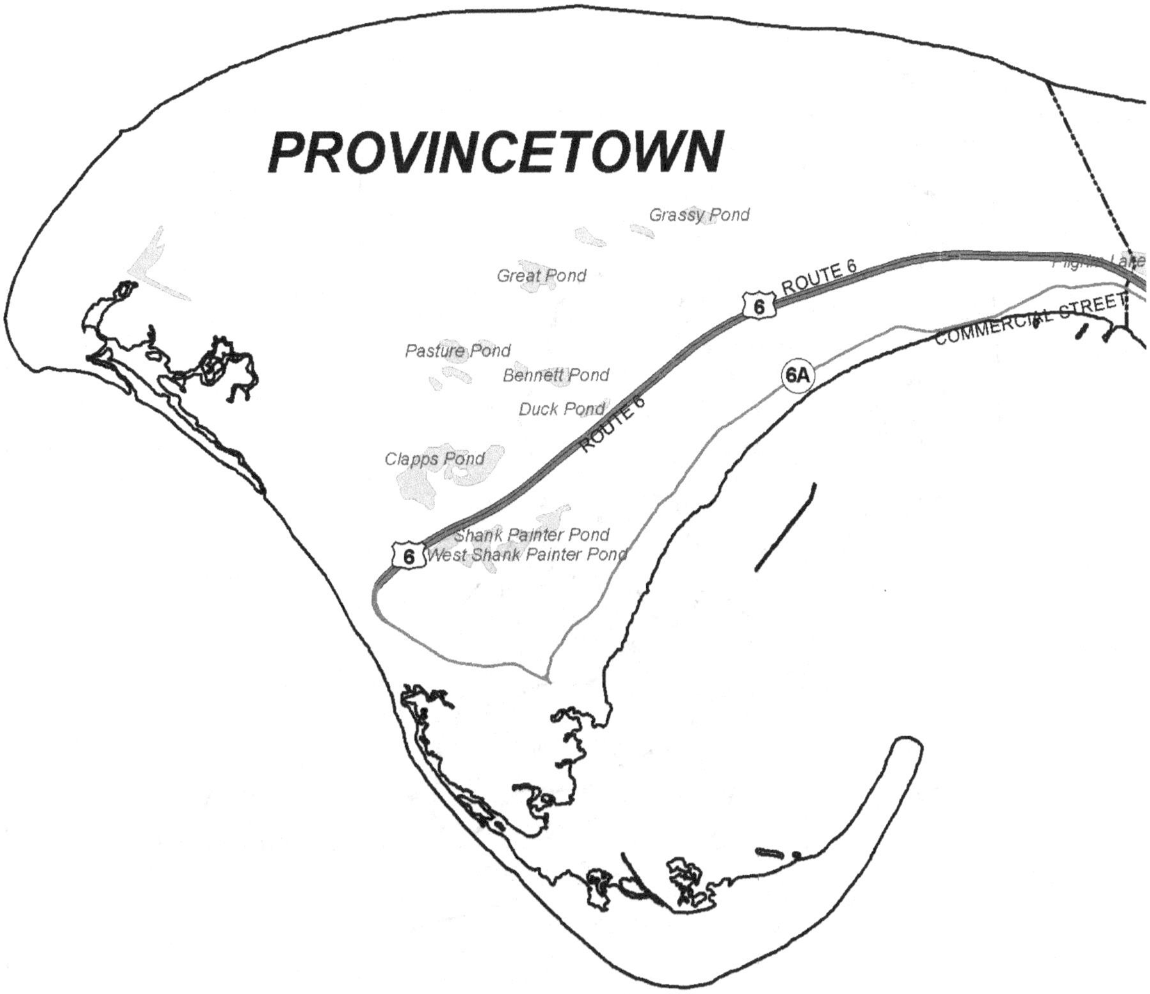

Note: NOTE: In geologic terms, Provincetown ponds are much younger than the rest of the Cape's ponds, forming after the growth of the Provincelands during the last 3,500 years. They are more properly classified as swamps or bogs.

CLAPPS POND
PROVINCETOWN

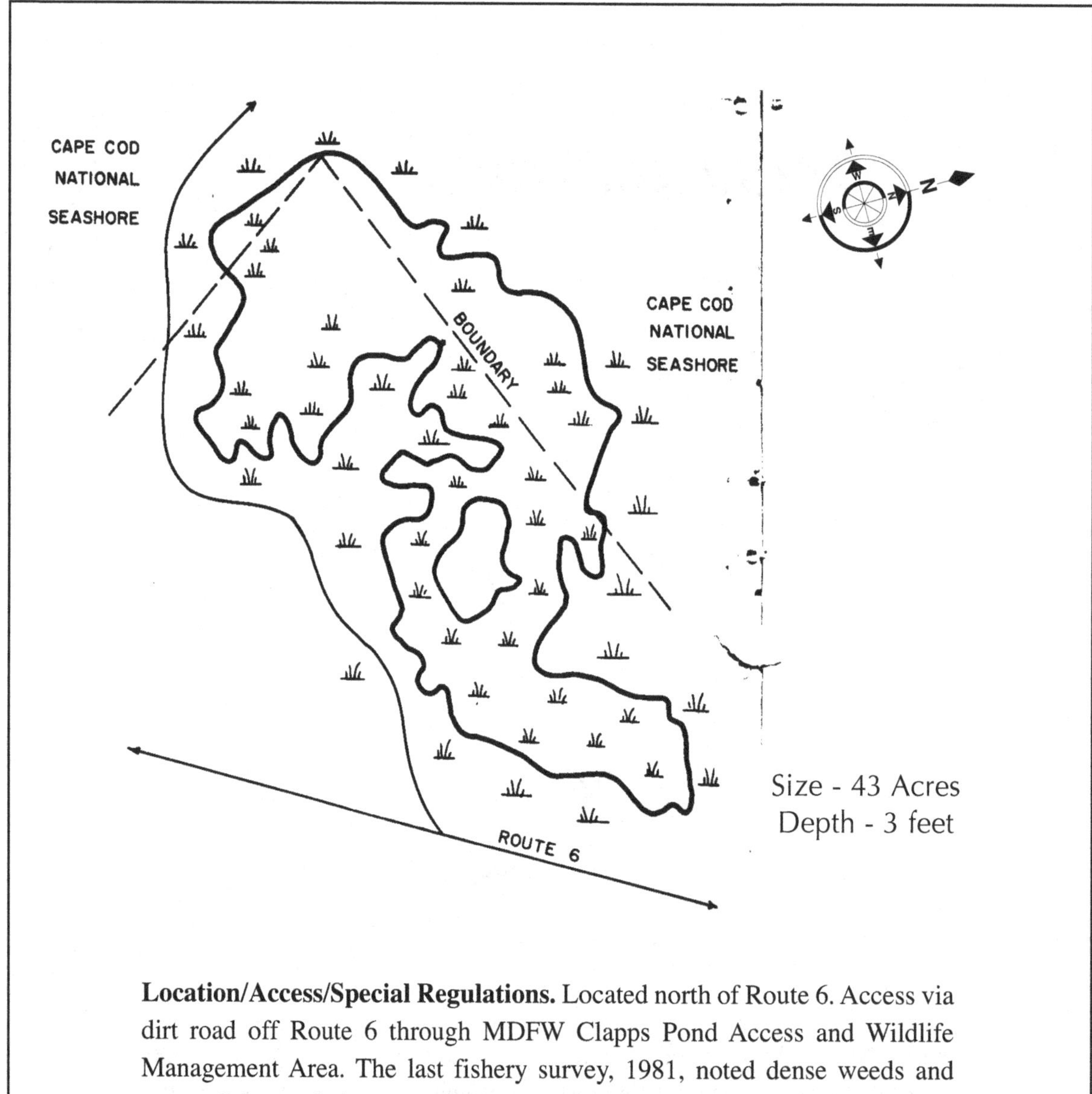

Location/Access/Special Regulations. Located north of Route 6. Access via dirt road off Route 6 through MDFW Clapps Pond Access and Wildlife Management Area. The last fishery survey, 1981, noted dense weeds and sparse fish population: pickerel,largemouth bass, pumpkinseed.

Yet another Cape Cod innermost water (Photo: J. Real Photos, jreal75@hotmail.com

Cast 23:

SANDWICH

Ponds & Lakes

Total Land Area (sq. miles) **42.61**

Total Area of Ponds (acres) **698**

Total numbers of Ponds **63**

Number of Ponds by size:

Size	Number
<1 acres:	32
1-5 acres:	17
5-10 acres:	4
10-20 acres:	3
20-50 acres:	2
50-100 acres:	3
>100 acres:	2

Pond groups:

Shawme Pond Watershed Association, Inc.
Sandwich Pond Monitoring Group

> *"If fishing interferes with your business, give up your business. The trout do not rise in Greenwood Cemetery."*
>
> Sparse Grey Hackle, Fishless Days (1954)

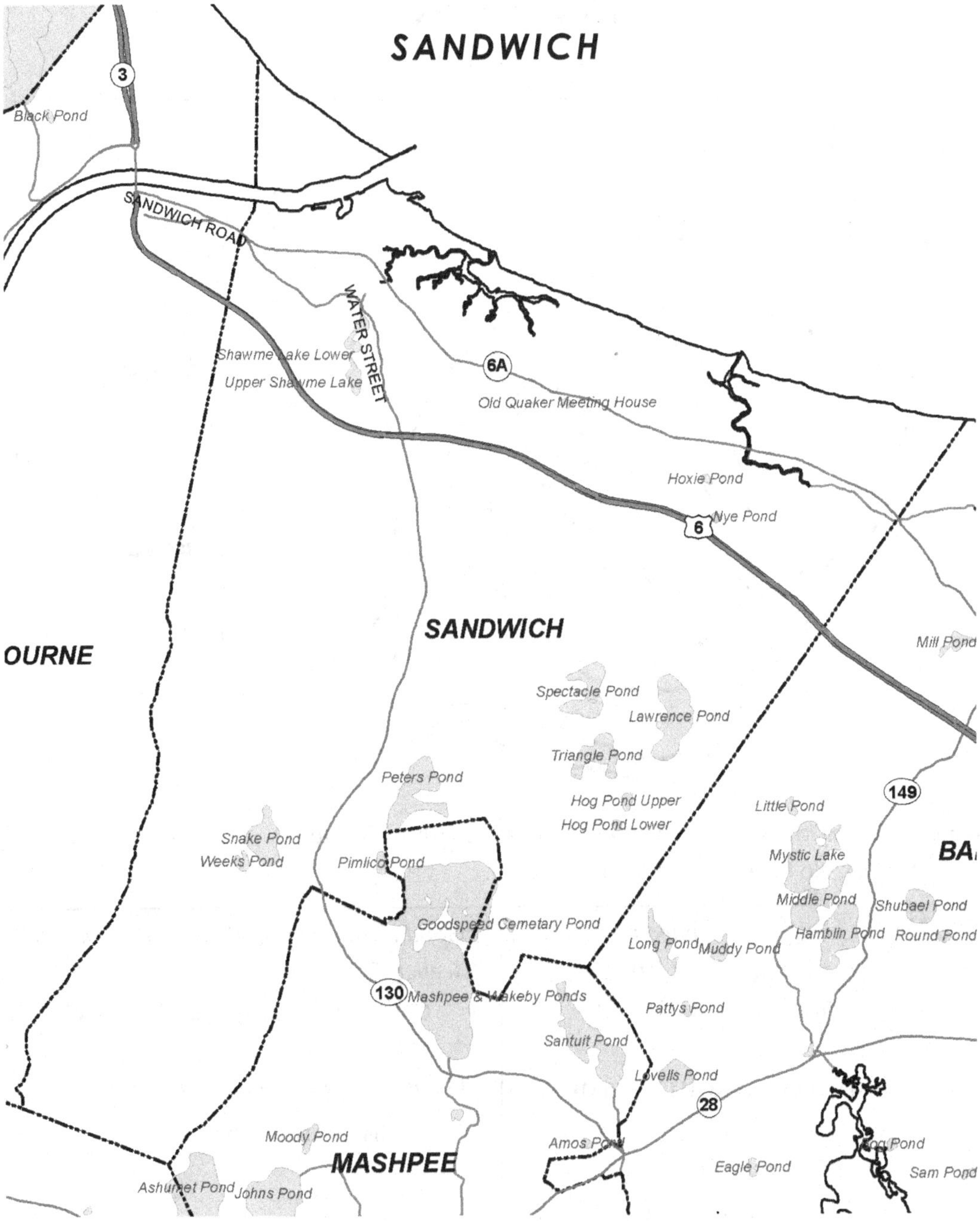

SANDWICH
Black Pond
SANDWICH ROAD
WATER STREET
Shawme Lake Lower
Upper Shawme Lake
6A
Old Quaker Meeting House
Hoxie Pond
Nye Pond
6
SANDWICH
OURNE
Mill Pond
Spectacle Pond
Lawrence Pond
Triangle Pond
Peters Pond
Hog Pond Upper
Hog Pond Lower
Little Pond
149
Snake Pond
Weeks Pond
Pimlico Pond
Mystic Lake
Middle Pond
Shubael Pond
Goodspeed Cemetary Pond
Long Pond
Muddy Pond
Hamblin Pond
Round Pond
130
Mashpee & Wakeby Ponds
Pattys Pond
Santuit Pond
Lovells Pond
28
Moody Pond
MASHPEE
Amos Pond
Eagle Pond
Sam Pond
Ashumet Pond
Johns Pond

HOXIE POND

SANDWICH

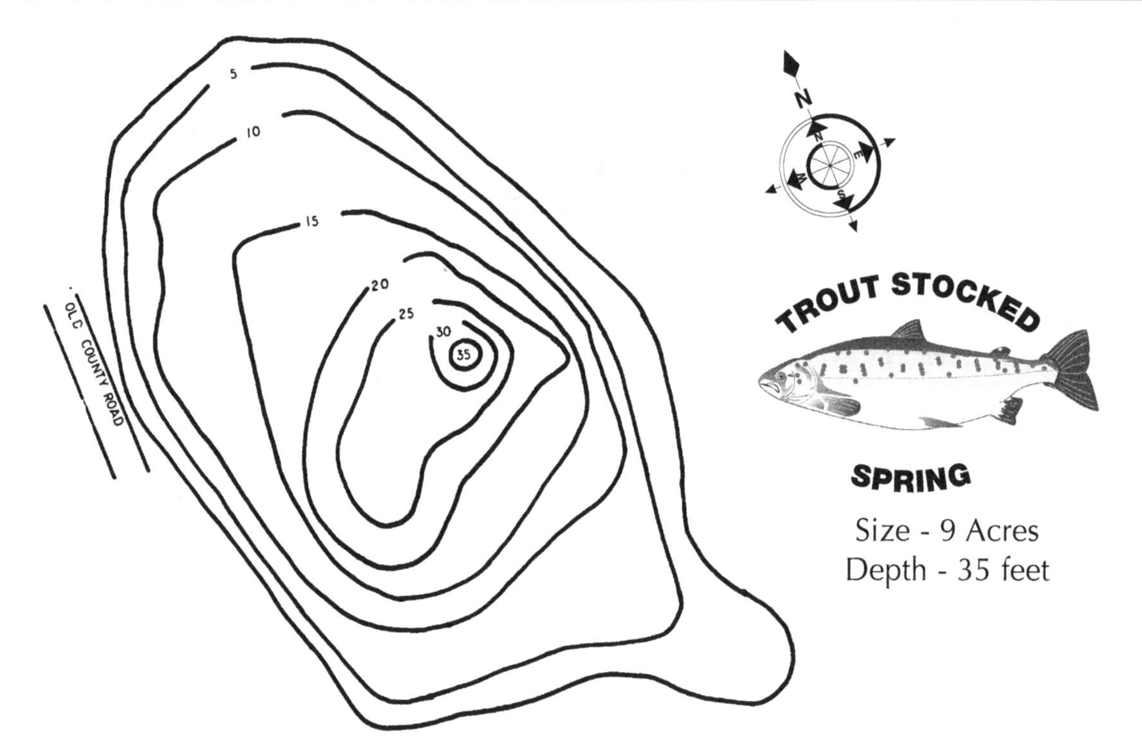

Location/Access/Special Regulations. Located north of Route 6A and east of Old Country Road. Walk in. No boat launch. Pond has outlet.

"Pond is too small for sustained use. Great trout pond in spring and good bass and panfish pond later in season. Best fly fished."

STAN MOAK, TROUT UNLIMITED

"Popular spring trout pond."

STEVE HURLEY, MDFW

"Good trout pond. Little fished. Good 'sleeper'".

GENE BOURQUE, EDITOR, ON THE WATER

"Good for trout. Try lures, powerbait."

JEFF CAPUTE, AWARD WINNING ANGLER

LAWRENCE POND

SANDWICH

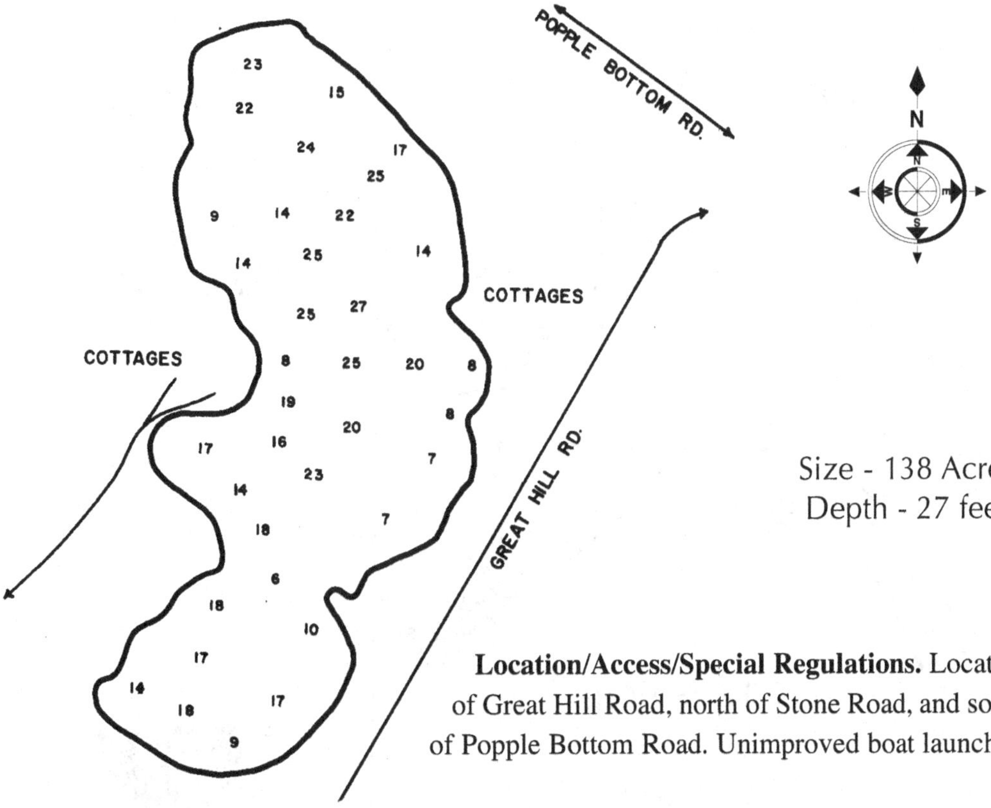

POPPLE BOTTOM RD.

COTTAGES

COTTAGES

GREAT HILL RD.

N

Size - 138 Acres
Depth - 27 feet

Location/Access/Special Regulations. Located west of Great Hill Road, north of Stone Road, and southwest of Popple Bottom Road. Unimproved boat launch.

> *"A good yellow perch pond. Fish worms or small shiners near bottom."*
>
> PETER MIRICK, EDITOR, MASSACHUSETTS WILDLIFE
>
> *"Good largemouth and smallmouth bass pond, also yellow perch and pumpkinseed."*
>
> STEVE HURLEY, MDFW

PETERS POND
SANDWICH

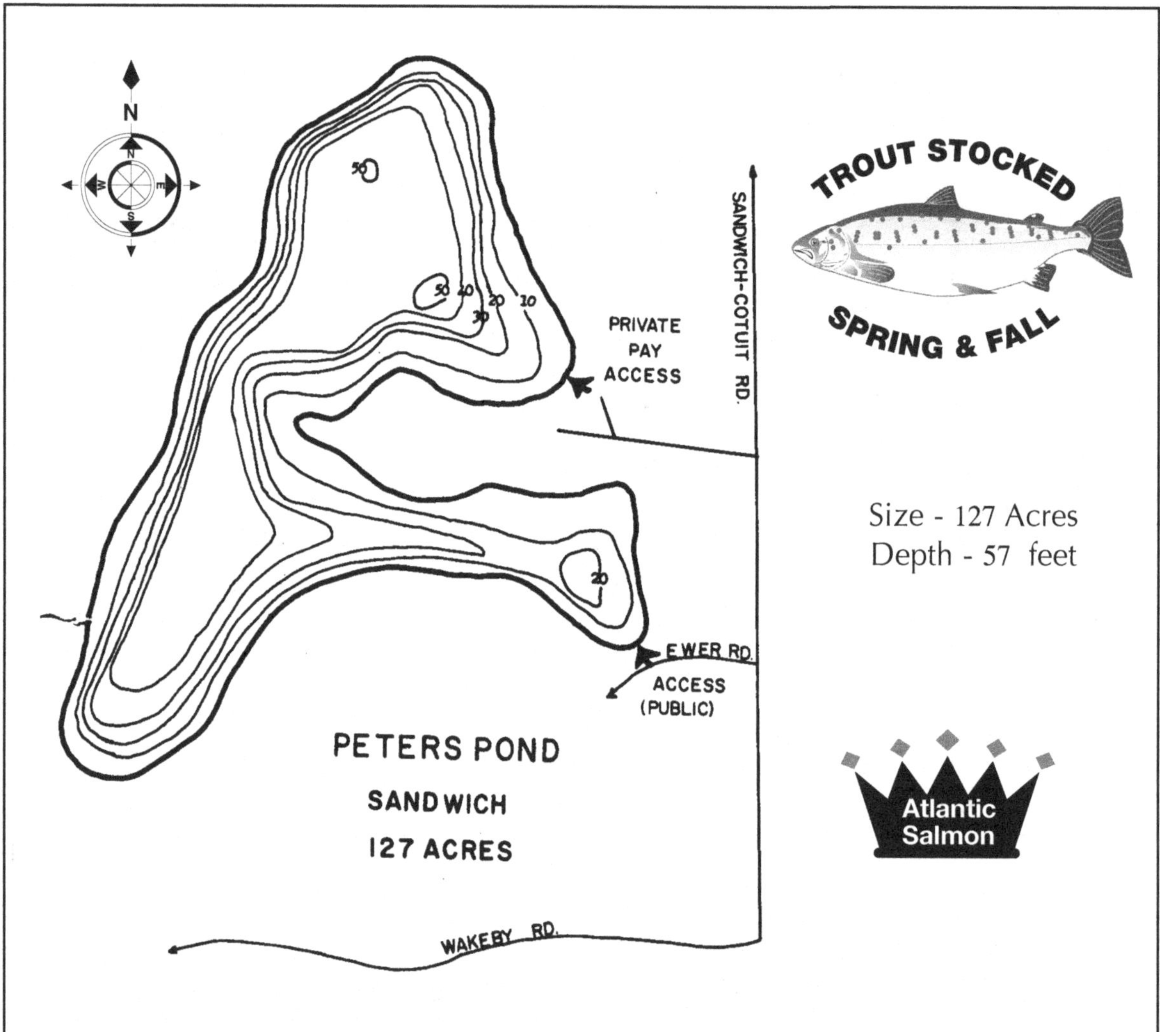

Location/Access/Special Regulations. Located between Cotuit Road and Route 130, just south of Quaker Meetinghouse Road. Access on southeastern shore via paved boat ramp off John Ewer Road, and a town right of way over a beach area at the southern end of pond. Also, private pay access off Sandwich-Cotuit Road.

PETERS POND: TIPS FROM EXPERTS

"Excellent pond for trout and even brood stock salmon. Best bet-lures, shiners."

GENE BOURQUE, EDITOR, ON THE WATER

"Best pond in Sandwich for trout. Use powerbait, live bait."

JEFF CAPUTE, AWARD WINNING ANGLER

"The best pond in town for trout and salmon. Excellent summer trout and salmon habitat. Good holdovers."

STEVE HURLEY, MDFW

"Known to hold very large fish. All methods work. Timing is critical. Please catch, photograph and release."

ROBERT JESSUP, THE SPORTING LIFE

"Good pond for trout and smallmouth. One fly catches them all: Olive Wooly Bugger."

CRAIG POOSIKIAN, CRAIG'S CUSTOM RODS

"Toss up for 'best' between trout and smallmouth. Grass shrimp are killers here. Stockies will strike any small gold spoons/spinners, streamers with silver and red."

PETER MIRICK, EDITOR, MASSACHUSETTS WILDLIFE

"Thought I was doing great with trout here on flies one day 'til old timer with worms beside me landed what was a new state record brook trout which he brought home to eat."

PETER BUDRYK, A FISHERMAN

PIMLICO POND

SANDWICH

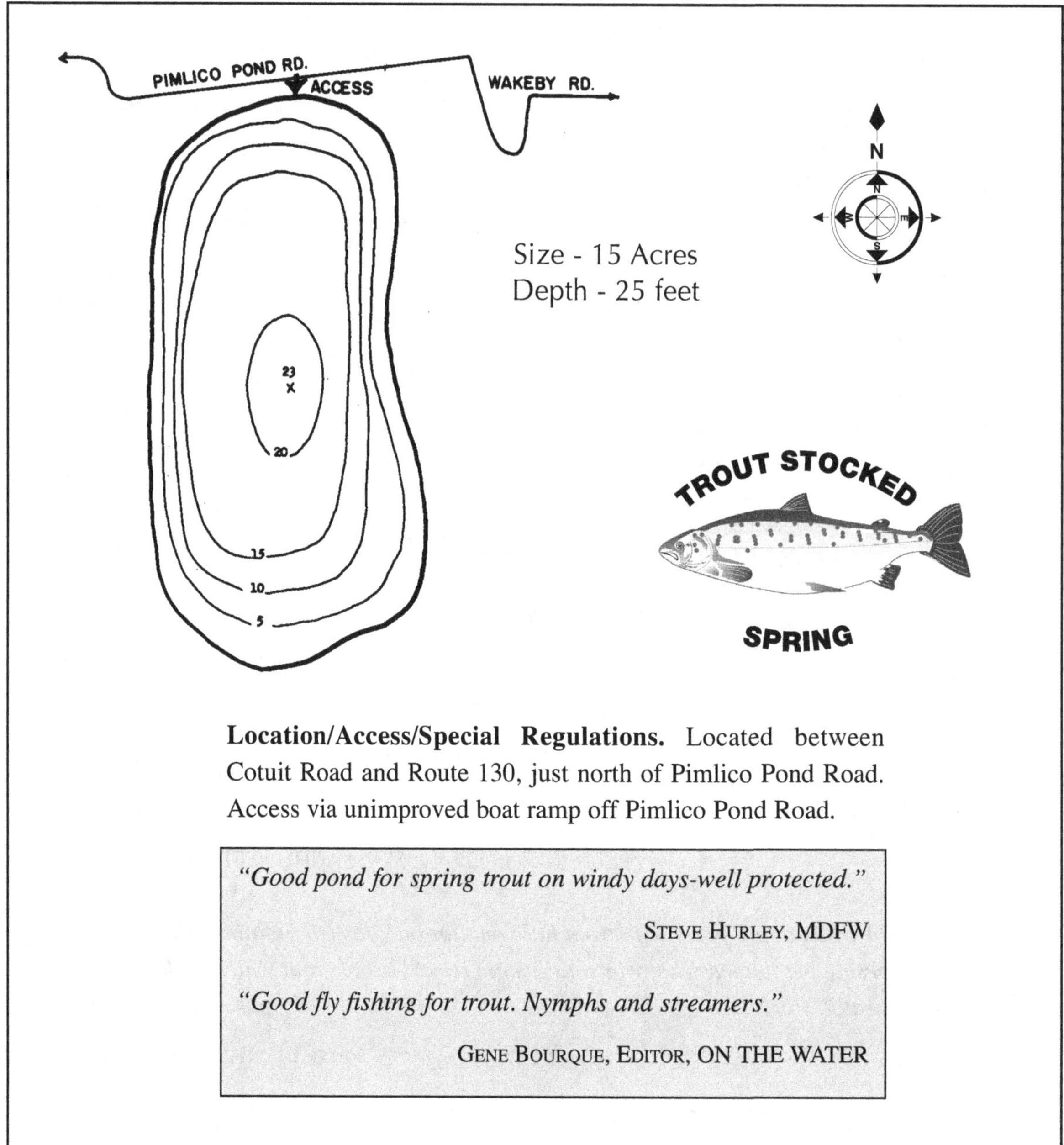

Location/Access/Special Regulations. Located between Cotuit Road and Route 130, just north of Pimlico Pond Road. Access via unimproved boat ramp off Pimlico Pond Road.

> *"Good pond for spring trout on windy days-well protected."*
>
> STEVE HURLEY, MDFW
>
> *"Good fly fishing for trout. Nymphs and streamers."*
>
> GENE BOURQUE, EDITOR, ON THE WATER

SHAWME LAKES - Upper & Lower

SANDWICH

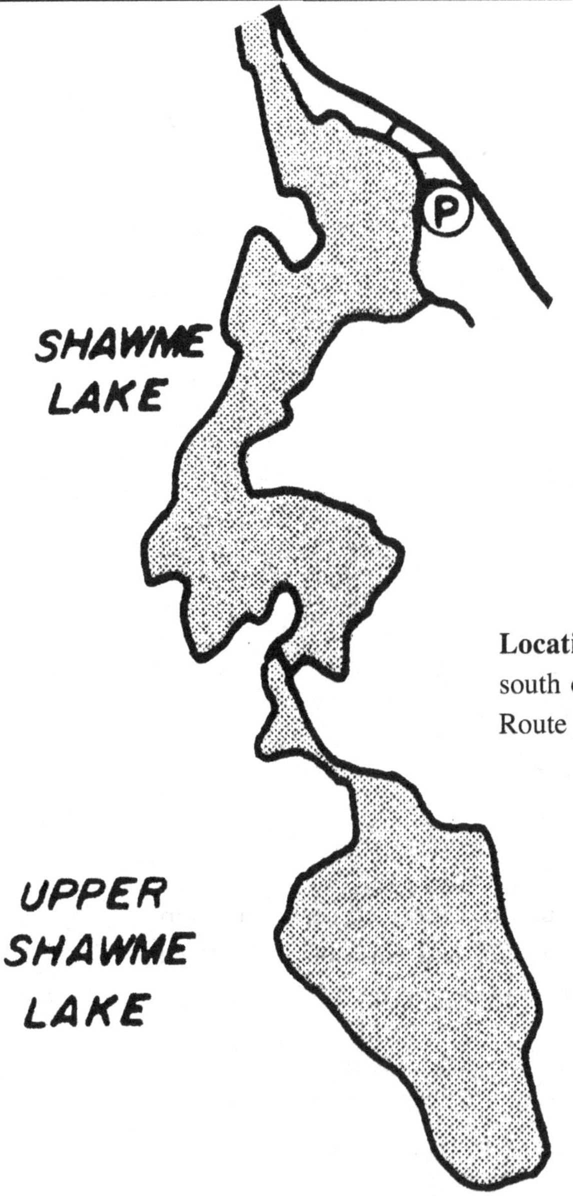

SHAWME LAKE

UPPER SHAWME LAKE

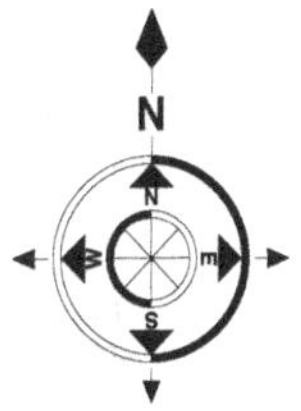

UPPER
Size - 23 Acres
Depth - 24 feet

LOWER
Size - 25 Acres
Depth - 16 feet

Location/Access/Special Regulations. Located south of Route 6A, north of Routh 6, and west of Route 130. Inlet and outlet.

> *"Fair largemouth bass fishing."*
>
> STEVE HURLEY, MDFW

SNAKE POND

SANDWICH

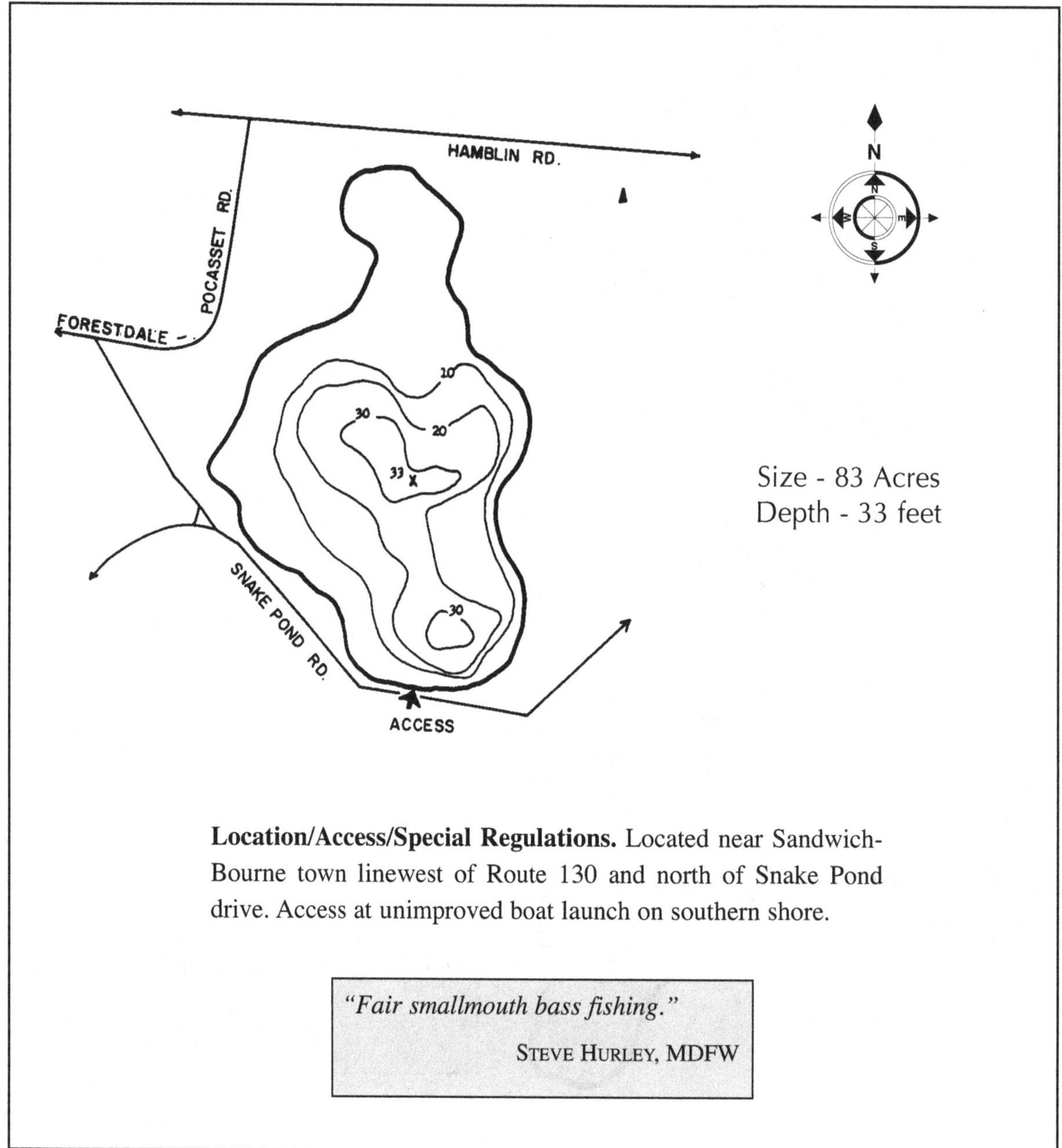

Size - 83 Acres
Depth - 33 feet

Location/Access/Special Regulations. Located near Sandwich-Bourne town linewest of Route 130 and north of Snake Pond drive. Access at unimproved boat launch on southern shore.

> *"Fair smallmouth bass fishing."*
>
> STEVE HURLEY, MDFW

SPECTACLE POND

SANDWICH

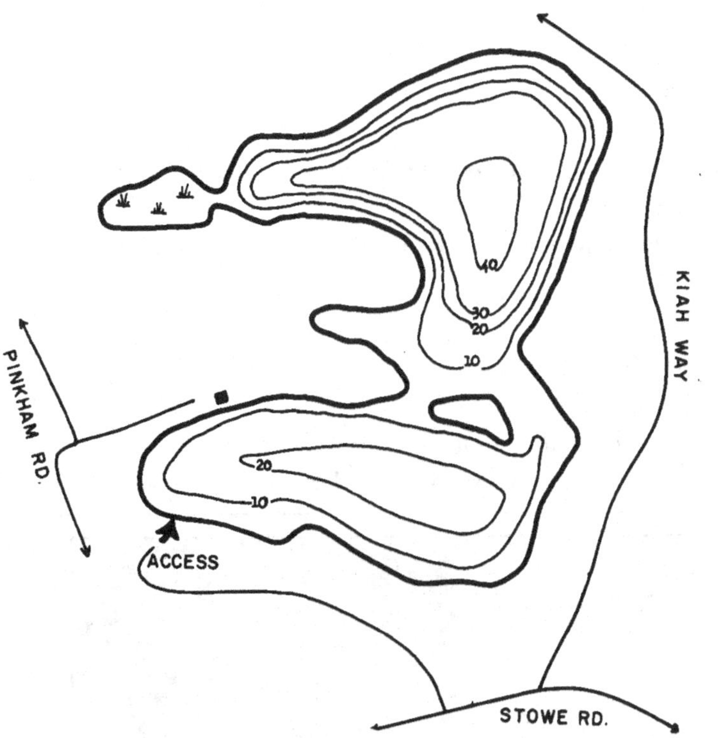
40
30
20
10
20
10
PINKHAM RD.
KIAH WAY
ACCESS
STOWE RD.

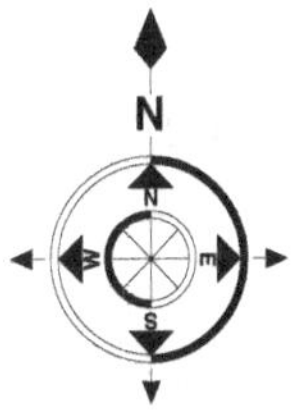
N

Size - 95 Acres
Depth - 43 feet

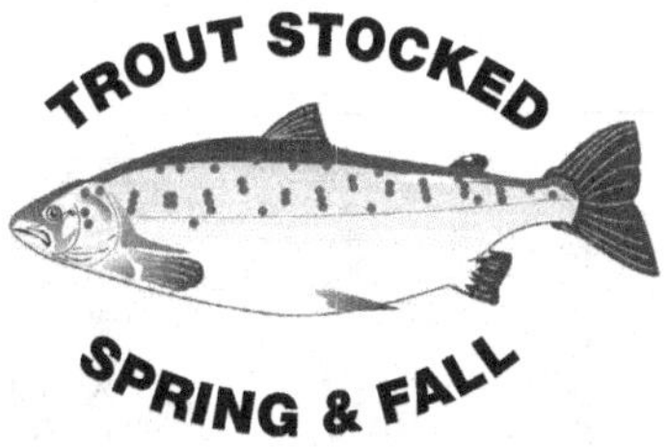
TROUT STOCKED
SPRING & FALL

Location/Access/Special Regulations. Located east of Pinkham Road, west of Kian Way, and north of Stowe Road. Access off Stowe road.

SPECTACLE POND: TIPS FROM PANEL OF EXPERTS

"Excellent trout fishing. Some big ones."

Rod Schou, Butterworth Maps

"Good trout fishing."

Steve Smith, MDFW

"Some large fish here."

Robert Jessup, The Sporting Life

"Always a favorite. Fish high for trout, low(near bottom) for perch. Will also produce a largemouth to 3 pounds now and then."

Peter Mirick, Editor, MASSACHUSETTS WILDLIFE

"Good for trout. Powerbait, live bait, worms."

Jeff Capute, Award Winning Angler

"Tough wading, but good fly fishing for trout with nymphs and streamers."

Gene Bourque, Editor, ON THE WATER

Mixed double limit of Cape Cod trout. "Holy didn't approve of extra. 'Everything depends on knowing how much,' she said, and 'Good is knowing when to stop'" *Beloved, Tony Morrison*

TRIANGLE POND

SANDWICH

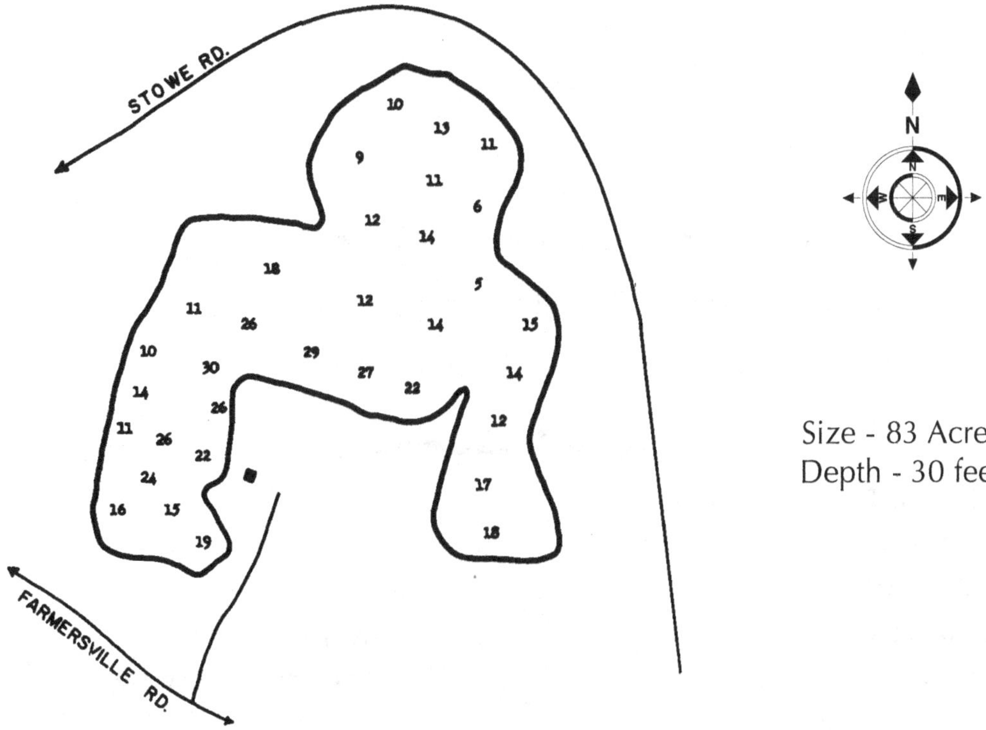

Size - 83 Acres
Depth - 30 feet

Location/Access/Special Regulations. Located south and west of Stowe Road and north of Farmersville Road.

> *"Pond holds bass, pickerel, and white perch."*
>
> ROD SCHOU, BUTTERWORTH MAPS
>
> *"Fair smallmouth bass fishing."*
>
> STEVE HURLEY, MDFW

Cast 24:

TRURO
Ponds & Lakes

Total Land Area (sq. miles) 35

Total Area of Ponds (acres) 140

Total numbers of Ponds 20

Number of Ponds by size:

<1 acres:	5
1-5 acres:	8
5-10 acres:	3
10-20 acres:	1
20-50 acres:	3
50-100 acres:	0
>100 acres:	0

Pond groups:
National Park Service

Craig Poosikian, Orleans, custom rod maker, member of book's panel of experts.

TRURO

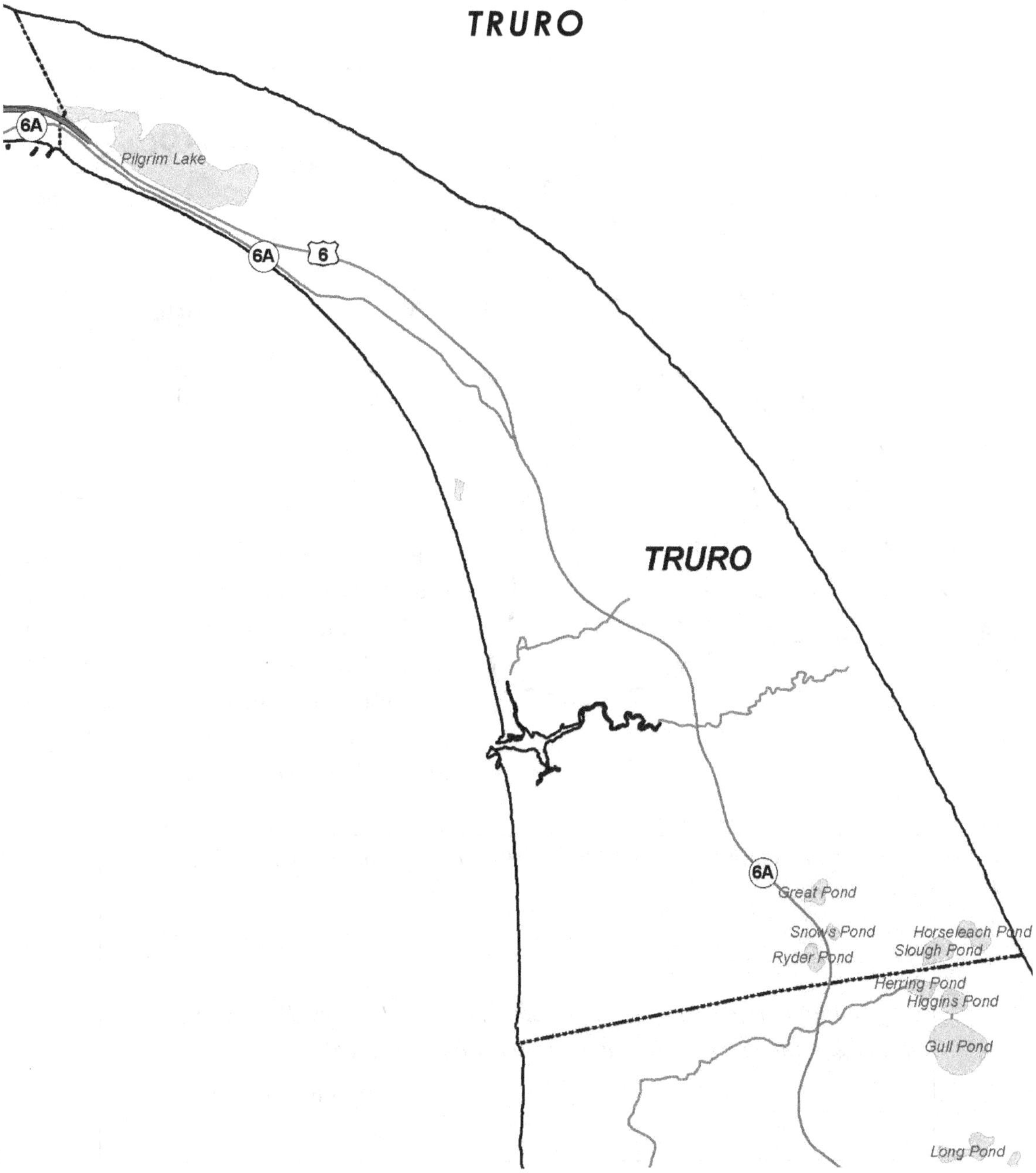

6A
Pilgrim Lake
6A
6
TRURO
6A
Great Pond
Snows Pond
Horseleach Pond
Ryder Pond
Slough Pond
Herring Pond
Higgins Pond
Gull Pond
Long Pond

GREAT POND

TRURO

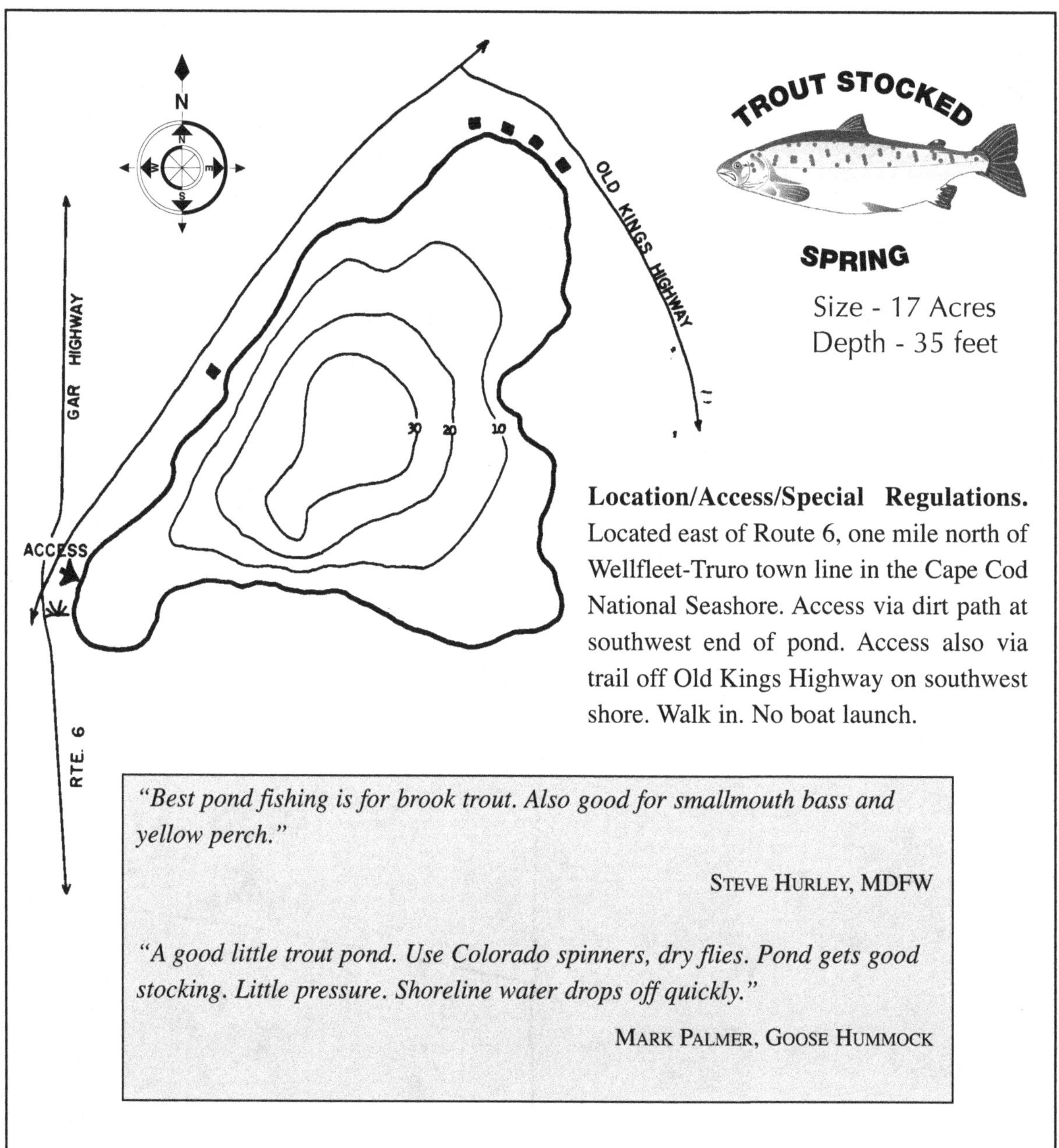

Size - 17 Acres
Depth - 35 feet

Location/Access/Special Regulations. Located east of Route 6, one mile north of Wellfleet-Truro town line in the Cape Cod National Seashore. Access via dirt path at southwest end of pond. Access also via trail off Old Kings Highway on southwest shore. Walk in. No boat launch.

"Best pond fishing is for brook trout. Also good for smallmouth bass and yellow perch."

STEVE HURLEY, MDFW

"A good little trout pond. Use Colorado spinners, dry flies. Pond gets good stocking. Little pressure. Shoreline water drops off quickly."

MARK PALMER, GOOSE HUMMOCK

HORSELEECH POND

Truro

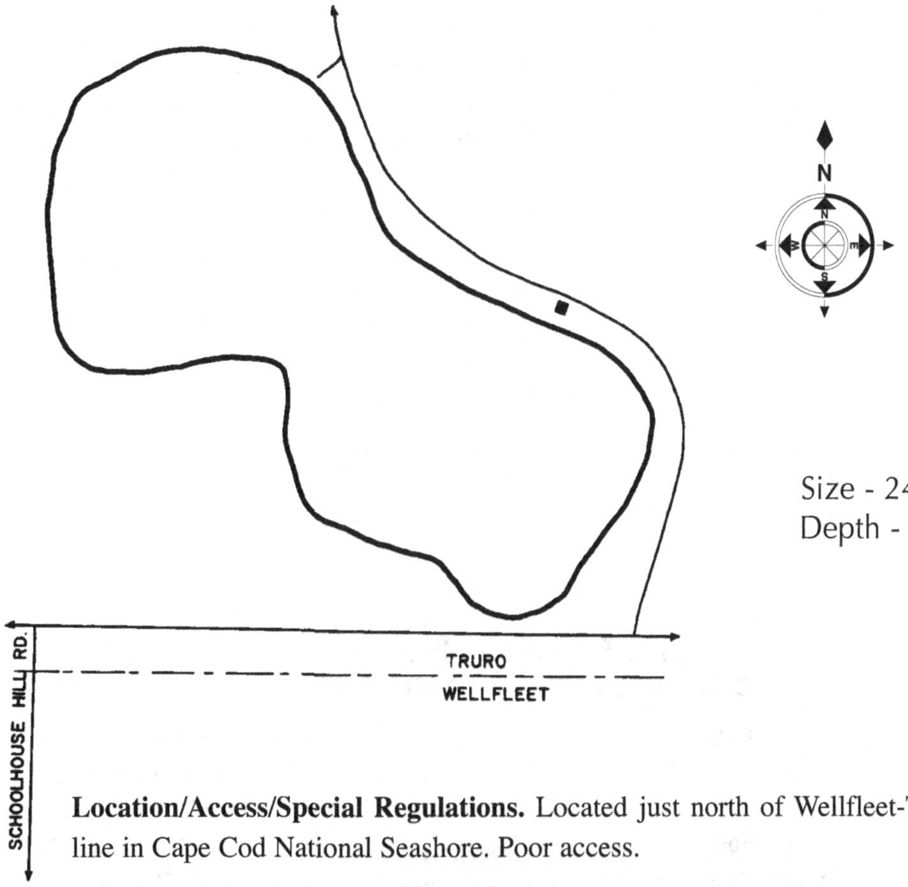

N

Size - 24 Acres
Depth - 16 feet

SCHOOLHOUSE HILL RD.

TRURO
WELLFLEET

Location/Access/Special Regulations. Located just north of Wellfleet-Truro town line in Cape Cod National Seashore. Poor access.

"Good largemouth bass pond. Use shiners or fish top water. Be patient. Big fish."

Mark Palmer, Goose Hummock

"Good largemouth bass pond."

Steve Hurley, MDFW

"A good bass pond with pickerel and white perch."

Rod Schou, Butterworth Maps

PILGRIM LAKE
TRURO

HAS BEEN RETURNED TO A SALTWATER POND

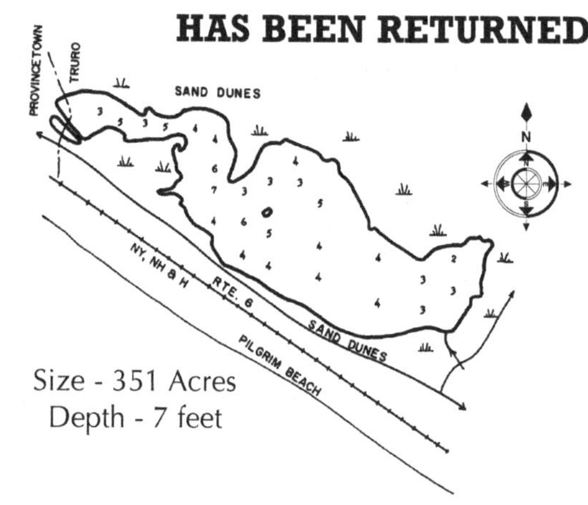

Size - 351 Acres
Depth - 7 feet

Location/Access/Special Regulations. Located among sand dunes off Route 6 in Cape Cod National Seashore.

"An excellent pond for giant carp. Use doughballs or worms on bottom or with a float. Find 'mudding' fish and cast, trying not to spook them. Then hold on to your ultra light outfit. They are a blast."

CRAIG POOSIKIAN,
CRAIG'S CUSTOM RODS

"Carp, white perch. Carp are dying off as lake is being restored to brackish water habitat by Cape Cod National Seashore."

STEVE HURLEY, MDFW

WHAT'S IN A NAME?
COLORFUL POND & LAKE NAMES

BARNSTABLE
- Aunt Bettys Pond
- Flowing Pond
- No Bottom Pond

BOURNE
- A2 Pond
- GP-3 Pond
- Little Halfway Pond
- Opening Pond

BREWSTER
- 1858 Pond
- Dark Bottom Pond
- No Bottom pond

CHATHAM
- Archies Pond
- Black Pond
- Blue Pond
- Hospital Pond
- Lovers Lake
- Pinkwink Pond
- White Pond

DENNIS
- Cash Pond
- Fund Pond
- Great Pond Plash
- Run Pond
- The Plashes

FALMOUTH
- Angel Mirror Pond
- Flashy Pond

HARWICH
- Kiddies Pond

MASHPEE
- Flying Squirrel Pond

ORLEANS
- Chigger Pond
- Uncle Harveys Pond
- Uncle Israels Pond
- Uncle Seths Pond
- Wash Pond

PROVINCETOWN
- Shank Painter Pond

SANDWICH
- Boiling Springs Pond
- Doughnut Pond
- Goodspeed Cemetery Pond

WELLFLEET
- Sewells Gutter

YARMOUTH
- Jabez Neds Pond

(Source: CCC, GIS Dept.)

Herring-baited angler into fast autumn action with largemouth bass on Cape Cod pond.

Cast 25:

WELLFLEET
Ponds & Lakes

Total Land Area (sq. miles) 20.47

Total Area of Ponds (acres) 330

Total numbers of Ponds 29

Number of Ponds by size:

<1 acres:	9
1-5 acres:	11
5-10 acres:	1
10-20 acres:	3
20-50 acres:	4
50-100 acres:	0
>100 acres:	1

Pond groups:
National Park Service

Fly fisher flicks feathered fake forward, feigning fish food.

WELLFLEET

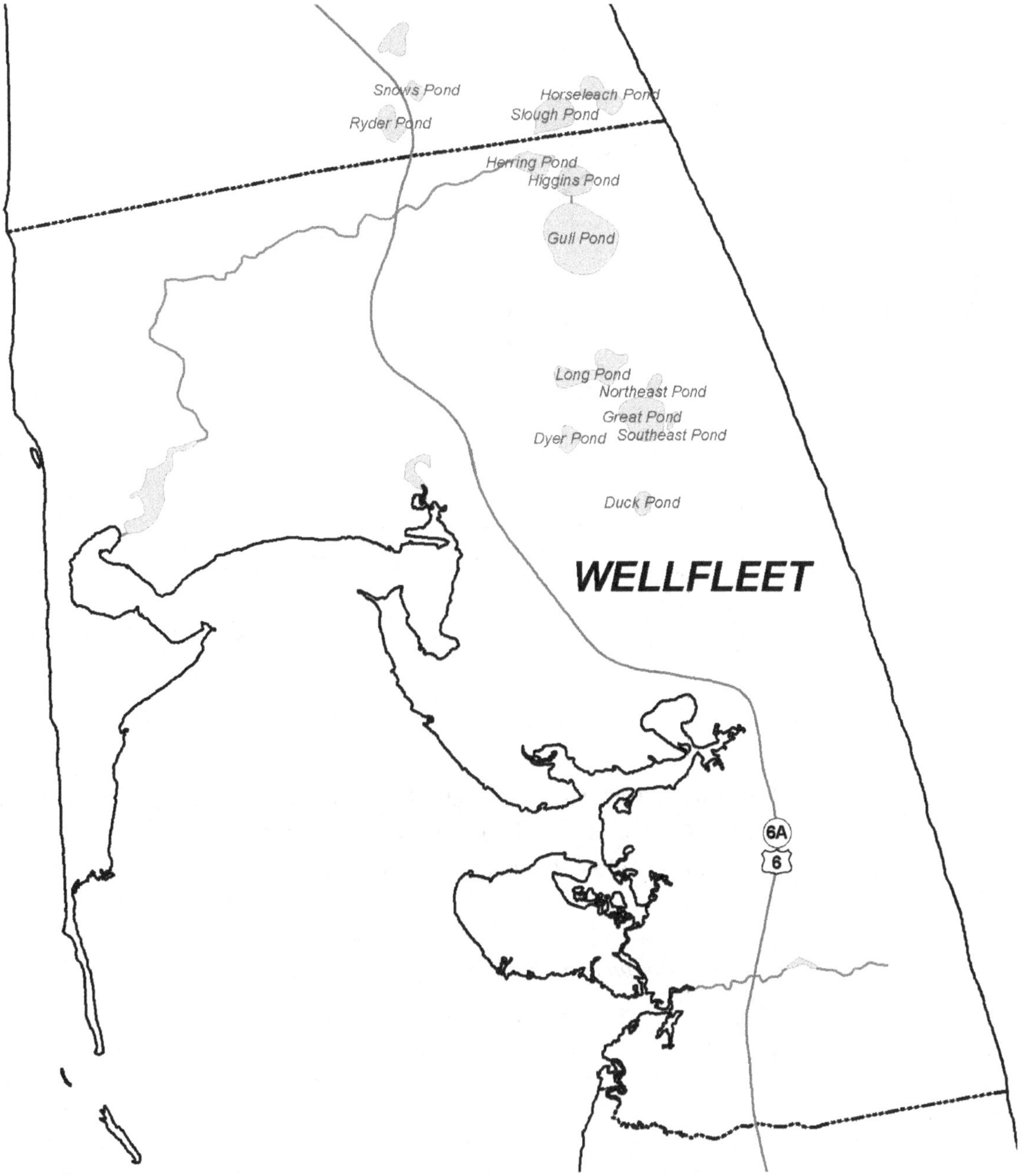

Snows Pond
Horseleach Pond
Slough Pond
Ryder Pond
Herring Pond
Higgins Pond
Gull Pond
Long Pond
Northeast Pond
Great Pond
Dyer Pond
Southeast Pond
Duck Pond
WELLFLEET
6A
6

GREAT POND
Wellfleet

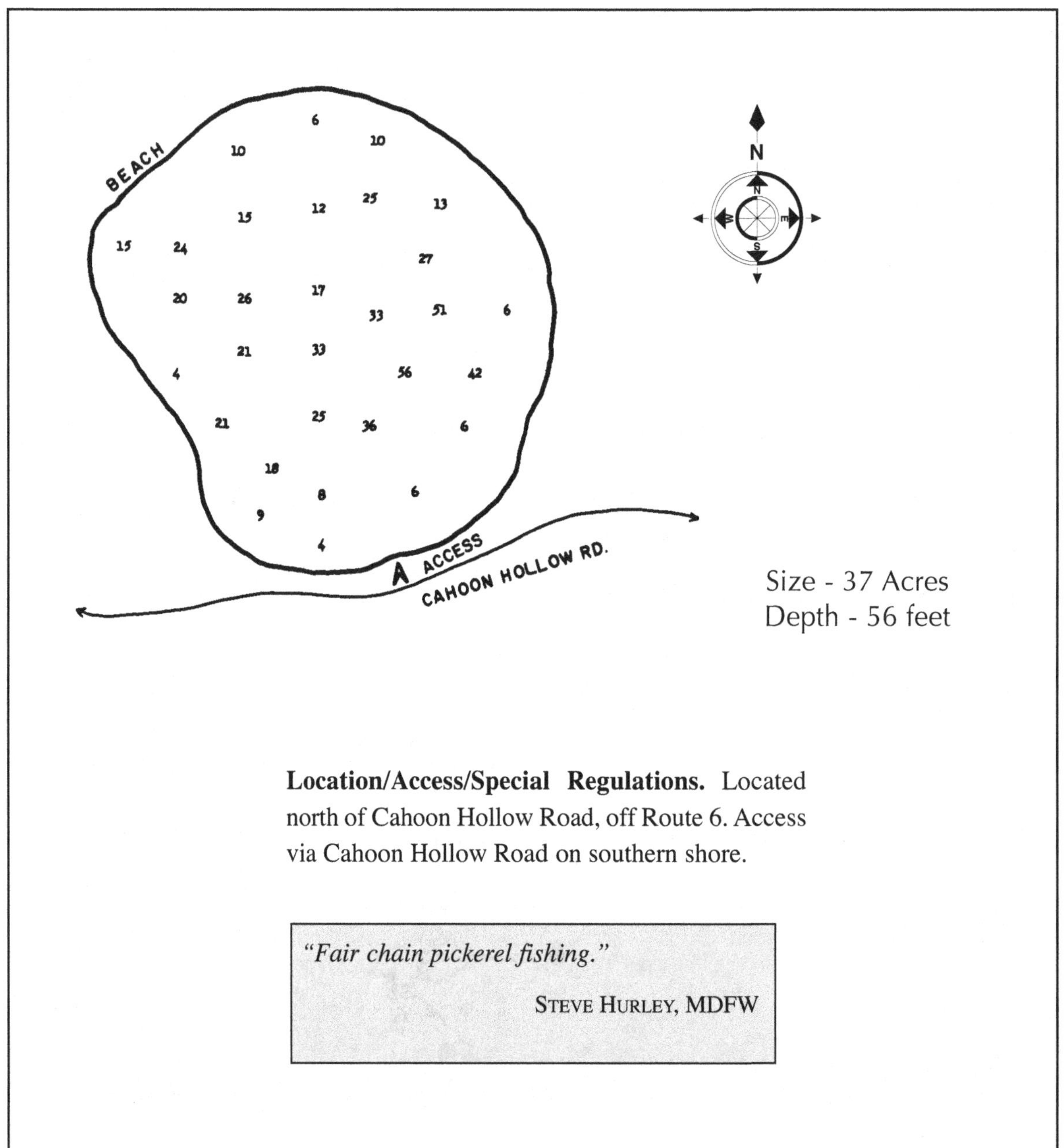

Location/Access/Special Regulations. Located north of Cahoon Hollow Road, off Route 6. Access via Cahoon Hollow Road on southern shore.

> *"Fair chain pickerel fishing."*
>
> Steve Hurley, MDFW

GULL POND

WELLFLEET

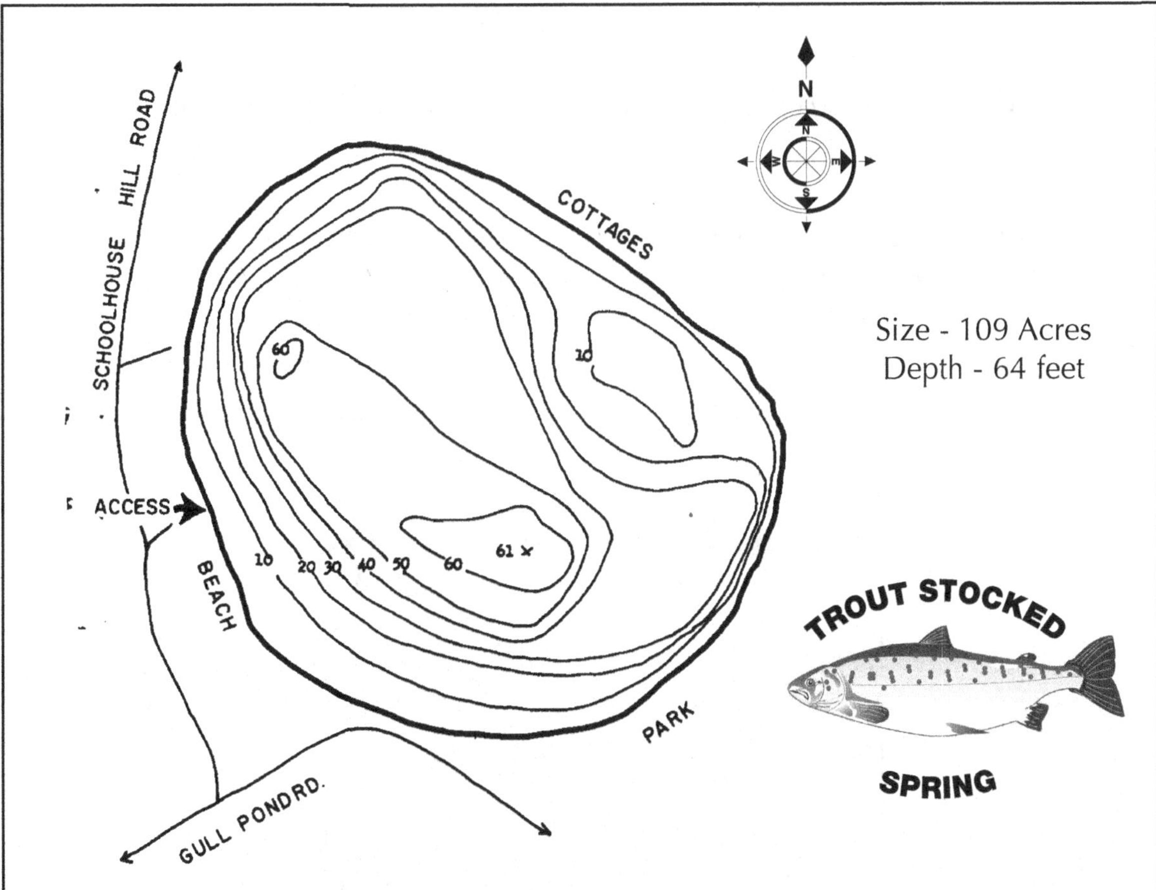

Location/Access/Special Regulations. Located off Gull Pond Road off Route 6. In Northeastern corner of Wellfleet in cape Cod National Seashore. Southernmost pond in a chain of interconnected ponds that connect to Herring River. Discharges water through a small inlet to Higgins Pond. Access via town beach on western shoreline. No outboard motors allowed. Launch area. Parking.

GULL POND: TIPS FROM PANEL OF EXPERTS

"An excellent pond for trout and smallmouth bass."

DAVID GILMORE, ACCLAIMED ANGLER

"An excellent trout pond. Try casting a Red Devil or a gold Thomas Cyclone."

ELLA SCHULTZ, EXPERIENCED ANGLER

"Excellent trout pond.best bet-cast shiners, crawlers, fly fish with Wooly Worms, Wooly Buggers. Big trout taken out of here. Lots of bait and doesn't get pressure it deserves. Fish with live bait by inlet."

MARK PALMER, GOOSE HUMMOCK

Take this road.

LONG POND

WELLFLEET

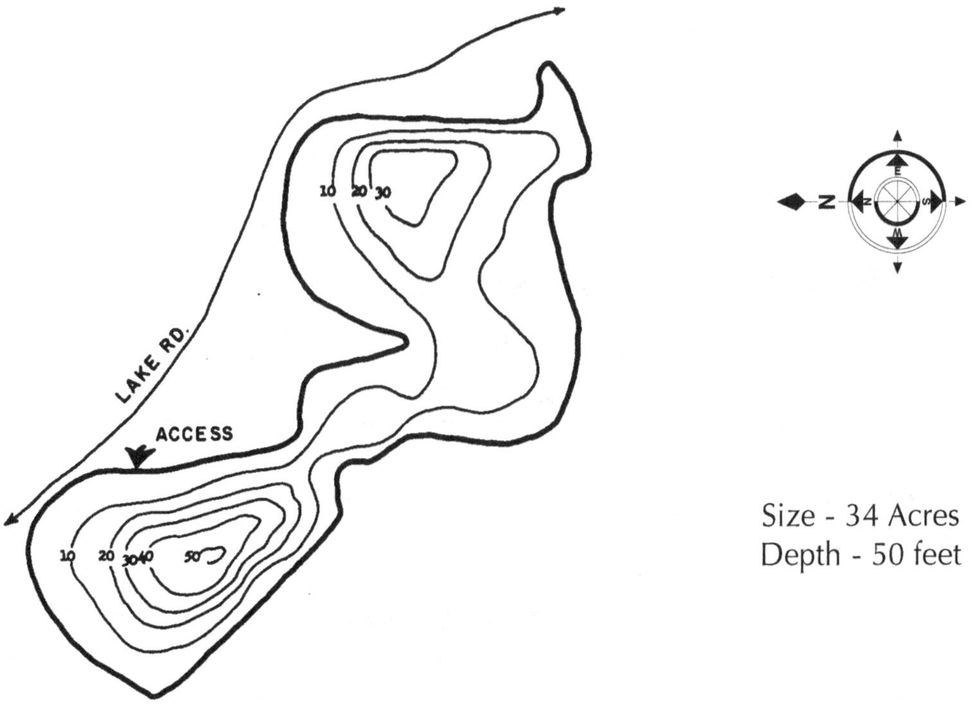

Size - 34 Acres
Depth - 50 feet

Location/Access/Special Regulations. Located in Cape Cod National Seashore south of Lake Road. Access via town beach on western shore, heavily used during summer months.

> *"Fair chain pickerel fishing."*
>
> STEVE HURLEY, MDFW

Cast 26:

YARMOUTH

Ponds & Lakes

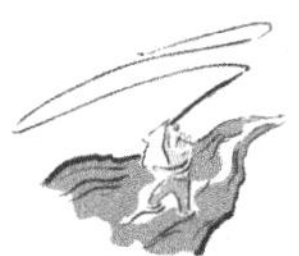

Total Land Area (sq. miles) → **24.13**

Total Area of Ponds (acres) → **440**

Total numbers of Ponds → **70**

Number of Ponds by size:

Size	Number
<1 acres:	28
1-5 acres:	23
5-10 acres:	9
10-20 acres:	3
20-50 acres:	6
50-100 acres:	1
>100 acres:	0

Pond groups:
None

> *"There must be some kind of equation to express the relation between the use of small dry flies and the use of truth. There are men alive today who have used them both, probably, but not at the same time."*
>
> John W. "Jack" Randolph, 1956

YARMOUTH

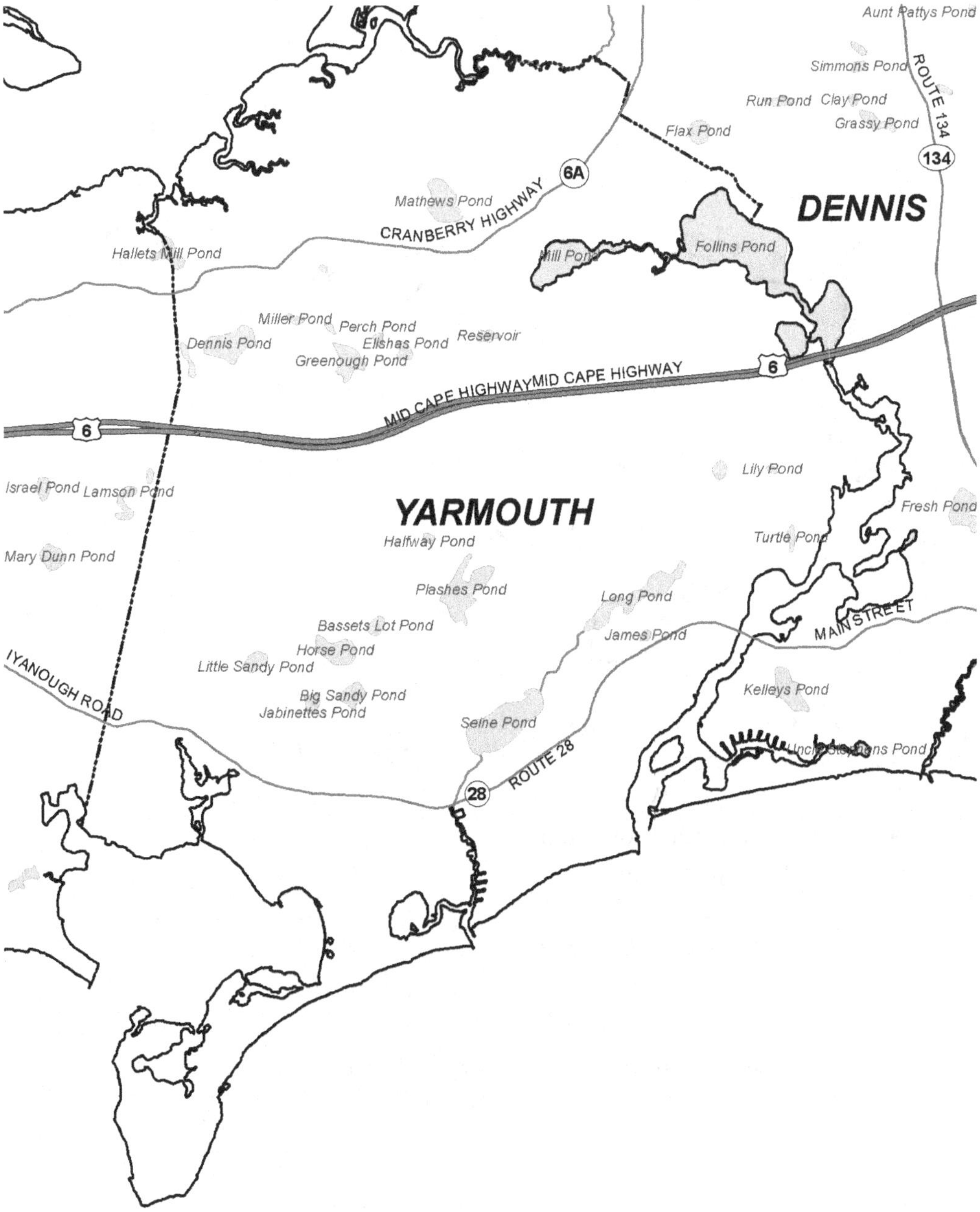

Aunt Pattys Pond
Simmons Pond
ROUTE 134
Run Pond
Clay Pond
Grassy Pond
Flax Pond
134
6A
Mathews Pond
CRANBERRY HIGHWAY
DENNIS
Hallets Mill Pond
Mill Pond
Follins Pond
Miller Pond
Perch Pond
Dennis Pond
Elishas Pond
Reservoir
Greenough Pond
MID CAPE HIGHWAYMID CAPE HIGHWAY
6
6
Lily Pond
Israel Pond
Lamson Pond
YARMOUTH
Fresh Pond
Halfway Pond
Turtle Pond
Mary Dunn Pond
Plashes Pond
Long Pond
MAIN STREET
Bassets Lot Pond
James Pond
Horse Pond
IYANOUGH ROAD
Little Sandy Pond
Kelleys Pond
Big Sandy Pond
Jabinettes Pond
Seine Pond
ROUTE 28
Uncle Stephens Pond
28

DENNIS POND

Yarmouth

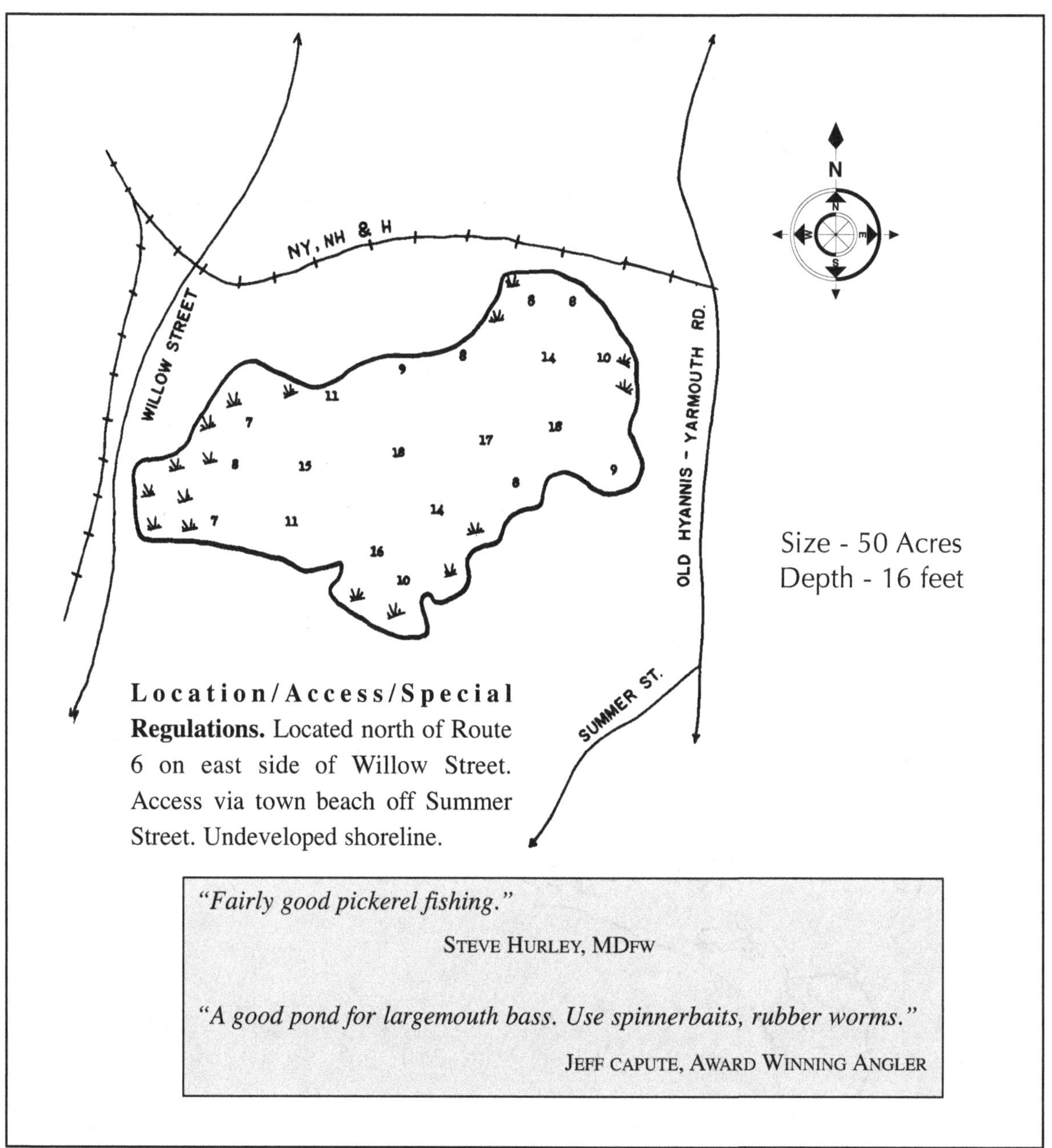

Size - 50 Acres
Depth - 16 feet

Location/Access/Special Regulations. Located north of Route 6 on east side of Willow Street. Access via town beach off Summer Street. Undeveloped shoreline.

"Fairly good pickerel fishing."

Steve Hurley, MDfw

"A good pond for largemouth bass. Use spinnerbaits, rubber worms."

Jeff capute, Award Winning Angler

GREENOUGH POND

YARMOUTH

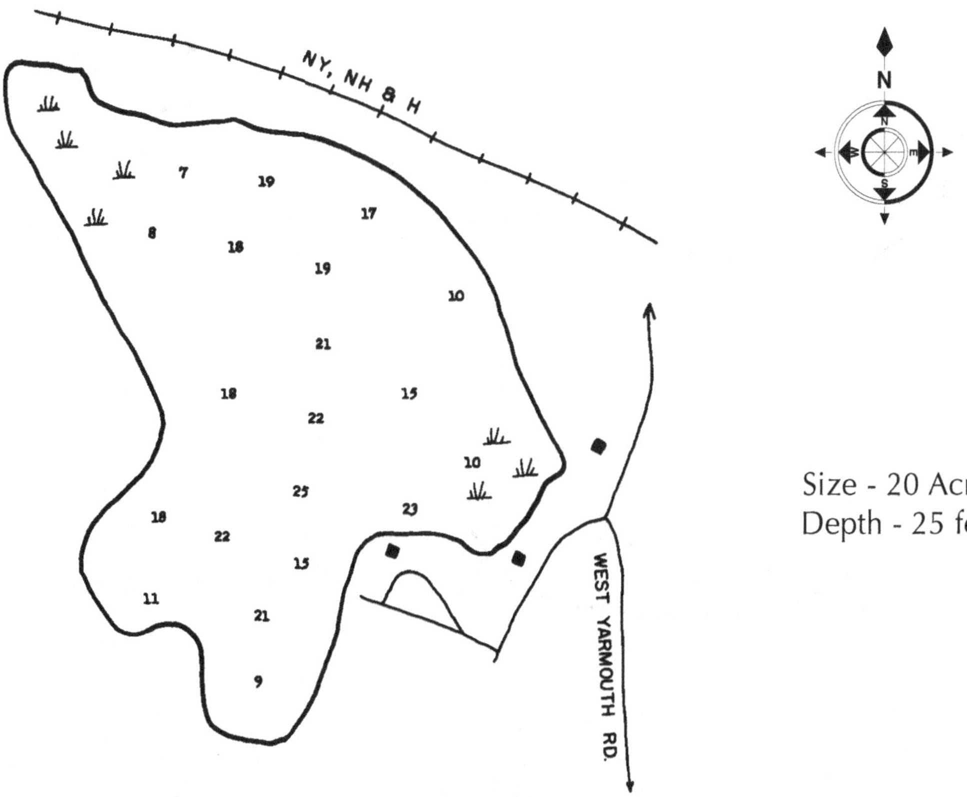

NY, NH & H

N

WEST YARMOUTH RD.

Size - 20 Acres
Depth - 25 feet

Location/Access/Special Regulations. Located north of Route 6, west of West yarmouth Road. Access off West Yarmouth Road.

> *"Chain pickerel. Not surveyed since 1961. Boy Scout Camp."*
>
> Steve Hurley, MDFW

HORSE POND
YARMOUTH

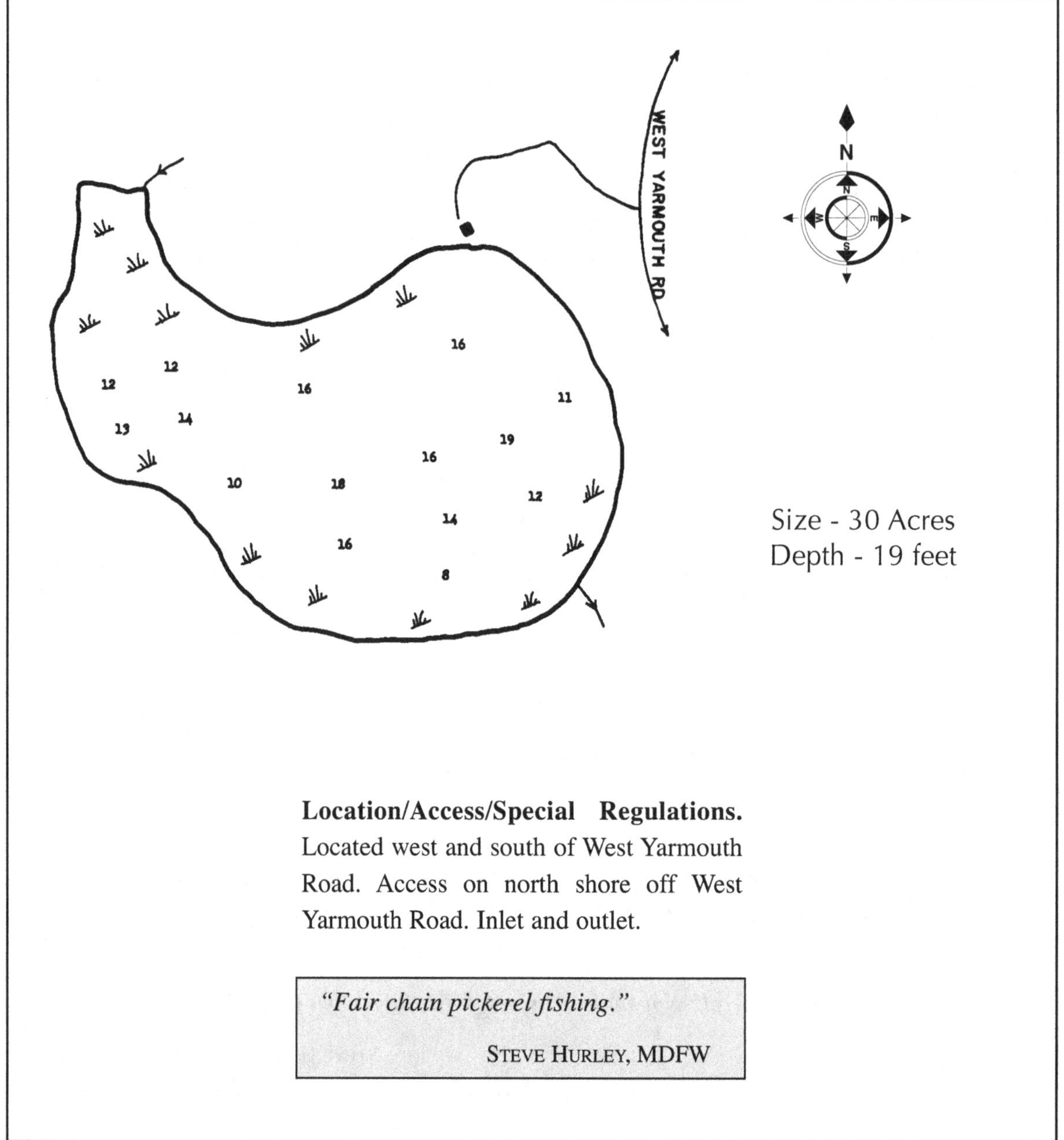

Size - 30 Acres
Depth - 19 feet

Location/Access/Special Regulations. Located west and south of West Yarmouth Road. Access on north shore off West Yarmouth Road. Inlet and outlet.

> *"Fair chain pickerel fishing."*
>
> STEVE HURLEY, MDFW

LONG POND

YARMOUTH

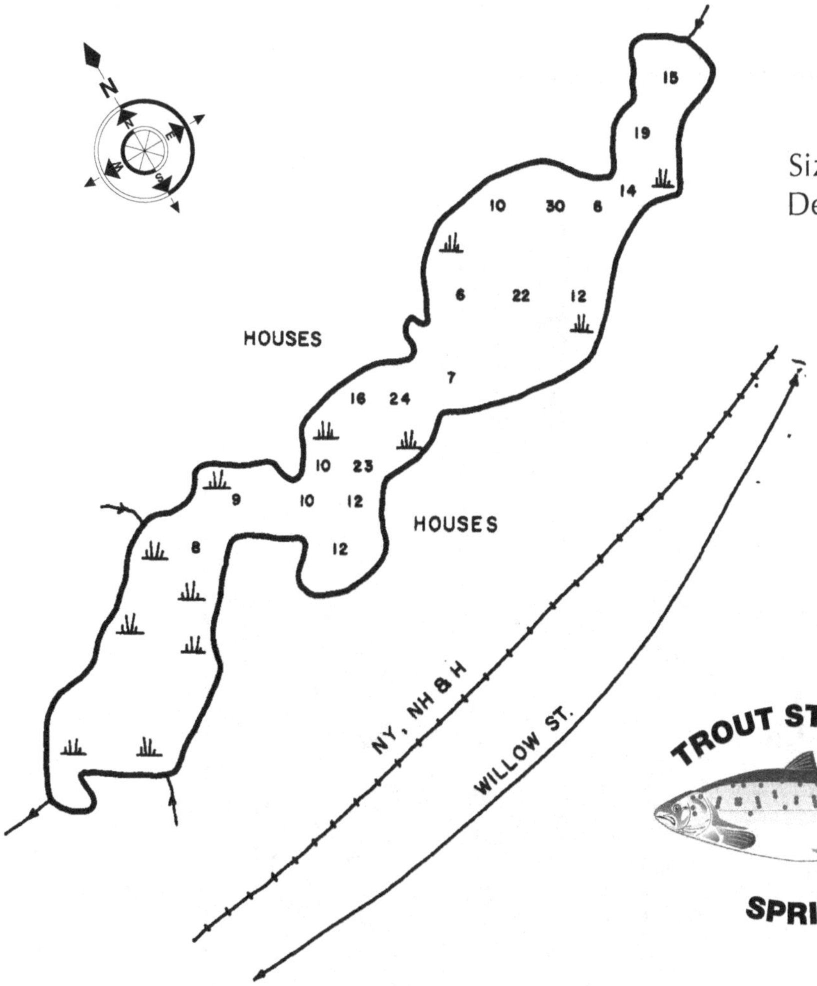

HOUSES

HOUSES

NY, NH & H

WILLOW ST.

Size - 57 Acres
Depth - 30 feet

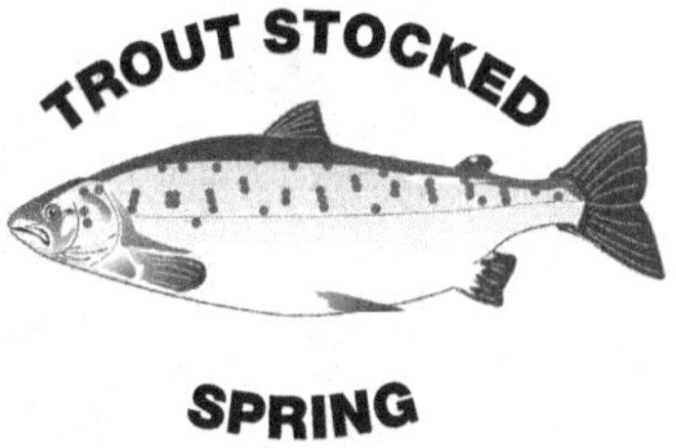

TROUT STOCKED

SPRING

Location/Access/Special Regulations. Located just north of Route 28 and west of Station Avenue. Access via town beach with concrete boat ramp on southwestern shore. Connected to Parker River by a herring run.

LONG POND (YARMOUTH): TIPS FROM PANEL OF EXPERTS

"A good pond for all panfish except crappie. Any lure, any bait works. I have seen more fish in this pond than any other pond or lake ever. They travel in mixed schools waiting to be caught."

CRAIG POOSIKIAN, CRAIG'S CUSTOM RODS

"An excellent pond for trout and largemouth bass."

STEVE HURLEY, MDFW

Monster yellow perch from Cape Cod pond. Kept and eaten with gusto. (Photo: Jeff Capute)

BIG SANDY POND

YARMOUTH

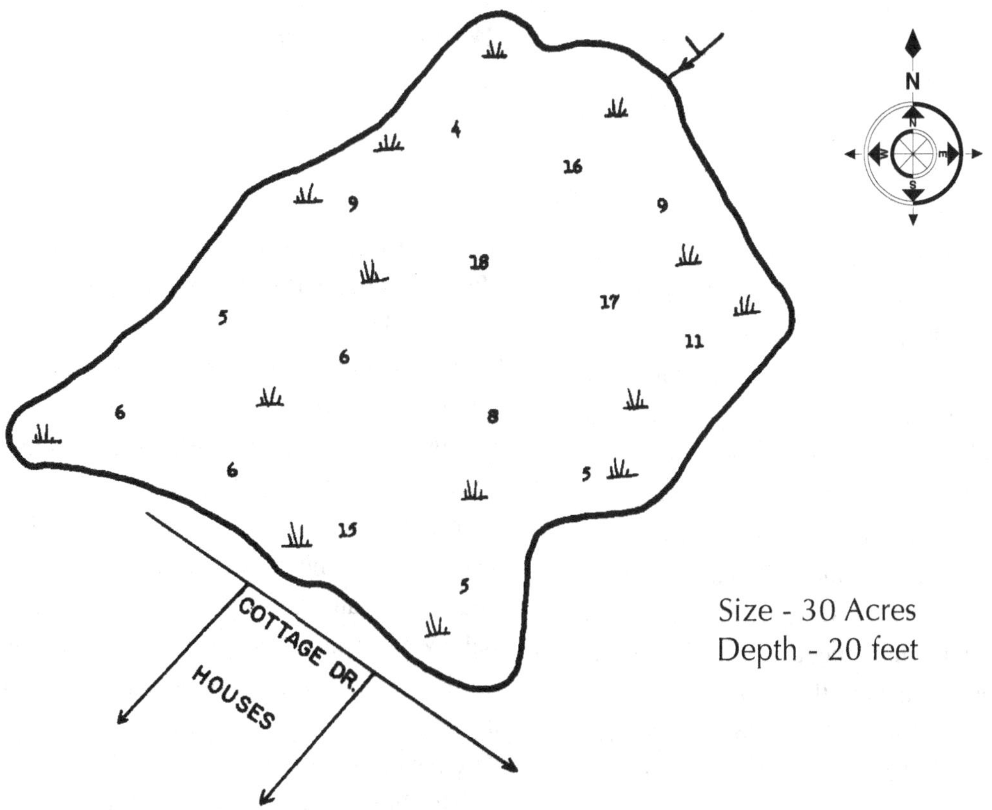

Size - 30 Acres
Depth - 20 feet

Location/Access/Special Regulations. Located north of Cottage Drive. Access via sub division off Cottage Drive. Inlet near northeast shore.

> *"A fair chain pickerel pond. No recent information available."*
>
> STEVE HURLEY, MDFW

Cast 27:
TESTOSTERONE/YAHOO/FIBBER ALERTS

A Message from a Woman to Men

I am a woman angler. I love to fish, probably for the same reasons you do. The quiet of the waters helps me find the quiet in myself. I also like to challenge myself to think like a fish. If I was a trout, where would I hide? What would make me come to the surface to grab some food? Am I not catching fish because they are smarter than I am? Mostly when I'm fishing, I'm not really caring if I catch a fish; I mostly just want to let my mind wander and take in the beauty of the woods and the sights and sounds of the water around me.

Unless one lives on a lake or stream, one has to leave the safety of home to indulge in this sport. The best sites are isolated and less frequently visited. For women, this suggests immediate danger. While we are young and learning all the necessary skills to be capable adult females, we unconsciously learn to assess situations and be on our guard in places where we sense danger. The woods is one of those places.

Why are women afraid in the woods? I hate to tell you this, but it is not the bogeyman, ghosts, or bears we fear lurking behind trees. It is men. Men who threaten our safety. Men who can rape us. Men who can hurt or kill us.

Remember the fear you felt when you watched the movie *Deliverance?* That's the fear I am talking about. It isn't fair and most men are not predatory, but the threat is real.

Therefore, I send out a plea to all men who fish. Welcome the women you meet in the woods. Humans aren't much different than animals. We unconsciously (or consciously) wait for signals that ease our minds, assure us we are safe.

Here are some tips:

- Use body language and small talk to acknowledge your equal status as anglers and lovers of nature.
- Don't comment on a woman's clothing or attractiveness.
- Talk about the sport, lures and bait.
- Leave and find your own spot.
- Try not to imply that you are a better angler; you might not be.

• **GO EASY ON THE ALCOHOL!** Alcohol makes people do stupid things and sends major danger signals to women. Drunk men are dangerous men.

Unfortunately I will never again go alone in search of a place to fish. I can carry a big knife and be as tough as can be, but there is probably nothing that will make me feel at ease in secluded places. But let's see if we can make a world where my daughter and other females can serenely commune with nature, think like a fish, and not worry about her fellow humans bringing her back to reality.

Liz Warner

(The author of this overture, sadly, like many other female anglers, has been the victim of harassment by men and virtually been deprived of the joy of fishing. No caring man wants his wife, daughter, mother or sister to be threatened in any way in their pursuit of this wonderful activity. ONLY MEN CAN ASSURE THAT THE WOODS AND THE WATERS ARE SAFE AND PLEASANT FOR EVERYONE. PB)

FISHING AND FIBBING

"All fishermen are liars. Except for you and me. And I have my doubts about you!" This is a commonly held and probably justifiable view of anglers as they relate to the slippery fish, truth. I myself confess to having had difficulty at times getting a firm grip on that flip-flopping critter.

> *"Fishermen are born honest, but they get over it."*
>
> ED ZERN, 1945

Having acknowledged I'm not on a pedestal of piscatorial purity looking down on the rest of the angling populace, I now ask you to understand an important aspect of this book as it relates to honesty. Unlike the Saturday morning sportfishing shows on TV on which the host, hostess, or guest hooks up with a fish on every cast, our fishing is done in real time. You and I cannot edit out the fishless casts from our trips. I believe it is important to your enjoyment of a fishing trip that this book, its praising of the bounty of the Cape's ponds, the many photographs of huge fish landed, and the tips provided that they do not give you the mind set that you will limit out every time you head out. No member of my panel does. I don't. You won't. If consistently catching large fish is the only standard by which an angler judges the quality of a fishing experience, frustration and disappointment will result.

Fishing success is relative to how we judge each experience. Every trip to a Cape Cod stillwater is an aesthetic joy, and every hook up with a fish, regardless of species or size, is a bonus that needs to be relished as the unique and wonderful experience it is. I guess that, like me, you do not go fishing only to catch fish.

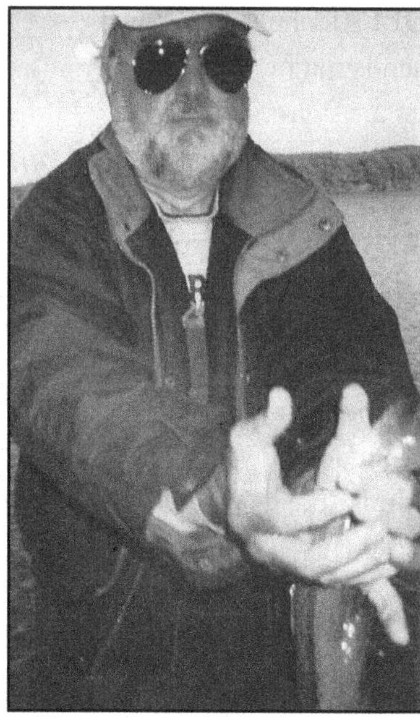

"Yes, Peter, that rainbow trout I lost at Gull Pond went 4, 6, maybe even 8 pounds. It was a giant!" "Some of us have a difficult time getting a firm grip on that flip-flopping critter, truth."

In fishing the lakes and ponds of Cape Cod my primary goal, I admit, is to catch fish, the bigger the better. Many times I catch nothing. Yet, regardless of the outcome of my previous trip, I eagerly anticipate my next trip, full of fresh hope that, this time, I am going to get a big one. And if I fail to hook up with any trophy fish, I will still bring back some pleasant memories of the lake's special beauty, the scent of pine, the thrill of an osprey's wild cry, and a spectacular sunset yet to be captured on canvas by any painter throughout history.

So, when you pack up to fish these ponds, together with your bait, tackle and, of course, your copy of this book, don't forget to bring along the right attitude. It will make a fishless day enjoyable. My wish is that this book will add some measure to your success and delight.

> *"Lyin' is lyin', be it about fish or money, and is forbid by Scripter. Billy Matison's got to give up fish-lyin' or he won't never get into the Kingdom."*
>
> ELLIS PARKER BUTLER, 1899

"You Da Man!"

Give a man a fish & he will eat for a day. Teach him to fish & he will sit in a boat & drink beer all day.

G. GILLESPIE *(Courtesy of Michael Rance, The Greeting place (888) 462-5830 www.thegreetingplace.com)*

> *"You can't say enough about fishing. Though the sport of kings, it's just what the deadbeat ordered."*
>
> THOMAS MCGUANE, IN SILENT SEASONS (1978)

Cast 28

BAITS, LURES, FLIES, RODS & REELS

"Simplify. Simplify. Simplify," said Thoreau. A thin bamboo pole, a line as long attached to the tip, and a small hook hidden in a garden worm could be all you need. But what you gotta have is another matter.

Such an abundance of freshwater fishing equipment is available that it would require numerous full length books to cover them. In fact, you can find many excellent books on the subject in your local library. Rather than my attempting to do the impossible and cover it here, I recommend that, at your leisure, and to the extent you are ready to explore the subject on your own, you pay a

American sport fishing icon, Lefty Kreh at home in Maryland, displaying a small portion of his collection of equipment in his basement.

visit to the library. You will be able to survey the range of books available and, if you find any you may want to own, you will then have a preview before you make a purchase.

Your choices of rods & reel will be among spin fishing, fly casting, & conventional bait casting gear, illustrated in the photos here.

Conventional, so-called "bait casting" outfit, which is also used to cast lures, not just bait.

Spin fishing rod & reel. "Spin casting" reels have a closed face on which the line spool is not visible.

Fly casting rod & reel.

Cast 29

TRIP LOG- THE MIND IS A LEAKY BAIT BUCKET

In the middle of a fishing trip on a Cape Cod pond, especially a successful one,it is very clear to us what the weather conditions are,with whom we are fishing, what areas of the lake we're working, and the specific bait, lure, fly and method that are producing. We may even remember some of the details months later. However, as time passes, one by one the details leak out, leaving us little memory to recapture a clear picture of a particular trip to a Cape stillwater.

The TRIP LOG on the next page is intended to help you remember some of the details of each of your trips. If you are faithful in taking a few minutes to record information at the end of the fishing day, it will be there to remind and inform you the next time you visit that spot. This can save you time and enable you to focus on those things that made a previous trip successful. The opposite, of course, is also valid. That is, your notes will remind you of techniques that were not productive. You can then move on to trying other methods, baits, and ares in the hope of hitting the right combination. Either way, keeping a trip log can not only make you a more successful angler, but also bring back some warm memories on a cold winter night.

Make copies of the log to use for each lake and pond you fish.

A beautiful rainbow trout caught & released in a Cape Cod pond. Will the angler remember the details that led to her success? For how long? (Photo: Michael Shelton)

POND: ____________________

TOWN: ____________________

TRIP LOG

DATE	TIME	COMPANIONS	METHODS	BAITS LURES, FLIES	CATCH TYPE, SIZE	AREAS	COMMENTS

POND: ____

TOWN: ____

TRIP LOG

DATE	TIME	COMPANIONS	METHODS	BAITS LURES, FLIES	CATCH TYPE, SIZE	AREAS	COMMENTS

POND: ______________________________

TOWN: ______________________________

TRIP LOG

DATE	TIME	COMPANIONS	METHODS	BAITS LURES, FLIES	CATCH TYPE, SIZE	AREAS	COMMENTS

Cast 30

S.O.S.
Save Our Stillwaters

Users of the ponds and lakes of Cape Cod-visitors, boaters, swimmers, birders, anglers-whether we are home owners or just passing through, have a responsibility to preserve and protect these important and vulnerable places. Are they indeed vulnerable? The Cape Cod Commission points out that most of the stillwaters "satisfactorily provide the majority of uses that most Cape Codders [and visitors] desire. Bacterial testing of ponds shows that these ponds generally provide healthy conditions for swimming. Fishing and boating are still popular, and recent property values and sales show that demand for pond front properties is only increasing."

This may sound comforting, but all is not what it seems. So what's the problem? The problem is the difference between appearance and reality. What we see on the surface, superficially observing the stillwaters, looks hunky dory. What we don't see, beyond mere surface, visual scanning, is the reality of the waters' conditions-their biological and chemical health.

Consider these findings in the Pond and Lake Atlas, May 2003 Final Report of the Cape Cod Commission Water Resources Office:

- Review of current USEPA nutrient thresholds and Cape Cod nutrient thresholds suggests that the water quality in Cape Cod ponds is **significantly impacted** by surrounding development.
- Between 74% and 93% of the Cape's ponds are **impacted**.
- Review of 2001 dissolved oxygen concentrations [vital for fish survival] and comparisons of 1948 and 2001 suggest that many of these pond ecosystems are not only **impacted,** but also **seriously impaired**.
- Approximately **45% of all the ponds and 89% of the deepest ponds are impaired.**

- **Trout** generally **do not have adequate habitats** to make it through a summer due to **a lack of oxygen** in the cold waters of deeper ponds.
- Occasional **large fish kills** or **algae blooms** are due to **excessive nutrients**.
- More nutrients generally favor bass fishing, but **half of the ponds** tested for **mercury** now have **health warnings** about consumption of fish tissue.
- These measures indicate **significant ecological problems.**

Appearance and reality: a person with cancer on the inside can look deceptively healthy on the outside. These waters we admire, swim, boat, and fish, are locked in a silent struggle for survival, and we are the cause of that frightening situation. What can and must we do to take responsibility and reverse the decline of Cape Cod's ponds and lakes and **S**ave **O**ur **S**tillwaters?

There are many individual, community, organizational, and collaborative steps we can take.

Individuals. NO ONE CAN DO EVERYTHING, BUT EVERYONE CAN DO SOMETHING.. It appears that most of the visible trash around lakes and ponds is left there by careless and irresponsible anglers. The first thing we can do is not be one ourselves. The second step we can take is to pick up the trash we see. Sadly, there's a lot of it; too much for one caring person to pick up. But we are not alone in our love of the beauty and our commitment to help.

Save supermarket and other small trash bags and store some of them in your vehicle and tackle box. Whenever you visit a lake or pond carry a bag with you rolled up in your pocket. Pick up some of those empty soda and beer containers, cardboard, plastic or styrofoam worm boxes, fishing line, lunch bags, sandwich wrappers, fishing tackle packaging, and anything else you run across that is a visual and ecological blight to the surroundings. Of course you may not be there specifically to clean up the area (though you could organize a shoreline clean up with your family or a group of like minded folks), but always make it a point to personally take out some trash. If each of us consistently picks up a little we will, collectively, pick up a lot.

Having a plastic bag with you is key. Without the bag to hold the trash you probably will not pick up what you see. I know I don't; I allow myself to feel frustrated, overwhelmed, angry, and finally, guilty. But not when I remember to carry a bag and do my part.

I figure there will always be thoughtless litterers; however, if I take personal responsibility I can better live with myself since integrity is doing the right thing even when no one is looking. And when

they are, perhaps the sight of increasing numbers of individuals schlepping trash from around the lakes and ponds will be contagious to youngsters and adults who observe it.

> **HOW MERCURY GETS INTO CAPE COD FISH**
>
> - When power plants burn coal for electricity, they emit mercury.
> - Rain washes some mercury out of the air onto land and into waterways-not only in areas near smoke stacks-rust belt states- but also far from the source - Cape Cod.
> - Fish absorb the mercury as it passes over their gills and as they feed on organisms containing mercury.
>
> As larger fish eat smaller fish, mercury concentrations increase; thus older, larger predator fish- bass in particular- have the highest concentrations of mercury.
>
> *(Adapted from "Fishing for Trouble", Public Interest Research Group)*

Community-Green lawns equal ruined ponds. Generally speaking, Cape Cod is a gigantic, bottomless sand box resting on top of water- fresh water, including Cape Cod's drinking water supply, which is directly below the sand box, held there by the hydrodynamics of the salt water surrounding the peninsula. The Cape's ponds and lakes are the blinking eyes of the underwater lenses. Everything we do while we are playing in this sand box above the fresh water has an impact on the drinking water below as well as on the interconnected ponds and lakes.

Carrying this image a little further, consider how we treat our own children's sand box. We protect it from cats who would urinate and defecate in it, causing not only an offense to the sands but also a health hazard for our children. We certainly would not allow gasoline, motor oil, or noxious chemicals into the sand box. That would poison our children as it destroys the sand box. But do we show the same concern, in the larger picture, for the rain run off from roads and the leaching of chemical lawn and garden fertilizers into the Cape's drinking water supply and its ponds and lakes?

Regardless of the distance of a Cape Cod home from a pond or lake, chemical fertilizers used on its lawns and gardens will eventually percolate through the thin, porous Cape sands, and, increased by rainfall, make their way into and contaminate the underground water and the stillwaters.

The high concentrations of phosphorous and nitrogen in comercial lawn and garden fertilizers then overfeed a pond's water plants that sprout, bloom, and multiply across the stillwater, extracting most of the life supporting oxygen needed by fish and other underwater creatures, as well as creating a weed choked environment unsuitable not only for fishing but also for virtually every other stillwater recreational activity. This is an unarguable fact backed up by the hard scientific research of the Cape Cod Commission report.

So do we have to give up our flowers and green lawns to avoid slimy green ponds? No. A solution lies in using organic fertilizers lower in phosphorous and nitrogen that will do the job without the damage to the ecosystem. Just as the relatively recently mandated Title 5 septic systems installed on the 90% of Cape homes that use them are a buffer between biological waste and the underground water supply, so too should laws, in the absence of voluntary compliance, ban the use of chemical fertilizers in the interest of fur-

"The sandbox that is Cape Cod is our children's sand box writ large. We abuse it at our peril."

A dead perch frames William Risko as he surveys the fish kill on Cedar Pond in Orleans which Ricko's property abuts. Dead fish started washing ashore there Tuesday evening. (Photo: Steve Heaslip, Cape Cod Times)

ther slowing the decline of Cape Cod's freshwaters.

In the absence of a law, to ignore a known organic solution for ameliorating the contamination of the Cape's underwater drinking water and our open stillwaters borders on criminal irrespossibility. The sand box that is Cape Cod is our children's sand box writ large. We abuse it at our own peril.

Institutional involvement. Several Cape area schools and organizations have involved themselves in efforts to monitor and remedy ecological problems confronting our freshwaters. Yet there are many others that can play a role. How better to tap into the idealism of youth and the leadership of educators than to make applicable and real the abstract theories of classroom science, biology, chemistry, citizenship, and other studies? Not only would such involvement create a constantly renewable citizen army that could help solve some of the problems of our stillwaters but it would also enhance meaningful learning by engaging students in problem solving, the highest objective of education.

If schools "adopted" the area ponds, orphaned, with no pond association to monitor their health, much good would result. (See the chapters in this book that list the towns, ponds and lakes, including whether or not the pond has an association.)

Collaborative. If you want to get started, contact the Cape Cod Commission Water Resources Office at (508) 362-3828, water@capecodcommission.org, or stop by their offices at 3225 Main Street in Barnstable.)

Ask them about the PALS program, the Cape Cod Pond and Lake Stewardship, an organized, up and running collaboration among some, not yet all, of the Cape's 15 towns that "was initiated and nurtured to achieve the goal of better understanding the status of Cape Cod ponds." Our lakes and ponds need you to become their PALS.

"In the end,
we will conserve only what we love,
we will love only what we understand,
we will understand only what we are taught."

BABA DIOUM,
SENEGALESE CONSERVATIONIST

REFERENCES

Ancher, Ted
BASS BETS, Boston Herald, 1993

Budryk, Peter
TROUT & SALMON LAKES of CT & How To Fish Them, Covered Bridge Press/Parnassus Imprints, 2000

Eichner, Edward; Cambareri, Thomas; Smith, Ben; Belfit, Gabrielle; McCaffery, Donna; Fenn, Margo
CAPE COD POND & LAKE ATLAS Final Report May 2003, Cape Cod Commission Water Resource Office, 2003

Evanoff, Vlad
THE FISHERMAN"S CATALOGUE, Doubleday Dolphin, 1977

Flynn, Owen
50 TROUT PONDS IN MA, New Hampshire Publishing Company, 1979

Koch, Maryjo
POND LAKE RIVER SEA, Swan Island Books, 1998

Larsen, Larry
MASTERING LARGEMOUTH BASS, North American Fishing Club, 1989

Mullen, James; Tompkins, William
TROUT POND MANAGEMENT IN MA, MA Division of Fisheries & Game, 1959

McClane, A.J., Editor
McCLANE'S NEW STANDARD FISHING ENCYCLOPEDIA, Gramercy Books, 1998

REFERENCES CONTINUED

McClane, A.J.
FIELD GUIDE TO FRESHWATER FISHES OF NORTH AMERICA, Holt, Rinehart, and Winston, 1974

Merwin, John, Editor
STILLWATER TROUT, Nick Lyon Books, 1980

Portnoy, J.W.; Winkler, M.J.; Sanford, P.R.; University of Wisconsin
KETTLE POND DATA ATLAS, Cape Cod National Seashore, National Park Service, 2001

Reid, George
POND LIFE, Western Publishing Company, 1967

Sternberg, Dick
ADVANCED BASS FISHING
HOW TO CATCH PANFISH
SECRETS OF THE BASS PROS, The Hunting & Fishing Library, Cowles Creative Publishing, 1995, 1999, 1989

Tucholke, Brian, Editor
AN ANGLER'S GUIDE TO TROUT FISHING IN MA, MA/RI Council of Trout Unlimited, 1988

> *"I have laid aside business, and gone a fishing."*
>
> IZAAC WALTON, THE COMPLEAT ANGLER, 1633

Postscript

Coty Benjamin Carreiro finally busted his way out of the water August 27. Much to the consternation of his father – you know how dads can be about their first kid – he went oystering with me at the tender age of three weeks old. We have an Oyster Festival here in Wellfleet in September. I needed oysters, I'd agreed to babysit, and so, ensconced in his plastic carryall gizmo, into the skiff he went.

It was kind of funny really. Midway through picking, I had to stop and pop a bottle into his mouth, wiping oyster mud off my hands as best I could. As I was about to shove off, a young deputy-assistant warden cam bounding across the flats to see I hadn't exceeded my limit; once he spotted Coty, he couldn't get me out of there fast enough. Since I had most likely exceeded my limit by just ever so little, I was more happy Coty was along.

Which says to me that it's looking good. I think Coty will grow into a fine fishing-shell fishing companion. I'll teach him to fish and I'll show him how to harvest shellfish. And most importantly, I'll show him how to tuck the shellfish money into the bank, because that's what'll pay for college. He's built like a little linebacker right now, but I'm betting it'll be his brains, not brawn, that will help him make his way in this world.

And the more one understands the really true essence of fishing, the sharper you know those brains will be. I can hardly wait to teach him the fisherman's knot.

GRANDMA MOLLY BENJAMIN, WELLFLEET

INDEX

INDEX CONTINUED

INDEX CONTINUED

Cape Cod Bait & Tackle Shops

(Source: Massachusetts Division of Marine Fisheries)

Bourne

One Shot Outdoor Sports, 41 Meetinghouse Lane, 508-833-3500
Budd's Bait and Tackle Shop, 5 Main Street, 508-759-6600
Cape Cod Charlie's, 340 Scenic Highway, 508-759-2611
Maco's Inc., 3253 Cranberry Highway, 508-759-9836
Red Top Sporting Goods, 265 Main Street, 508-759-3371

Falmouth

Eastman's Sport and Tackle, 150 Main Street, 508-548-6900
Falmouth Bait & Tackle, 258 Teaticket Hwy., 508-457-0700
Green Pond Fish'n Gear, 348 Rt. 28, 508-548-2573
Maco's at Green Pond, 366 Menauhant Road, 508-457-4155
Harborside Sport & Tackle, 56 Scranton Avenue, 508-548-0143

Sandwich

Canal Marine, 20 Freezer Rd., 508-888-0096
Forestdale Bait & Tackle, 48 Rt. 130, Forestdale, 508-539-8952
Sandwich Ship Supply, 68 Tupper Road, 508-888-0200
SAS Bait & Tackle, Rt. 130 #374, 508-420-8328

Mashpee

The Sporting Life, Mashpee Commons, 508-539-0007

Cotuit

Cotuit Bait and Tackle, 4424 Route 28, 508-428-2111

Barnstable

Barnstable Marine Service, Barnstable Harbor, 508-362-3811

Osterville

Osterville Angler's Club, 72 Crosby Circle, 508-420-4336

Hyannis

The Powder Horn Outfitters, 210 Barnstable Road, 508-775-8975
Sports Port, 149 West Main Steet, 508-775-3096
Hyannis Angler's Club, 235 Ocean St., 508-951-9692

Yarmouth

Riverview Bait and Tackle, 1273 Route 28, 508-394-1036
Truman's Bait & Tackle, 608 Route 28, 508-771-3470

Dennis

Bass River Bait and Tackle, 42 Main Street, 508-394-8666
Fishermen's Outfitter, 311 Main Street, 508-398-4125
North Side Marina Sesuit Road, 508-385-3936
Sesuit Creek Outfitters, 22 Bridge Street, 508-385-1912

Harwich

Fishing the Cape, Harwich Commons, 508-432-1200
Kildee Hill Bait & Tackle, 390 Main Street, 508-430-8009
Sunrise Bait & Tackle, 306 Route 28, 508-430-4117

Chatham

Cape Fisherman's Supply, 67 Depot Road, 800-588-8650
Drew's Sport Shop, 1137 Main Street, 508-945-0964
Top Rod, 1082 Orleans Road, 508-945-2256

Orleans

Bait Shack, 4 Bay Ridge Lane, 508-240-1575
Goose Hummock Shop, 15 Route 6A, 508-255-0455
The Hook-Up, 85 Lowell Road, 508-240-0778

Eastham

Blackbeard's Bait & Tackle Shop, 50 Brackett Rd., 508-240-3369

Wellfleet

Black Duck Sports Shop, Main Street, 508-349-9801
Bay Sails Marine, 2568 Route 6, 508-349-3840
Gone Fishin', 2616 Route 6, 508-349-0592

Provincetown

Flyer's Boat Rental, 131A Commercial Street, 508-487-0898
Nelson's Bait & Tackle, 43 Race Point Road, 508-487-0034

Truro

Pamet Bait and Tackle, 8 Truro Center Rd., 508-349-3228